PsycEssentials

PsycEssentials

A Pocket Resource for Mental Health Practitioners

Janet L. Sonne

American Psychological Association • *Washington, DC*

Published by
American Psychological Association
750 First Street, NE
Washington, DC 20002
www.apa.org

To order
APA Order Department
P.O. Box 92984
Washington, DC 20090-2984
Tel: (800) 374-2721; Direct: (202) 336-5510
Fax: (202) 336-5502; TDD/TTY: (202) 336-6123
Online: www.apa.org/pubs/books
E-mail: order@apa.org

In the U.K., Europe, Africa, and the Middle East, copies may be ordered from
American Psychological Association
3 Henrietta Street
Covent Garden, London
WC2E 8LU England

Typeset in Stone Serif by Circle Graphics, Inc., Columbia, MD

Printer: Edwards Brothers, Inc., Ann Arbor, MI
Cover Designer: Naylor Design, Washington, DC

The opinions and statements published are the responsibility of the authors, and such opinions and statements do not necessarily represent the policies of the American Psychological Association.

Library of Congress Cataloging-in-Publication Data

Sonne, Janet L.
  PsycEssentials : a pocket resource for mental health practitioners / Janet L. Sonne. — 1st ed.
      p. cm.
  Includes bibliographical references and index.
  ISBN-13: 978-1-4338-1117-3
  ISBN-10: 1-4338-1117-0
  1. Psychiatry—Handbooks, manuals, etc. I. American Psychological Association. II. Title. III. Title: Psychological essentials.
  RC456.S66 2012
  616.89—dc23
                              2011034272

British Library Cataloguing-in-Publication Data
A CIP record is available from the British Library.

Printed in the United States of America
First Edition

Contents

Acknowledgments

This book represents the invaluable contributions of many people to my life and to my education and career as a psychologist—those who taught, guided, pushed, and supported me. Among many other things, my father, John Hubbard, taught me to honor and develop the skills of thorough research and concise writing. My mother, Diana Hubbard, urged me to stay open to even the most improbable possibilities. My siblings and friends encouraged me to explore all that life has to offer and appreciate the process—Julian, Jim, Susan, my Stanford roommates, Karen Holmes, the Wheel Women, and the Riverside ladies. Teachers, supervisors, and colleagues infused me with a passion for learning about psychology, to cherish the complexity of the human condition, and to think both "outside of the box" and for myself—Philip Zimbardo PhD, Robert Sears, PhD, Daphne Bugenthal, PhD, Braddie Dooley, PhD, and Mark Haviland, PhD. I am particularly grateful to Ken Pope, PhD, for his many years of mentoring and nourishing my commitment to the practice of ethical psychology and for his promptings to move outside of my comfort zone and participate in professional activities beyond my private practice or graduate school offices. I also want to thank Brandt Caudill, Esq., Joe George, PhD, Esq., Michele Licht, Esq., Gary Schoener, MEq., and Jeff Younggren, PhD, for the many opportunities they have shared with me to ponder and articulate the ethical and legal responsibilities of clinical psychologists. I acknowledge, too, the tremendous contributions of my graduate and medical students, and psychology and psychiatry supervisees to the project. Their thoughtful questions and our pursuits of answers inspired the creation of this resource.

No book reaches print without the understanding and collaborative hard work of the publications staff. I deeply appreciate the warm reception, creativity, and meticulous care offered by Susan Reynolds, Mary Lynn Skutley, Daniel Brachtesende, Tyler Aune, Ron Teeter, and Debbie Felder of APA Books.

Finally, I am grateful to my husband, Alan Sonne, and my children, Kate Sonne Myler and Chris Sonne, for their unfailing support and general cheerleading during the months I was glued to my desk chair and computer. Al is my earth and my sky; he has provided my footing and encouraged my reaching throughout our marriage. Kate and Chris always have delighted me with their enthusiasm for experiencing and learning—their many, many "why's"...and perhaps more importantly, their "why not's."

PsycEssentials

Introduction

A wise colleague once commented that "the next-best thing to knowing answers to questions is knowing how to find those answers." From the time I first entered graduate school, I have been confronted with thousands of questions regarding the practice of clinical psychology whose answers I either did not know or could not remember. My training and experience over the course of many years have afforded me the knowledge I have needed to answer many of those questions, at least the first time they arose. And those same years have embedded some answers so deeply that I can quickly and easily recall them. Yet I will never have the depth of knowledge or the recall ability necessary to anticipate and be able to answer all of the questions on my own. And I suspect that I am not alone.

Mental health practice is a constantly growing and evolving field. New questions arise constantly because new domains of adaptive and maladaptive psychological functioning and new assessment and intervention techniques are introduced by ongoing clinical observation and empirical research. For example, my training in graduate school in the screening assessment of possible neuropsychological impairment in patients was limited to an introduction to the Bender–Gestalt to "rule out organicity." Over the past few decades, there have been significant advances in the understanding of the nature and process of brain dysfunction in specific domains such as attention and memory. And those advances have resulted in the development of a number of specialized measures that may be used to screen for suspected deficits. When I was a graduate student, I would not have even known to ask (much less answer) the question "What is a good measure to screen for possible executive functioning impairment in this patient?"

Furthermore, the answers to familiar, recurring questions change. Consider, for example, the following question: "What are the possible diagnoses I should consider when my patient presents with psychotic symptoms?" When that question came up during my graduate school training, I must admit (at the very real risk of disclosing my age) that I referred to the second edition of the *Diagnostic and Statistical Manual of Mental Disorders* (2nd ed.; *DSM–II*) for answers. During my career, I have witnessed four revisions of the *DSM*. With each major revision, I changed how I answered the same question. Think about another question: "What is my legal responsibility should I suspect that my patient presents a viable potential danger to another person?" I was trained and have worked my entire career in California. But although I did not have to adjust to different state laws, I was confronted by changes in California law regarding the criteria that prompt mandatory reporting to law enforcement and any reasonably identifiable victims.

In an effort to keep pace with the explosion of information in the mental health professions; changes in clinical, ethical, and legal standards; and my only-human memory capabilities, I have purchased and dog-eared many books, attended and filed notes from numerous continuing education courses, and learned to search the web. But herein lies a basic problem. When a question arises regarding a patient whom I have just seen or am about to see in session, I actually may have a great resource that will likely help me arrive at an answer. Unfortunately, I may also have to spend precious time trying to remember which exact book, file folder, or website holds that one piece of information I need. Then, if I can determine that the information I need is in a specific book or folder, I typically spend more time trying to figure out whether the material is sitting at my home office or at my clinical office or whether I let a colleague or student borrow it.

The Purpose of This Resource

The idea for this resource came one day as I browsed through a medical school bookstore. I noticed that the bookshelves were stocked with a wide variety of pocket-sized reference books for medical and nursing students and practitioners containing up-to-date bits of information they commonly need to assess, diagnose, and treat their patients—all in one place. More recently I have observed physicians pull these little gems out of their coat pockets or exam room drawers to check, even during their face-to-face contacts with patients.

PsycEssentials is intended to provide a similar resource specifically for mental health practitioners, including psychologists, psychiatrists, marriage and family therapists, and social workers. To my knowledge, this resource is unique in its objective, its format, and its contents. My objective was to gather a broad range of information that clinicians commonly need and use in their practices and present it in a simple, clear, user-friendly format for quick reference. The resource is not intended to cover everything for everyone. Nor is it intended to provide an in-depth study of each topic. Instead, my hope was to give mental health practitioners with varied levels of experience, working in diverse disciplines and across a range of theoretical orientations, a "jump start" on developing answers to the myriad of questions posed by their professional interactions with clients. If the answer to the clinician's question is not contained in these pages, I hope that the reader at least gains some insight into where some information may be obtained.

The Chapters in This Resource

PsycEssentials is divided into 18 chapters. The order of the first 14 chapters is intended to reflect a "typical" chronological process with a client—from the initial session through assessment and diagnosis to treatment and termination. The final four chapters include information regarding questions that may arise for the clinician at any point in the professional relationship. Each chapter contains a text introduction followed by information in an outline form. At the end of most chapters, I provide references for readers to consider as they formulate their answers.

Chapters 1 through 4 present material regarding the process and content of the initial assessment of a client. Chapter 1 begins with a brief introduction regarding the purpose and the process of an initial clinical assessment interview. A comprehensive outline for an intake interview follows; the clinician is encouraged to decide what elements of the outline are appropriate for each client as well as the proper timing for gathering specific information. Chapter 2 includes a list of several standardized screening measures for psychological dysfunctions and disorders. The list begins with measures of cognitive functioning (separated into intelligence and neuropsychological screening measures) and achievement. Measures for the assessment of multiple Axis I symptoms and disorders and of single Axis I symptoms and disorders follow. The list concludes with screening measures for Axis II personality disorders (all in alphabetical order). The description for each measure includes the client age range for which the test is appropriate; whether the test is client self-report, other report, or clinician rated; the general type(s) of information provided by the measure; where the measure may be obtained; whether administration, scoring, and/or report software is available; and whether the measure is available in languages other than English.

Chapter 3 contains a list of structured and semistructured interview formats for the assessment of Axis I and Axis II disorders. Interviews for multiple Axis I symptoms or disorders are presented first, then for single Axis I symptoms or disorders, and finally for Axis II personality disorders (all in alphabetical order). The description for each measure includes the client age range, the information generated by each interview, where the interview may be obtained, whether software is available, and whether the measure is available in languages other than English. Chapter 4 includes guides for the completion of a child mental status examination (MSE) and an adult or elderly client MSE. Each guideline lists the major categories of the MSE and the elements of each category with some examples of element descriptors. Special notes are included to prompt the clinician to consider conducting further assessment should the MSE indicate impairment (e.g., possible dementia screening with evidence of impaired memory or executive functioning or a full suicide risk assessment if current ideation is detected).

Chapters 5 through 7 contain information regarding more extensive assessment of the client. Chapter 5 contains a list of some of the most common psychological assessment measures. The measures are presented alphabetically within categories. The categories begin with cognitive functioning (separated into intelligence and neuropsychological measures) and achievement. Then measures of motor, behavioral, emotional, and social development are outlined (separated into general measures and measures of Asperger's syndrome and autism). The list concludes with measures of multiple Axis I and/or Axis II characteristics and symptoms and then of single symptoms and disorders. The description of each measure includes the appropriate client age range; the format of administration (client report vs. clinician or other rated); the general types of information provided; where the test may be obtained; whether there is administration, scoring, and/or report software available; and whether the measure is available in Spanish.

Chapter 6 contains guidelines for the clinical assessment of client self-harm and interpersonally violent thoughts and behaviors. Assessments for self-harm are differentiated into two types: evaluations of nonsuicidal and suicidal self-injury. The guidelines include outlines for clinical interview assessment of self-harm and other harm (including some references to structured interview formats for nonsuicidal self-injury) and lists of paper-and-pencil measures to aid the clinician in the evaluation of each type of harm (including information regarding appropriate client ages, the types of information elicited, where the measure may be obtained, and whether software is available). Chapter 7 describes five steps for the assessment and management of clients at potential risk of self-harm (again including separate evaluations for nonsuicidal and suicidal self-injury) or interpersonal violence. Outlines for the structured clinical evaluations of risk and protective factors for each type of potential harm are described, followed by lists of available actuarial measures. There are separate outlines for the suicide risk assessments (and available actuarial measures) for children and adolescents, adults, and elderly clients. Following the outlines, descriptions for the estimations of risk (low, moderate, or high) are provided. Then, strategies for the acute management of clients at significant risk and for longer term treatment are presented. The chapter ends with a list of elements to include in the documentation of the client's risk evaluation and management.

Chapters 8 through 10 contain information regarding clinicians' legal duties when they suspect that a client is either the victim or perpetrator of child abuse (Chapter 8) or the abuse of an elderly, dependent, or disabled adult (Chapter 9) or that the client presents a more general threat of harm to another (Chapter 10). Each chapter includes a brief introductory description of the history underlying the general reporting duties of mental health professionals; a table with national resources (including telephone numbers and websites); and a state-by-state listing of relevant statutes, report contact information, and additional web resources.

Chapter 11 contains an outline of three basic sequential steps to help the clinician determine a diagnosis for a client: (1) differentiating symptoms that are the direct physiological effect of a general medical condition from those due to a psychological disorder, (2) differentiating symptoms due to substance intoxication and/or withdrawal from those due to a psychological disorder, and (3) differentiating among various psychological disorders that capture the presenting symptoms once a general medical condition and substance use have been ruled out. The clinician is guided through Steps 1 and 2 with lists of medical conditions and substances associated with common presenting symptoms. Then at Step 3, the chapter includes a list of presenting symptoms and possible diagnoses for the clinician to consider. At each step, references to potential *DSM* (4th ed., text revision; *DSM–IV–TR*) diagnoses are provided, including page numbers in the *DSM–IV–TR* associated with each diagnosis.

Chapters 12 through 14 include information regarding intervention. Chapter 12 contains an outline of recommendations for engaging in evidence-based practice and annotated lists of web and print resources of empirically supported assessments and treatments. The resources include references and links to specific intervention protocols and treatment manuals. Chapter 13 contains two tables of common psychotropic medications, prescribed and over-the-counter. Each table includes information regarding the disorders for which the medication is typically used; typical dosage levels for children, adolescents, adults, and elderly clients; and common side effects, serious complications, withdrawal warnings, and cautions. Chapter 14 contains recommendations for clinicians for the promotion of positive termination of psychotherapy with clients.

Chapters 15 through 18 cover various issues that arise for mental health practitioners throughout the course of their work with clients. Chapter 15 is focused on records and record keeping. Citations and Internet links are listed for ethical guidelines and standards and some federal legal requirements (Health Insurance Portability and Accountability Act [HIPAA], Medicare, and Medicaid) regarding mental health record keeping. The chapter ends with an outline of content elements that client records may contain, highlighting those required by HIPAA. Chapter 16 contains lists of web resources that mental health practitioners from several disciplines (psychologists, psychiatrists, marriage and family therapists, and social workers) may access to address questions regarding current ethical and legal standards and guidelines for practice. The lists include links to national and state professional organizations, state licensing boards, various professional practice guidelines for specific disorders and client groups, and HIPAA information. Chapter 17 includes additional resources intended to assist the clinician with the development of strategies for self-care (e.g., developing a professional support network and engagement in activities that build and sustain the clinician's well-being) and management of adverse events (e.g., the practitioner's sudden illness, disability, or death, or a client's suicide). Chapter 18 contains resources that clinicians may offer to clients and their significant others for a range of medical, psychological, and social problems they face, including HIV, AIDS, sexually transmitted diseases, cancer, clergy abuse, homelessness, rape, and surviving the suicide of a loved one.

This resource reflects many of the questions that have challenged me during my 28-year experience as a clinical psychologist in academic, research, clinical, and forensic settings. Many of the questions evolved in my own work with clients. But I have grappled with many more in my work as a teacher and supervisor of clinicians in training; as a consultant to other mental health professionals regarding clinical, ethical, and legal dilemmas in their practices; as a member of state and national ethics committees; and as an expert witness in civil and administrative proceedings regarding the standard of care for mental health professionals. Clinicians' work is a complex endeavor. I hope that *PsycEssentials* may provide clinicians with some initial answers to questions and resources for further exploration.

CHAPTER 1

Initial Clinical Assessment Interview

The initial clinical assessment interview consists of the exchange of information between the client (and/or the client's significant others) and the therapist. The quality of that exchange can affect the development of a collaborative working relationship between the therapist and client as well as the adequacy of the therapist's diagnostic assessment of the client, the understanding of the client's interpersonal style and motivation level for therapy, and the formulation of an appropriate treatment plan.

Much of the information provided to the client is transmitted verbally by the therapist, but the client also receives information by reading documents provided by the therapist (e.g., informed consent form, notifications required by the Health Insurance Portability and Accountability Act regarding privacy and security) and by observing the therapist's behavior and office milieu. Likewise, much of the information elicited from the client is communicated verbally. However, the therapist also gathers information from the client's nonverbal behavior, the verbal reports of others who may be present, and any pertinent documents or records (e.g., reports from other health professionals, school records).

The quality and the quantity of information offered by the client depend in part on his or her perception of and response to the verbal and nonverbal information provided by the therapist in the first few minutes (or even the first few seconds) of the interview. The therapist who exhibits a calm, accepting demeanor and communicates respect for and an interest in the client creates a comfortable setting in which the client is more likely to disclose issues of concern.

An outline for an initial clinical assessment interview is presented in the section that follows, with guidelines and prompts for gathering specific information. Notes are included for special concerns for child, adolescent, and elderly clients. The order of the content topics is a fairly traditional one. However, the outline covers the client's health and substance use and abuse histories and current statuses at the beginning to reflect the priority that information commands in diagnostic assessment. The *Diagnostic and Statistical Manual of Mental Disorders* (4th ed., text revision; American Psychiatric Association, 2000) states, for example, that general medical conditions and substance-related conditions must be ruled out as the causes of psychological symptoms before other disorders may be considered.

It is important to note that this outline presents a format for a comprehensive initial clinical assessment of a client. The clinician must decide what elements of the extensive content outlined are appropriate for each individual client. Keep in mind, however, that a thorough intake assessment provides essential information for accurate diagnosis and efficient and effective treatment planning. The therapist also should determine the proper timing of the information gathering in each circumstance. For most clients, the information contained in this initial assessment may be elicited verbally over one or more early sessions. The information may also be gathered by giving the client a written questionnaire to be completed before the first session and then reviewed at the beginning of treatment. And the clinician always should be mindful of how cultural factors may impact the process of the interview interaction.

The clinician may refer to the references listed at the end of this chapter for a few examples of detailed discussions of clinical interviewing. The resources contain guidelines for developing rapport with clients, sample questions that the practitioner can ask to obtain specific information from clients, diversity considerations, model interview documentation forms and reports, and other very helpful material (Fontes, 2008; Ivey, 1993; Morrison, 2007; Sommers-Flanagan & Sommers-Flanagan, 2009; Zuckerman, 2008).

Initial Clinical Assessment Interview Outline

- ➢ Identifying information
  - Client's name, age, birth date, gender, ethnic and cultural identity, religious identity, primary language spoken, other language(s) spoken, current address, persons with whom the client is living, current home phone and cell phone number, the client's preferred means of contact (i.e., home address, home phone, cell phone), person with whom the client authorizes contact in case of an emergency and that person's phone number, and the referral source
    - ○ If the client is a child, adolescent, or elderly person, the name of the legal representative or conservator (e.g., parent, guardian) and that individual's preferred means of contact
- ➢ Presenting problem
  - Client's description of the concerns that prompted the initial visit
    - ○ Current symptoms, including positive symptoms (excesses in emotions, perceptions, cognitions, behavior, e.g., increase in depressed mood, manic symptoms, hallucinations, racing thoughts) and negative symptoms (deficits in emotions, perceptions, cognitions, behavior, e.g., anhedonia, loss of volition, poor attention span)
    - ○ Chronological history of present symptoms (e.g., when the symptoms started, how they evolved, whether the intensity has changed over time)
      - ◆ Note any possible precipitating factors
      - ◆ Note any possible contributing factors (e.g., acute or chronic medical condition or substance abuse)
    - ○ Current thoughts of nonsuicidal self-injury (e.g., cutting, burning) and/or any recent acts of nonsuicidal self-injury (If such symptoms are present, conduct a full assessment; see Chapter 6, this resource.)
    - ○ Current thoughts of suicide and/or recent suicidal acts (If present, conduct a full assessment; see Chapter 6, this resource.)

- ○ Current thoughts of harming others and/or recent behaviors that were intended to or did harm others (If present, conduct a full assessment; see Chapter 6, this resource.)
  - ▪ Note: If the client is a child, adolescent, or elderly person, also obtain a description and history of the current concerns from a representative or significant other (primary caretaker).
- ➢ Recent treatment efforts for same symptoms
  - ▪ Recent inpatient treatment
    - ○ Name and contact information of inpatient facility/ facilities and treating professional
    - ○ Length of stay
    - ○ Diagnosis given by treatment staff
    - ○ Authorization from client to contact, consult with, and/or obtain records from treatment staff
  - ▪ Recent or current outpatient psychotherapy
    - ○ Name and contact information of therapist(s)
    - ○ Length of each engagement
    - ○ Diagnosis given by therapist(s)
    - ○ Authorization from client to contact, consult with, and/or obtain records from therapist(s)
  - ▪ Recent or current use of psychotropic medications
    - ○ Name of medication(s), dose(s), and side effects
    - ○ Name and contact information of physician(s) who prescribed
    - ○ Length of time on medication(s)
    - ○ Diagnosis given by the physician(s)
    - ○ Authorization from client to contact, consult with, and/or obtain records from physician(s)
- ➢ Past psychological history
  - ▪ Chronological history of prior psychological symptoms, including prior experience with symptoms similar to those the client is currently experiencing, as well as with any other psychological symptoms
  - ▪ Past thoughts of nonsuicidal self-injury (e.g., cutting, burning) and/or any past acts of nonsuicidal self-injury (If such symptoms are present, conduct a full assessment; see Chapter 6, this resource.)

- Past thoughts of suicide and/or past suicidal acts (If present, conduct a full assessment; see Chapter 6, this resource.)
- Past thoughts of harming others and/or past behaviors that have harmed others (If present, conduct a full assessment; see Chapter 6, this resource).
- Chronological history of prior psychological or psychiatric treatment, including dates, location, with whom (obtain contact information), for what problems, for how long, and whether the treatment was helpful
    - Outpatient individual, conjoint, or family therapy
    - Outpatient group therapy
    - Outpatient self-help groups (e.g., Alcoholics Anonymous, Al-Anon)
    - Emergency room visits
    - Day treatment or partial hospital
    - Inpatient treatment (including inpatient substance abuse treatment program)
    - Prescribed medication
    - Over-the-counter medications (e.g., St. John's wort)
    - Electroconvulsive treatment or other medical intervention
    - Authorization from client to contact, consult with, and/or obtain records from prior treating professionals
- Current health status
    - Name and contact information of current general physician
        - Details of last physical exam, any remarkable results
        - Details of last visit with a physician, any remarkable results
        - Authorization (if appropriate) to contact, consult with, and/or obtain records from physician
    - Acute health problems (e.g., recent illness, recent injury with pain)
        - Treatment efforts, including dates, location, with whom (obtain contact information), for what problems, for how long, whether the treatment was helpful, and side effects from any medications

- ○ Authorization (if appropriate) to contact, consult with, and/or obtain records
  - ▪ Acute concerns with physical functions (e.g., eating problems, weight loss or gain, vomiting or laxative abuse, sleep disruptions, changes in energy level, changes in libido or sexual functioning)
  - ▪ Chronic health problems and/or physical disabilities (e.g., HIV/AIDS, hyper- or hypothyroidism, cancer, chronic fatigue, fibromyalgia, chronic pain, vision or hearing impairments)
    - ○ Treatment efforts, including dates, location, with whom (obtain contact information), for what problems, for how long, whether the treatment was helpful, and side effects from any medications
    - ○ Authorization (if appropriate) to contact, consult with, and/or obtain records
- ➢ Health history
  - ▪ Chronological history of health and/or physical problems that have been resolved and do not affect current functioning, including when each first occurred, when each was resolved, and any treatments
  - ▪ Chronological history of hospitalizations or emergency room visits for physical reasons (e.g., surgeries, traumatic injuries, delivery of child [note type of delivery]), including the location of the hospitalization or emergency room visit and the date, reason, length of stay, and outcome
- ➢ Recreational substance use/abuse history and current status
  - ▪ Note: A complete assessment of the client's current and past recreational substance use is essential for accurate assessment and diagnosis and appropriate treatment planning. For example, as the clinician considers potential diagnoses, an initial concern is whether the presenting psychological symptoms may be due to the client's use of, acute intoxication from, and/or withdrawal from a substance. Furthermore, many symptom presentations are complicated by the effects of the client's substance use. Also, the potential efficacy, and possible dangers, of proposed treatment interventions are often associated with substance use or abuse.

- Substance use inventory for each of the following substances (if used), including method of ingestion (e.g., oral, intravenous, nasal), amount (per use), frequency, age at first use and last use, whether the client used the substance within the last 48 hours and within the past 30 days
  - Alcohol
  - Amphetamines (e.g., methamphetamine, methylphenidate or "diet pills")
  - Caffeine (e.g., coffee, tea, Red Bull soda, over-the-counter medications or weight loss aids)
  - Cannabis (e.g., marijuana, hashish)
  - Cocaine
  - Hallucinogens (e.g., LSD, PCP, "Ecstasy," mescaline)
  - Inhalants (e.g., glue, gasoline, spray paint, paint thinners)
  - Nicotine (e.g., all forms of tobacco, nicotine gum or patch)
  - Opioid (e.g., heroin, morphine, codeine, hydrocodone, oxycodone, fentanyl, methadone)
  - Sedative, hypnotic, or anxiolytic (e.g., benzodiazepines, carbamates, barbiturates, sleep medications, prescription antianxiety medications)
  - Other (e.g., anabolic steroids, nitrite inhalants, nitrous oxide, over-the-counter and prescription medications, e.g., antihistamines)
- Circumstances of substance use
  - Most recent use
    - When and where
    - Which substance
    - Circumstances
  - Typical use
    - When and where
    - Which substance (preferred substance?)
    - Reasons (e.g., addiction, taste, sensation, escape, fun, increase self-confidence, self-soothing)
- Consequences of substance use
  - Problems with family or friends
  - Problems with school
  - Problems on the job

- o Problems with the law (e.g., driving under the influence or driving while intoxicated, arrest)
- o Problem with adverse reaction (e.g., blackout); note substance
- o Any experience of overdose; note substance and outcome
  - ■ Attempts to cut down or stop
    - o When and under what circumstances
    - o Outcome (e.g., successful for a while and then relapse, never successful)
    - o Ever experience withdrawal symptoms (e.g., shakiness, sweating, nausea, sleeplessness, headache, seizure, delusions or hallucinations)
- ➤ Family history of medical and/or psychological problems including history of self-harm or other harm
  - ■ Name and relationship of family member
  - ■ Type of medical or psychological problem (diagnosis)
  - ■ Treatment, including medication, and response to treatment
- ➤ Early developmental history (0–5 years)
  - ■ Note: The early developmental history of a client can provide some clues to potential biological, psychological, and/or social and cultural factors that may contribute to the client's current presentation. Although some clients may not know the information requested, most have some details of their early history. For child, adolescent, or elderly clients, the information may be solicited from a caregiver or significant other.
  - ■ Circumstances of the client's mother's pregnancy with the client and the client's birth
    - o Pregnancy planned or unplanned, wanted or unwanted
    - o Client's mother's physical condition at time of pregnancy
    - o Any prenatal complications for fetus
    - o Circumstances of birth (e.g., breech, vaginal or cesarean section)
    - o Birth trauma (e.g., anoxia)

- o Perinatal complications for the mother (e.g., excessive bleeding) or the infant (e.g., breathing difficulties)
  - o Separations of client as a newborn or infant from the mother
- Problems with the client's developmental milestones (motor development, speech, toilet training)
- Client's temperament as a child (e.g., easy, difficult, slow to warm up)
- Early behavioral problems (disturbed sleep, enuresis or encopresis, aggressive behavior, separation anxiety)
- ➤ Social history and current status
  - Familial relationships
    - o Identification and quality of familial relationships (including names and ages; whether alive or deceased; quality of relationship for client as a child, adolescent, and currently)
      - ◆ Mother, stepmother, adoptive mother
      - ◆ Father, stepfather, adoptive father
      - ◆ Siblings (full, half, step, adopted)
      - ◆ Paternal and maternal grandparents
      - ◆ Spouse(s), partner(s)
      - ◆ Children (biological, step, adopted)
      - ◆ Grandchildren (biological, step, adopted)
      - ◆ Other familial relationships of importance to the client
  - Social relationships
    - o Nature and quality of social relationships as a child, adolescent, and young adult (as appropriate for client's age)
      - ◆ With same gender
      - ◆ With opposite gender
      - ◆ Social interactional style of client as a child, adolescent, and young adult (e.g., outgoing, shy)
    - o Nature and quality of current social relationships
      - ◆ With same gender
      - ◆ With opposite gender
      - ◆ Current social interactional style (e.g., outgoing, shy)

- Dating and sexual relationships
  - ◆ Age started dating
  - ◆ Age when first physically intimate
  - ◆ Age when first experienced sexual intercourse
  - ◆ Current sexual orientation
  - ◆ History of same-gender sexual intimacies, including when and circumstances
- History of a socially traumatic events (e.g., bullying; rejection by a loved one; racial, ethnic, cultural, or sexual orientation discrimination)

➢ Spiritual and religious history and current status
  - Childhood spiritual or religious affiliation
  - Current spiritual or religious affiliation
    - Any conflict with family or significant other regarding current affiliation or nonaffiliation

➢ Education history
  - School history, including name and location of school, dates attended, grades attended, public or private, typical grades or grade point average, graduation dates, degree or certificate earned
    - Preschool
    - Kindergarten
    - Elementary school
    - Middle school
    - High school
    - Occupational school
    - 2-year college
    - 4-year college
    - Graduate or professional school
    - Other certifications (e.g., pilot's license)
  - Special education experiences (learning disabilities, gifted classes)
  - History of repeating a grade
  - History of behavior or academic problems in school

➢ Employment history and current status
  - Current employment
    - Full or part time
    - Job description
    - Date hired
    - If unemployed, date and circumstances of job loss

  o If unemployed, source of support (spouse, family, disability, Social Security, military benefits, retirement)
  ▪ Chronological history of major jobs, including dates, type of job, full or part time, reason for leaving position (e.g., laid off, fired, pregnancy, better position)
➤ Military experience
  ▪ Branch of military
  ▪ Drafted or enlisted (when entered service)
  ▪ Type of military experience (where and when served)
  ▪ Discharge (when, type, rank at discharge)
➤ Legal history and current status
  ▪ Legal involvements, including dates, nature, and outcome
    o Traffic (including driving under the influence and driving while intoxicated)
    o Civil
    o Criminal
      ◆ Dates of any probation or parole
      ◆ History of offenses involving potential harm to others
    o Administrative (e.g., professional licensing complaint)
➤ Leisure and recreation
  ▪ Hobbies (e.g., art, reading, crafts), including how often per week client engages in activity
  ▪ Physical activities (e.g., golf, swimming, cycling), including how often per week client engages in activity
➤ History of compulsive or habitual behaviors and current status
  ▪ Note: Assessment of compulsive or habitual behaviors (in addition to substance abuse) in the client's history or current life circumstances is often neglected in clinical interviews. That information, however, also affects the clinician's accurate diagnosis and appropriate treatment planning.
  ▪ Compulsive or habitual behaviors, including description of activity, frequency per week and hours per day in past or currently
    o Gambling

- ○ Pornography (print, video, Internet)
- ○ Video or Internet games
- ○ Sex (phone, Internet, prostitutes)
- ○ Eating
- ○ Other

➤ Trauma history

- ■ Note: A complete history of traumatic events is essential for the accurate diagnosis and treatment of each client. The experience of trauma can be the basis of a psychological disorder, can complicate other psychological disorders, and has direct implications for the types and goals of treatment. Studies indicate, however, that traumatic events (e.g., child, elder, or vulnerable person abuse) are more prevalent than is reported by the victims (or significant others) to protective agencies or to health care professionals. It is crucial, therefore, that the clinician assume an active role in obtaining a trauma history.
- ■ Note: Interviewing a client about traumatic experiences requires a delicate understanding of appropriate timing and pacing of the process. Some clients enter the clinician's office with the desire and expectation that such topics will be explored; some may even have been referred to the clinician because of prior disclosure of a traumatic experience. Other clients, however, may be quite uncomfortable with discussion of such experiences and may even resist exploration by the clinician.
- ■ Note: The clinician who determines that a client has experienced abuse assumes a professional responsibility to protect the welfare of that individual. That responsibility can extend to a legal mandate when the client is a child or an elderly (or otherwise legally protected) adult. State laws vary regarding the definition of what constitutes abuse, whether it is mandatory or permissible that the clinician report the abuse to a protective agency, and the requirements for that report. Chapters 8 and 9 contain citations of state legal standards for the reporting of child abuse and elder or vulnerable adult abuse for mental health professionals.

- Traumatic experiences inventory for each of the following types of traumas, including a list of the age of the client at the time of the trauma, the nature of the trauma (with the identification of the perpetrator if applicable), whether the client experienced any physical injury, other outcomes for the client, and whether the experience precipitated any legal proceedings involving the client
  - Natural or man-made disaster (e.g., flood, tornado, tsunami, earthquake)
  - Vehicle accident (plane, car)
  - Verbal abuse (including childhood experience of bullying)
  - Physical abuse or attack (including childhood experience of bullying)
  - Physical neglect (can be self-neglect in the case of an elderly client)
  - Sexual abuse (e.g., rape, incest)
  - Domestic violence (observed or involved)

References

American Psychiatric Association. (2000). *Diagnostic and statistical manual of mental disorders* (4th ed., text revision). Washington, DC: Author.

Fontes, L. A. (2008). *Interviewing clients across cultures: A practitioner's guide.* New York, NY: Guilford Press.

Ivey, A. E. (1993). *Intentional interviewing and counseling* (3rd ed.). Pacific Grove, CA: Brooks/Cole.

Morrison, J. (2007). *The first interview* (3rd ed.). New York, NY: Guilford Press.

Sommers-Flanagan, R., & Sommers-Flanagan, J. (2009). *Clinical interviewing* (4th ed.). Hoboken, NJ: Wiley.

Zuckerman, E. L. (2008). *The paper office: Forms, guidelines, and resources to make your practice work ethically, legally, and profitably* (4th ed.). New York, NY: Guilford Press.

Chapter 2

Standardized Screening Measures

Standardized screening measures are typically administered either before or during an initial clinical assessment session to guide the interview process, clarify the client's symptom presentation, and help generate hypotheses regarding possible diagnoses. Such measures are particularly useful when the client presents a complex symptom picture (e.g., possible multiple comorbid conditions) and/or has difficulty articulating concerns to the clinician. Several screening measures for *Diagnostic and Statistical Manual of Mental Disorders* (4th ed., text revision; *DSM–IV–TR*; American Psychiatric Association, 2000) Axis I and Axis II disorder symptoms are described in the sections that follow. The measures listed were selected from a review of screening tests with standardized norms; the list is not intended to be exhaustive.

Cognitive Functioning: Intelligence Screening Measures

➢ Kaufman Brief Intelligence Test, Second Edition (KBIT–2)
  ■ Ages 4–90 years
  ■ Clinician administered, easel-based tasks
  ■ Provides verbal (crystallized) and nonverbal (fluid) scores and a composite IQ score
  ■ Conormed with Kaufman Test of Educational Achievement—II (KTEA–II) for ages 26–90 years

- Available from PsychCorp (http://www.psychcorp. com), Western Psychological Services (http://www. wpspublish.com)
- ➢ Reynolds Intellectual Screening Test (RIST)
  - Ages 3–94 years
  - Clinician-administered measure with stimulus book
  - Provides a RIST Index score ($M = 100$, $SD = 15$) from one verbal and one nonverbal Reynolds Intellectual Assessment Scales subtest as an overall estimate of general intelligence (g)
  - Available from Psychological Assessment Resources (PAR; http://www4.parinc.com)
    - ○ Scoring, feedback, and interpretive report software available
  - Available from MHS (http://www.mhs.com); PRO-ED Inc. (http://www.proedinc.com); Western Psychological Services (http://www.wpspublish.com)
- ➢ Shipley—2
  - Ages 7–89 years
  - Clinician administered, paper-and-pencil administration
  - Provides a quick estimate of overall cognitive functioning and an index of discrepancy between crystallized and fluid reasoning abilities
  - Available from MHS (http://www.mhs.com), PAR (http://www4.parinc.com), Western Psychological Services (http://www.wpspublish.com)
    - ○ Administration and scoring software available
- ➢ Test of Nonverbal Intelligence, Fourth Edition (TONI–4)
  - Ages 6–89 years, 11 months
  - Clinician-administered measure with stimulus book
  - Uses simple oral or pantomime instructions requiring test taker to answer with simple gestures
  - Provides a norm-referenced, language-free assessment of intelligence, aptitude, abstract reasoning, and problem solving in percentile ranks and deviation quotients
  - Available from PAR (http://www4.parinc.com), PsychCorp (http://www.psychcorp.com)
    - ○ Two equivalent forms
    - ○ Examiner instructions in seven major languages in addition to English

> Wechsler Abbreviated Scale of Intelligence (WASI; two-subtest form or four-subtest form)
  - Ages 6–89 years, 11 months
  - Clinician-administered measure with stimuli and manipulatives
  - Provides an estimate of general cognitive ability (full-scale IQ score) using two subtests (Vocabulary and Matrix Reasoning) or four subtests (Vocabulary, Similarities, Block Design, and Matrix Reasoning)
  - Available from PsychCorp (http://www.psychcorp.com)

Cognitive Functioning: Neuropsychological Screening Measures

> Beery–Buktenica Developmental Test of Visual–Motor Integration—Fifth Edition (Beery VMI–5)
  - Ages 2–18 years, 11 months
  - Clinician-guided tasks
  - Provides a screening measure of visual–motor deficits in several domains (basic gross motor, fine motor, visual, and visual–fine motor development)
  - Available from PRO-ED Inc. (http://www.proedinc.com)
    ○ Short and full forms
    ○ Supplemental visual perception and motor coordination tests
> Bender–Gestalt—II
  - Ages 3–85+ years
  - Clinician-administered measure with stimulus cards
  - Koppitz Developmental Scoring System provides a measure of visual–motor integration
  - Provides standard scores, percentiles, age equivalents, and specialized scores
  - Available from MHS (http://www.mhs.com), Western Psychological Services (http://www.wpspublish.com)
> Cognistat
  - Ages 12 years and older
  - Clinician-administered with stimulus booklet and tokens
  - Assesses neurocognitive functioning in three general areas (level of consciousness, attention span, orientation)

and five ability areas (language, constructional ability, calculation skills, memory, and reasoning/judgment)
- Available from PAR (http://www.parinc.com)

➢ Comprehensive Trail-Making Test (CTMT)
- Ages 8–74 years, 11 months
- Clinician-administered, paper-and-pencil tasks (five tasks)
- Provides composite score based on detection of neuro-psychological deficits (e.g., frontal lobe, attention and set-shifting impairments) in T scores ($M = 50$, $SD = 10$) and percentile ranks
- Available from PRO-ED Inc. (http://www.proedinc.com), Western Psychological Services (http://www.wpspublish.com)

➢ Dementia Rating Scale-2 (DRS-2)
- Ages 55–89 years and older
- Clinician-administered, 36 tasks and 32 stimuli
- Assesses overall cognitive functioning at lower ability levels; total score; five subscale scores (Attention, Initiation/Perseveration, Construction, Conceptualization, and Memory)
- Available from PAR (http://www4.parinc.com)
  ○ Alternate form available
  ○ Scoring and report software available

➢ Frontal Systems Behavior Scales (FrSBe)
- Ages 18–95 years
- Client self-report and family member or caregiver report, paper-and-pencil administration
- Three subscale scores: Apathy, Disinhibition, Executive Dysfunction; total score for behavioral problems associated with frontal lobe damage
- Available from PAR (http://www4.parinc.com)

➢ Mini-Mental State Examination—2 Brief Version (MMSE–2–BV)
- Adult
- Clinician-administered set of cognitive tasks (16 items)
- Provides a quantitative measure of cognitive functioning in raw and T scores
- Available from PAR (http://www4.parinc.com)
  ○ Scoring and report software available

- Available from MHS (http://www.mhs.com)
  - Two alternate forms for retesting
  - Pocket-sized card with administration, scoring, and interpretation information
  - Also available in a standard version (30 items) and expanded version (90 items)
- ➤ Montreal Cognitive Assessment (MoCA)
  - Older adult (normed on patients about 72 years and older)
  - Clinician-administered, paper-and-pencil administration with stimulus pictures
  - Screens for mild cognitive impairment in several different domains: attention and concentration, executive functioning, memory, language, visuoconstructional skills, conceptual thinking, calculations, and orientation
  - Available from http://www.mocatest.org
    - Instructions and test forms available in several languages
- ➤ Neuropsychological Impairment Scale (NIS)
  - Ages 18–88 years
  - Client self-report and other report, paper-and-pencil administration
  - Four validity checks, three summary scores (Global Measure of Impairment, Total Items Circled, Symptom Intensity Measure), seven subscale scores
  - Available from Western Psychological Services (http://www.wpspublish.com)
    - Scoring software available
    - Separate form for physically impaired elderly clients
- ➤ Repeatable Battery for the Assessment of Neuropsychological Status (RBANS)
  - Ages 20–89 years, 11 months
  - Clinician-administered with stimulus booklet
  - Assesses early signs of dementia in elderly clients and other impairments in younger adults; 12 subtests organized into five index scores (immediate memory, visuospatial/constructional, language, attention, and delayed memory) and a total score

- Available from PsychCorp (http://www.psychcorp.com)
  - Alternate form available for repeat testing
  - Spanish-language version is available with no normative data; also available in several other languages for research and pharmaceutical trials in electronic format

Achievement Screening Measures

> Basic Achievement Skills Inventory (BASI) Survey Version
- Ages 8–80 years
- Clinician-administered measure
- Screens for academic strengths and weaknesses using BASI math and verbal subtests
- Available from PsychCorp (http://www.psychcorp.com)
  - Scoring and report software available
> Kaufman Test of Educational Achievement, Second Edition (KTEA–II) Brief Form
- Ages 4 years, 6 months–90 years
- Clinician-administered measure
- Reading, math, and writing subtest scores; battery composite score
- Conormed with KBIT–II Brief Form for ages 26–90 years
- Available from PsychCorp (http://www.psychcorp.com)

Multiple Axis I Symptoms and Disorders Screening Measures

> Adolescent Symptom Inventory—4 (ASI–4)
- Ages 12–18 years
- Parent and teacher report, paper-and-pencil rating scales
- Screens for symptoms of common *DSM–IV–TR* adolescent psychological disorders using criterion-related screening cutoff scores plus norm-based symptom severity scores
- Available from Western Psychological Services (http://www.wpspublish.com)
> Behavioral and Emotional Screening System (part of the BASC–2)
- Preschool to Grade 12
- Client self-report and parent report, paper-and-pencil administration

- Validity indices, total scores with corresponding level of risk for behavioral and emotional issues
- Uses T scores and percentiles
- Available from PsychCorp (http://www.psychcorp.com)
  - Scoring and report software available
  - Spanish form

> Brief Symptom Inventory (BSI; short form of the Symptom Checklist—90—Revised; SCL–90–R)
  - Ages 13 years and older
  - Client self-report, paper-and-pencil administration
  - Same nine primary symptom areas and three global indices as SCL–90–R
  - Available from PsychCorp (http://www.psychcorp.com)
    - Audio compact disc or computer administration available
    - Scoring and report mail-in service and software available
    - Spanish form

> Child Symptom Inventory—4 (CSI–4)
  - Ages 5–12 years
  - Parent and teacher report, paper-and-pencil rating scales
  - Screens for symptoms of common *DSM–IV–TR* childhood psychological disorders
  - Uses criterion-related screening cutoff scores plus norm-based symptom severity scores
  - Available from Western Psychological Services (http://www.wpspublish.com)

> Clinical Assessment Scales for the Elderly—Short Form (CASE–SF)
  - Ages 55–90 years
  - Client self-report and caregiver report, paper-and-pencil administration
  - Screens for Axis I disorders
  - Available from PAR (http://www4.parinc.com)

> Early Childhood Inventory—4 (ECI–4)
  - Ages 3–5 years
  - Parent and teacher report, paper-and-pencil rating scales
  - Screen for symptoms of common *DSM–IV–TR* early childhood psychological disorders

- Uses criterion-related screening cutoff scores plus norm-based symptom severity scores
- Also provides a global impression of child's early developmental skills (e.g., speech and language abilities, motor coordination, social skills)
- Available from Western Psychological Services (http://www.wpspublish.com)

➢ Personality Assessment Screener (PAS)
- Ages 18 years and older
- Client self-report, paper-and-pencil administration
- Ten individual clinical element scores (Negative Affect, Health Problems, Social Withdrawal, Suicidal Thinking, Alcohol Problem, Acting Out, Psychotic Features, Hostile Control, Alienation, Anger Control), PAS total score
- All element scores transformed into probability (p) scores reflecting probability of problematic profile on full PAI
- Available from PAR (http://www4.parinc.com)

➢ Problem Behavior Inventory: Adolescent Symptom Screening Form
- Adolescent
- Client self-report, paper-and-pencil checklist
- Identifies more than 100 *DSM–IV–TR*-related symptoms, including V codes
- Available from Western Psychological Services (http://www.wpspublish.com)

➢ Problem Behavior Inventory: Adult Symptom Screening Form
- Adult
- Client self-report, paper-and-pencil checklist
- Identifies more than 100 *DSM–IV–TR*-related symptoms, including V codes
- Available from Western Psychological Services (http://www.wpspublish.com)

➢ Psychiatric Diagnostic Screening Questionnaire (PDSQ)
- Ages 18 years and older
- Client self-report, paper-and-pencil administration
- Thirteen *DSM–IV–TR* disorder scales with cutoff scores (Major Depression, Generalized Anxiety Disorder, Panic Disorder, Posttraumatic Stress Disorder [PTSD],

Alcohol Abuse/Dependence, Drug Abuse/Dependence, Psychosis, Bulimia/Binge Eating Disorder, Somatization Disorder, Obsessive–Compulsive Disorder, Social Phobia, Hypochondriasis, Agoraphobia), total score, critical items
- Available from Western Psychological Services (http://www.wpspublish.com)

> Symptom Assessment—45 Questionnaire (SA–45)
- Ages 13 years and older
- Client self-report, paper-and-pencil administration
- Eight primary symptom areas, two global indices of distress
- Available from MHS (http://www.mhs.com)
   o Administration and scoring software available

> Symptom Checklist—90—Revised (SCL–90–R)
- Ages 13 years and older
- Client self-report, paper-and-pencil measure
- Nine primary symptom dimensions (Somatization, Obsessive Compulsive, Interpersonal Sensitivity, Depression, Anxiety, Hostility, Phobic Anxiety, Paranoid Ideation, Psychoticism), Global Severity Index scores, Positive Symptom Distress Index score, Positive Symptom Total
- Uses normalized T scores
- Available from PsychCorp (http://www.psychcorp.com)
   o Audio compact disc or computer administration available
   o Scoring and report mail-in service and software available
   o Spanish form

Attention-Deficit Disorder and Attention-Deficit/Hyperactivity Disorder Screening Measures

> ADHD Symptom Checklist—4 (ADHD–SC4)
- Ages 3–18 years
- Parent and teacher report, paper-and-pencil checklist
- Measures symptoms of attention-deficit/hyperactivity disorder (ADHD), Peer Conflict Scale, Stimulant Side Effects Checklist

- Available from Western Psychological Services (http://www.wpspublish.com)

> Attention-Deficit/Hyperactivity Disorder Test (ADHDT)
  - Ages 3–23 years
  - Parent or teacher completed, paper-and-pencil rating scale
  - Three subtests (Hyperactivity, Impulsivity, Inattention)
  - Uses percentiles and standard scores, full scale percentile and ADHD quotient
  - Available from PRO-ED Inc. (http://www.proedinc.com), Western Psychological Services (http://www.wpspublish.com)

> Conners' Adult ADHD Rating Scales Screening Versions (CAARS–S:SV, CAARS–O:SV)
  - Ages 18 years and older
  - Client self-report and other report
  - *DSM–IV–TR* ADHD symptom subscales (Inattention/Memory Problems, Hyperactivity/Restlessness, Impulsivity/Emotional Lability, Problems With Self-Control), ADHD Index
  - Available from MHS (http://www.mhs.com)
    - Administration and scoring online service and software
  - Available from PAR (http://www4.parinc.com)

Anger Screening Measures

> Beck Anger Inventory for Youth (BANI–Y)
  - Ages 7–18 years
  - Client self-report, paper-and-pencil administration
  - Measures anger affect and cognitions associated with anger as well as common comorbid symptoms such as depression
  - Uses T scores ($M = 50$, $SD = 10$)
  - Available from PsychCorp (http://www.psychcorp.com)

Anxiety Screening Measures

> Adult Manifest Anxiety Scale (AMAS)
  - Ages 19–59 years (AMAS–A), 60 years and older (AMAS–E), students enrolled in college (AMAS–C)

- Three separate client self-report measures, paper-and-pencil administration
- Four subscales for AMAS–A: Worry/Oversensitivity, Social, Concerns/Stress, Physiological Anxiety; total score; uses normalized T scores
- Four subscales for AMAS–E: Worry/Oversensitivity, Social, Concerns/Stress, Fear of Aging; total score; uses normalized T scores
- Five subscales of AMAS–C: Worry/Oversensitivity, Social, Concerns/Stress, Physiological Anxiety, Test Anxiety; total score; uses normalized T scores
- Available from Western Psychological Services (http://www.wpspublish.com)

➢ Beck Anxiety Inventory (BAI)
  - Ages 17–80 years
  - Client self-report, paper-and-pencil administration
  - Four factor scores (Subjective, Neurophysiological, Panic, Autonomic), Total Anxiety score ranging from 0 to 63
  - Uses T scores
  - Available from PsychCorp (http://www.psychcorp.com)
    ○ Computer administration available
    ○ Administration, scoring, and report software available
    ○ Spanish print form

➢ Beck Anxiety Inventory for Youth (BAI–Y)
  - Ages 7–18 years
  - Client self-report, paper-and-pencil administration
  - Measures anxious cognitions and feelings, somatic or vegetative symptoms, social anxiety symptoms, specific fears, and concerns about physical or psychological integrity
  - Uses T scores
  - Available from PsychCorp (http://www.psychcorp.com)

➢ Revised Children's Manifest Anxiety Scale: Second Edition (RCMAS–2)
  - Ages 6–19 years
  - Client self-report, paper-and-pencil administration
  - Two validity scales, three clinical scales (Physiological Anxiety, Worry, Social Anxiety), Total Anxiety score

- Available from PRO-ED Inc. (http://www.proedinc.com)
- Also available from Western Psychological Services (http://www.wpspublish.com)
  - Audio compact disc administration
  - Ten-item short form also available

Bipolar Disorder Screening Measures

> Pediatric Behavior Rating Scale (PBRS)
  - Ages 3–18 years
  - Parent- and teacher-report rating scales
  - Assists in identification of severe emotional disturbance, specifically early onset bipolar disorder, validity (Inconsistency) scale, score summaries, critical items
  - Uses T scores and percentiles
  - Available from PAR (http://www4.parinc.com)
    - Scoring and report program (Pediatric Behavior Rating Scale Scoring Program) available

Conduct Disorder Screening Measures

> Beck Disruptive Behavior Inventory for Youth (BDBI–Y)
  - Ages 7–18
  - Client self-report, paper-and-pencil administration
  - Assesses conduct disorder and oppositional defiant symptoms (aggression toward people or animals, destruction of property, deceitfulness and theft, serious rule infractions, arguing and defiance with adults, deliberate annoyance, blaming others, and feeling annoyed by or vindictive toward others)
  - Uses T scores ($M = 50$, $SD = 10$)
  - Available from PsychCorp (http://www.psychcorp.com)
> Conduct Disorder Scale (CDS)
  - Ages 5–22 years
  - Parent, sibling, teacher, or other report; paper-and-pencil administration
  - Four subscales (Aggressive Conduct, Nonaggressive Conduct, Deceitfulness and Theft, Rule Violations), uses standard scores
  - Available from PRO-ED Inc. (http://www.proedinc.com)

Depression and Suicidal Ideation Screening Measures

> Beck Depression Inventory—II (BDI–II)
>   - Ages 13–80 years
>   - Client self-report, paper-and-pencil administration
>   - Measures somatic, cognitive, and affective symptoms of depression, Total Depression score ranging from 0 to 63
>   - Uses T scores
>   - Available from PsychCorp (http://www.psychcorp.com)
>   o Administration, scoring, and report software available
>   o Spanish print form
> Beck Depression Inventory for Youth (BDI–Y)
>   - Ages 7–18 years
>   - Client self-report, paper-and-pencil administration
>   - Measures symptoms of depression related to negative thoughts about self, life, and the future; feelings of sadness and guilt; and vegetative and somatic problems
>   - Uses T scores
>   - Available from PsychCorp (http://www.psychcorp.com)
> Children's Depression Inventory (CDI)
>   - Ages 7–17 years
>   - Client self-report, paper-and-pencil administration
>   - Five factor scores (Negative Mood, Interpersonal Problems, Ineffectiveness, Anhedonia, Negative Self-Esteem), total score
>   - Available from PsychCorp (http://www.psychcorp.com)
>   - Available from Western Psychological Services (http://www.wpspublish.com)
>   o Also offers 10-item short form
>   o Offers 17-item parent-report and 12-item teacher-report forms that yield a total score and two subscale scores (Emotional Problems and Functional Problems)
>   - Available from MHS (http://www.mhs.com)
>   o Administration, scoring, and report online services and software
> Postpartum Depression Screening Scale (PDSS)
>   - New mother of any age
>   - Client self-report, paper-and-pencil administration
>   - Overall severity score falling into one of three areas (normal adjustment, significant symptoms of postpartum

depression, positive screen for major postpartum depression); scores in seven symptoms areas (Sleeping/Eating Disturbances, Anxiety/Insecurity, Emotional Lability, Mental Confusion, Loss of Self, Guilt/Shame, Suicidal Thoughts)
- Available from Western Psychological Services (http://www.wpspublish.com)
  - Spanish form
> Reynolds Child Depression Scale, Second Edition (RCDS–2)
- Ages 7–13 years
- Client self-report, paper-and-pencil administration
- Total score for depression symptoms
- Uses T scores and percentile ranges for the total standardization sample by gender, by grade, and by gender for each grade; highlights critical items
> Reynolds Adolescent Depression Scale, Second Edition (RADS–2)
- Ages 11–20 years
- Client self-report, paper-and-pencil administration
- Four subscale scores (Dysphoric Mood, Anhedonia/Negative Affect, Negative Self-Evaluation, Somatic Complaints), Depression total score
- Uses T scores and clinical cutoff scores
- Available from PAR (http://www4.parinc.com)
  - Also offers 10-item short form
> Reynolds Depression Screening Inventory (RDSI)
- Ages 18–89 years
- Client self-report, paper-and-pencil administration
- Assesses *DSM–IV–TR* symptom criteria for Major Depressive Disorder, using empirically derived cutoff scores to identify those at risk for more serious diagnoses of depression
- Available from PAR (http://www4.parinc.com)

Developmental Delays and Disorders Screening Measures

> Bayley—III Screening Test
- Ages 1–42 months
- Clinician administered, paper-and-pencil administration

- Provides cutoff scores by age for cognitive, language, and motor skills
- Available from PsychCorp (http://www.psychcorp.com)
> Brief Infant–Toddler Social and Emotional Assessment (BITSEA)
  - Ages 12–35 months
  - Parent and child-care provider report, paper-and-pencil administration
  - Consists of most discriminating ITSEA items (see Chapter 5, this resource) to detect social and emotional problems
  - Available from PsychCorp (http://www.psychcorp.com)
    - Spanish form
> Pervasive Developmental Disorders Screening Test—II (PDDST–II)
  - Ages 1–4 years
  - Parent or caregiver report, paper-and-pencil administration
  - Helps differentiate children with autism spectrum disorder, pervasive developmental delay, or Asperger's disorder from those with other developmental problems
  - Available from PsychCorp (http://www.psychcorp.com)
    - Three response forms, each designed for a specific clinical setting (Primary Care Screener, Developmental Clinic Screener, Autism Clinic Severity Screener)
    - Spanish form

Eating Disorders Screening Measures

> Eating Inventory (EI)
  - Ages 17 years and older
  - Client self-report, paper-and-pencil administration
  - Three dimensions of eating behavior (Cognitive Restraint of Eating, Disinhibition, Hunger)
  - Uses mean and standard deviations of each dimension for normal and obese groups
  - Available from PsychCorp (http://www.psychcorp.com)

Posttraumatic Stress Disorder and Trauma Symptom Screening Measures

> Davidson Trauma Scale (DTS)
  - Ages 18 years and older
  - Client self-report, paper-and-pencil administration
  - Assesses *DSM–IV–TR* criteria for PTSD in three key areas (Intrusion, Avoidance/Numbing, Hyperarousal)
  - Available from MHS (http://www.mhs.com)
> Posttraumatic Stress Diagnostic Scale (PDS)
  - Ages 18–65 years
  - Client self-report, paper-and-pencil administration
  - Assesses *DSM–IV–TR* PTSD diagnostic criteria, Symptom Severity score, Symptom Severity rating, Level of Impairment of Functioning
  - Available from PsychCorp (http://www.psychcorp.com)
    ○ Administration, scoring, and report software available

Substance Abuse Screening Measures

> Adolescent Substance Abuse Subtle Screening Inventory—A2 (SASSI–A2)
  - Ages 12–18 years
  - Client self-report, paper and pencil administration
  - Five scales (Validity Check, Family and Friends Risk scale, Attitudes Toward Substance Use, Symptoms of Substance Misuse, Secondary Classification scale)
  - Available from MHS (http://www.mhs.com)
    ○ Administration, scoring, and report software available
  - Available from PAR (http://www4.parinc.com)
> Personal Experience Screening Questionnaire (PESQ)
  - Ages 12–18 years
  - Client self-report, paper-and-pencil administration
  - Three sections (Problem Severity, Psychosocial Items, Drug Use History), using cutoff scores to indicate need for more comprehensive chemical dependency evaluation
  - Available from Western Psychological Services (http://www.wpspublish.com)

> Personal Experience Screening Questionnaire for Adults (PESQ–A)
>   - Ages 19 years and older
>   - Client self-report, paper-and-pencil administration
>   - Three sections (Problem Severity, Defensiveness and Psychosocial Indicators, Recent Drug Use)
>   - Available from Western Psychological Services (http://www.wpspublish.com)
> Substance Abuse Subtle Screening Inventory (SASSI–3)
>   - Ages 18 years and older
>   - Client self-report, paper-and-pencil administration
>   - Subscales provide information regarding attitude toward assessment, defensiveness, emotional pain, ability to acknowledge problems, and risk of legal problems
>   - Available from MHS (http://www.mhs.com)
>   o Administration, scoring, and report software available
>   - Available from PAR (http://www4.parinc.com)
>   o Spanish form

Traumatic Events Screening Measures

> Childhood Trauma Questionnaire: A Retrospective Self-Report
>   - Ages 12 and older
>   - Client self-report, paper-and-pencil administration
>   - Designed to detect likely cases of child physical, sexual, and emotional abuse and neglect
>   - Available from PsychCorp (http://www.psychcorp.com)
> Traumatic Life Events Questionnaire (TLEQ)
>   - Ages 18 years and older
>   - Client self-report, paper-and-pencil administration
>   - Assesses current and prior exposure to 21 types of potentially traumatic events
>   - Available from Western Psychological Services (http://www.wpspublish.com)

Axis II Personality Disorders Screening Measures

> Axis II Personality Checklist (A–II)
>   - Older teens and adults
>   - Client self-report, paper-and-pencil checklist

- Items are transferred to an interview guide that contains critical items, a consistency check, and groupings of items that correspond to criteria for *DSM–IV–TR* personality disorders.
- Available from Western Psychological Services (http://www.wpspublish.com)

> Hare Psychopathy Checklist: Screening Version (PCL:SV)
- Ages 18 years and older
- Clinician-rated checklist based on 45-min structured interview and collateral review
- Normed for forensic nonpsychiatric, forensic psychiatric, civil psychiatric, noncriminal nonpsychiatric populations
- Available from PsychCorp (http://www.psychcorp.com)

> International Personality Disorder Examination (IPDE) Screening Questionnaire
- Ages 18 years and older
- Client self-report, paper-and-pencil administration
- Evaluates presence of criteria for *DSM–IV–TR* personality disorders
- Available from PAR (http://www4.parinc.com)

> Inventory of Altered Self-Capacities (IASC)
- Ages 18 years and older
- Client self-report, paper-and-pencil administration
- Seven scales reflecting difficulties in relatedness, identity, and affect control
- Available from PAR (http://www4.parinc.com)

Reference

American Psychiatric Association. (2000). *Diagnostic and statistical manual of mental disorders* (4th ed., text revision). Washington, DC: Author.

CHAPTER 3

Structured and Semistructured Interviews

Structured and semistructured interviews were developed to address the lack of uniformity and standardization in traditional clinical intake interviews and the resulting lack of precision in the evaluation of the nature and extent of clients' psychological symptoms. The primary advantages of structured and semistructured interviews are the increased reliability and validity of the diagnoses given to clients. There are disadvantages, however. Because such interviews are often highly detailed, information centered (as opposed to client centered), and directive, they can interfere with the building of initial rapport with the client. In addition, the interviews usually take a significant amount of time to administer. In clinical settings, therefore, it is suggested that structured or semistructured interviews (or sections of interviews) be used to augment and clarify information gained from the initial clinical interview and initial screening or full assessment measures to ensure the clinician's careful consideration of all criteria necessary for specific diagnoses. Several structured and semistructured interviews for *Diagnostic and Statistical Manual of Mental Disorders* (4th ed., text revision; *DSM–IV–TR*; American Psychiatric Association, 2000) Axis I and Axis II diagnoses are described in the sections that follow. For the most part, the interviews were chosen for this list on the basis of a review of published measures to ensure some professional oversight and standardization as well as reasonable availability.

Multiple Axis I Symptom and Disorder Interviews

> Diagnostic Interview for Children and Adolescents—IV (DICA–IV)
> - Ages 6–17 years
> - Software based self- and parent-report structured interview to assess a broad spectrum of *DSM–IV–TR* disorders
> - Available from MHS (http://www.mhs.com)
> Structured Clinical Interview for *DSM–IV* Axis I Disorders: Clinician Version (SCID–I:CV)
> - Ages 18 years and older
> - Structured interview format that includes full diagnostic criteria and corresponding interview questions for major Axis I diagnoses
> - Available from MHS (http://www.mhs.com)

Attention-Deficit Disorder and Attention-Deficit/Hyperactivity Disorder Interviews

> Conners' Adult ADHD Diagnostic Interview for *DSM–IV* (CAADID)
> - Ages 18 years and older
> - Structured interview designed to assist in *DSM–IV* diagnosis of adult ADHD
> - Available from MHS (http://www.mhs.com)

Developmental Disorder Interviews

> Autism Diagnostic Interview—Revised (ADI–R)
> - Mental age > 2 years
> - Structured interview of parent or caregiver of client to assess autism and other autism spectrum disorders, focusing on three domains: Language/Communication; Reciprocal Social Interactions; Restricted, Repetitive, and Stereotyped Behaviors and Interests
> - Available from Psychological Assessment Resources (PAR; http://www4.parinc.com), MHS (http://www.mhs.com)

- Available from Western Psychological Services (http://www.wpspublish.com)
  - Scoring software available
  - Spanish form

Dissociative Disorder Interviews

> Structured Clinical Interview for *DSM–IV* Dissociative Disorders—Revised (SCID–D)
  - Adult
  - Structured interview format to assist in diagnosis of several *DSM–IV* dissociative disorders and acute stress disorder
  - Available from MHS (http://www.mhs.com)

Posttraumatic Stress Disorder Interviews

> Clinician-Administered PTSD Scale for Children and Adolescents (CAPS–CA)
  - Ages 8–15 years
  - Clinician-conducted interview (36 questions) designed to detect the presence and severity of 17 posttraumatic stress disorder (PTSD) symptoms
  - Available from Western Psychological Services (http://www.wpspublish.com)
> Clinician-Administered PTSD Scale (CAPS)
  - Ages 16 years and older
  - Clinician-conducted interview (30 questions) designed to detect the presence and severity of current or lifetime PTSD symptoms
  - Available from Western Psychological Services (http://www.wpspublish.com)

Axis II Personality Disorder Interviews

> Hare Psychopathy Checklist—Revised Second Edition (PCL–R, 2nd Ed.)
  - Ages 18 years and older
  - Clinician-rated form based on structured interview and collateral review designed to detect psychopathic personality disorders in adult forensic populations

- Available from MHS (http://www.mhs.com)
  - Scoring and profile report software available
- Available from PsychCorp (http://www.psychcorp.com)
> Hare Psychopathy Checklist: Youth Version (PCL:YV)
  - Ages 12–18 years
  - Clinician-rated structured interview and collateral review designed to detect potential patterns of anti-social traits and acts in adolescents
  - Available from MHS (https://www.mhs.com)
> International Personality Disorder Examination (IPDE) Semistructured Interview
  - Ages 18 years and older
  - Semistructured interview that assigns a definite, probable, or negative diagnosis for each of the 11 *DSM–IV–TR* personality disorders
  - Available from PAR (http://www4.parinc.com)
> Structured Clinical Interview for *DSM–IV* Axis II Disorders: Clinician Version (SCID–II:CV)
  - Ages 18 years and older
  - Structured interview format that includes full diagnostic criteria and corresponding interview questions for Axis II personality disorders
  - Available from MHS (http://www.mhs.com)

Reference

American Psychiatric Association. (2000). *Diagnostic and statistical manual of mental disorders* (4th ed., text revision). Washington, DC: Author.

CHAPTER 4

Mental Status Examination

The mental status examination (MSE) provides a structured summary of the interviewer's observations and impressions of the client's psychological status at the time of the initial clinical assessment interview. The interviewer's observations and impressions serve as foundational information from which diagnostic hypotheses may be derived and considered. The MSE also may identify risk factors for self-harm or other harm. Finally, the findings of the initial MSE can serve as a baseline against which future assessments of the client's psychological status may be compared.

The MSE has its historical roots in psychiatry and remains one of the core "domains of clinical evaluation" of adult patients according to American Psychiatric Association guidelines (American Psychiatric Association, 2006). However, the MSE has been adapted for the assessment of children and adolescents (e.g., Goodman & Sours, 1998), and mental health professionals from other disciplines use the MSE as an essential tool for their assessments; its use is particularly common in medical or psychiatric settings. The comprehensive MSE is used to evaluate various domains of the client's functioning, including appearance, behavior, cognition, speech, mood, affect, thought process, thought content, perceptions, insight, and judgment. As noted previously, the MSE is more comprehensive than the Mini-Mental State Examination (Folstein, Folstein, & McHugh, 1975; now available in a revised version, the Mini-Mental Status Examination—2), which is a screening measure for cognitive impairment.

Information for completion of the MSE is gathered by the professional throughout the assessment interview(s). The data typically are divided into the domain areas noted previously (or similar areas) when the clinician integrates the information and documents the MSE in the client's chart. Two guides for the documentation of the MSE are presented in the sections that follow—one for a child MSE and one for an adult and elderly client MSE (with notes for use with an elderly client). It is important to note that the topic areas of the MSE contain behavioral elements that are not mutually exclusive; some behaviors observed may provide information for more than one topic area of the MSE. As such, these guides are not intended to be used as a sequential checklist of information to be gathered during the interaction with the client. References are provided for those interested in further discussions of the domains and documentation of the MSE (Goodman & Sours, 1998; Robinson, 2008; Trzepacz & Baker, 1993; Zuckerman, 2005, 2008).

Clinicians are cautioned to carefully consider use of the MSE with culturally diverse clients. Evaluations of the meaning of the clinician's observations are dependent on the cultural norms on which the observations are based (Paniagua, 2001). Sommers-Flanagan and Sommers-Flanagan (2009) presented a very helpful table of examples of observations that may lead an interviewer from one culture to an invalid conclusion regarding a client from a different culture.

Child Mental Status Examination Guide

The child MSE is grounded in the developmental meaning of the child's appearance, cognitions, emotions, and behavior, that is, whether a specific presentation is age appropriate. It is not unusual for a child to evidence several different maturational levels during the time span of one assessment interview. Therefore, the therapist should be familiar with developmental norms for various attributes and behaviors to make accurate assessments.

Data for the MSE of children often come more from the clinician's observation of the client's nonverbal behavior than verbal productions. Some young clients lack the cognitive and verbal skills to communicate their psychological concerns; some are reticent or unwilling to talk. As such, the interviewer should incorporate opportunities for the child to engage in free play activities during the interview. How the child plays provides a wealth of information about each of the MSE categories in the outline that follows.

➢ General appearance
  ▪ Age: appears stated age, appears younger, appears older
  ▪ Height: within normal limits (WNL), taller than expected for age or gender, shorter than expected for age or gender
  ▪ Weight: WNL; overweight, underweight
  ▪ Racial or ethnic origin
    ○ White, non-Hispanic; Hispanic; African American; Asian; Native American
    ○ Is appearance consistent with reported racial or ethnic origin?
  ▪ Body part anomalies: WNL, head anomaly, facial anomaly, other anomaly
  ▪ Bruising
    ○ Absent or present
      ◆ If present, description and location
      ◆ If present, intentionally self-inflicted?
      ◆ If present, intentionally other inflicted?
  ▪ Wounds, scars, other body markings (e.g., piercings, tattoos)
    ○ Absent or present
      ◆ If present, description and location
      ◆ If wounds or scars present, intentionally self-inflicted?
      ◆ If wounds or scars present, intentionally other inflicted?
  ▪ Grooming and clothing
    ○ Quality: well groomed, fair grooming, poor grooming
    ○ Cleanliness of clothing
    ○ Age appropriateness of clothing
    ○ Weather appropriateness of clothing
    ○ Notes regarding gender identity reflected in clothing

- ➢ Behavior
  - ▪ Engagement in interview: WNL, quickly engaged, slow to warm up, never engaged
    - ○ Notes regarding temperament type
    - ○ Notes regarding social maturity
  - ▪ Activity level: WNL, hyperactive with trigger, hyperactive overall, hypoactive
  - ▪ Coordination: WNL, unusual gait, balance problem, fine motor problem
  - ▪ Unusual behaviors or mannerisms
    - ○ Absent or present
    - ○ If present, describe (e.g., biting nails or lip, tic, compulsion, sexualized behavior, spinning, hand flapping, rocking, hair pulling, holding breath)
  - ▪ Relational behavior
    - ○ Ease of separation from caretaker: WNL, some anxiety, significant anxiety, could not separate, complete absence of anxiety with separation
    - ○ Relating to interviewer: WNL, poor eye contact, consistently distant or reticent, uncomfortable with physical proximity, unusually rapid connection, sought physical proximity
    - ○ Tone of relating: cooperative vs. oppositional or testing limits, serious vs. playful, confident vs. withdrawn or shy, involved vs. aloof, pleasant vs. provocative or hostile, compliant vs. controlling, solicitous vs. demanding
  - ▪ Behavior characteristics
    - ○ Self-direction
    - ○ Goal setting
    - ○ Goal persistence (without perseveration)
    - ○ Frustration tolerance
    - ○ Creativity
    - ○ Organization skills
- ➢ Cognition
  - ▪ Alertness: WNL, hyperalert, hypoalert, confused, other
  - ▪ Attention: WNL, unusually intense focus, limited span in free play but can focus, limited span overall, markedly impaired ability to focus
  - ▪ Fund of knowledge: WNL, exceptional, deficient

➢ Speech
  ▪ Receptive capacities: WNL, hearing difficulty, comprehension difficulty
  ▪ Expressive capacities
    ○ Quantity: WNL, restricted quantity, used gestures instead of speech
    ○ Quality: WNL, articulation problem, pitch problem, volume problem, rhythm problem, immature syntax, immature concept formation, unusual words or phrases
➢ Emotional responses
  ▪ Quality: flat, happy, silly, sad, fearful, anxious, angry, hostile, aggressive, irritable, crying, frustrated
  ▪ Mode of expression: verbal, behavioral
  ▪ Range of expression: constricted, variable or normal, labile
  ▪ Appropriateness
  ▪ Recovery capacity: WNL, mature, impaired
➢ Thoughts and perceptions
  ▪ Note: Children can express seemingly bizarre thought content or perceptions and exhibit unusual thought processes for a variety of reasons beyond reflecting a psychiatric disorder (e.g., to provoke or distance the interviewer). The interviewer must be able to determine whether the child is able to differentiate between primary- and secondary-process thinking.
  ▪ Thought content
    ○ Fantasies
      ◆ Note bizarre content
      ◆ Note affective quality
    ○ Preoccupations or concerns
    ○ Nonsuicidal self-injury thoughts
      ◆ None elicited
      ◆ If elicited, note current or past
      ◆ If elicited, conduct full assessment (see Chapter 6, this resource)
    ○ Suicidal thoughts
      ◆ None elicited
      ◆ If elicited, note current or past
      ◆ If elicited, conduct full assessment (see Chapter 6, this resource)

- Thoughts of harming others
  - None elicited
  - If elicited, note current or past
  - If elicited, conduct full assessment (see Chapter 6, this resource)
- Hopes and desires
  - Thought process: WNL, concrete, abstract capacity
  - Note unusual perseveration
- Perceptions
  - Self-perception (e.g., body image)
  - Perception of others (e.g., suspiciousness)
  - Hallucinations (auditory, visual, olfactory, gustatory, tactile, somatic)

Adult and Elderly Client Mental Status Examination Guide

- General appearance
  - Age: appears stated age, appears younger, appears older
  - Height: WNL, taller than expected for age or gender, shorter than expected for age or gender
  - Weight: WNL, overweight, underweight
  - Racial or ethnic origin
    - White, non-Hispanic; Hispanic; African American; Asian; Native American
    - Is appearance consistent with reported racial or ethnic origin?
  - Body part anomalies: WNL, head anomaly, facial anomaly, other anomaly
  - Bruising
    - Absent or present
      - If present, description and location
      - If present, intentionally self-inflicted?
      - If present, intentionally other inflicted?
  - Wounds, scars, other body markings (e.g., piercings, tattoos)
    - Absent or present
      - If present, description and location
      - If wounds or scars present, intentionally self-inflicted?

- ◆ If wounds or scars present, intentionally other inflicted?
  - ■ Grooming and clothing
    - ○ Quality (e.g., well groomed, fair grooming, poor grooming)
    - ○ Cleanliness
    - ○ Age appropriateness
    - ○ Weather appropriateness
    - ○ Situation appropriateness
    - ○ Does client need assistance with grooming or clothing?

➢ Behavior
- ■ Posture: slumped, rigid, relaxed
- ■ Coordination: WNL, unusual gait, balance problem, fine motor problem
  - ○ Is assistance needed with moving (e.g., walker, wheelchair, aide)?
- ■ Unusual behaviors or mannerisms
  - ○ Absent or present
  - ○ If present, describe (e.g., restlessness, fidgeting, constricted body movements)
- ■ Relational behavior with the interviewer
  - ○ WNL, poor eye contact, consistently distant or reticent, uncomfortable with physical proximity, intense eye contact, unusually rapid connection, sought physical proximity
  - ○ Tone of relating (e.g., cooperative vs. oppositional, open vs. guarded, serious vs. light-hearted, confident vs. shy, involved vs. aloof, pleasant vs. provocative or hostile, compliant vs. controlling)
  - ○ Attitude (e.g., cooperative, open, guarded, resistant, hostile, controlling)

➢ Cognition
- ■ Alertness: WNL, hyperalert, hypoalert, confused, other
- ■ Orientation
  - ○ Person: WNL, impaired
  - ○ Place: WNL, impaired
  - ○ Time: WNL, impaired
  - ○ Purpose: WNL, impaired

- Attention and concentration: WNL, impaired
- Short-term memory: WNL, impaired
- General fund of knowledge: WNL, impaired
- Abstract thinking ability: WNL, impaired
- Problem-solving ability: WNL, impaired
- Is a screening for possible dementia indicated (e.g., with impaired memory or executive functioning)?
  - (See descriptions of measures in Chapter 2, this resource; e.g., the Mini-Mental State Examination—2, the Frontal Systems Behavior Scale)
- ➢ Speech
  - Receptive capacities: WNL, hearing difficulty, comprehension difficulty
  - Expressive capacities
    - Quantity: WNL, restricted quantity (e.g., mute or impoverished), excessive quantity
    - Quality: WNL, volume problem, rate problem (e.g., pressured speech), rhythm problem, tone problem, spontaneity problem, fluency problem, clarity problem
- ➢ Mood
  - Quality of pervasive, sustained internal emotional state (e.g., depression, hopelessness, anhedonia, dysphoria, irritability, euthymia, elevated mood, euphoria, mood swings, alexithymia)
- ➢ Affect
  - Quality of client's external expression of present emotional state (e.g., flat, pleasant, smiling, laughing, serious, tearful, fearful, tense, angry)
  - Range (e.g., constricted, variable or normal, labile)
  - Appropriateness
  - Recovery capacity: WNL, impaired
- ➢ Thought
  - Thought content
    - Delusions
      - ◆ Type: persecutory, grandiose, jealous, erotomanic, somatic, delusion of reference, delusion of control
      - ◆ Quality: systematized, unsystematized, mood congruent, mood incongruent

- Preoccupations
  - Type: hypochondria, obsession, compulsion, phobia
- Nonsuicidal self-injury thoughts
  - If elicited, note current or past
  - If elicited, conduct full assessment (see Chapter 6, this resource)
- Suicidal thoughts
  - If elicited, note current or past
  - If elicited, conduct full assessment (see Chapter 6, this resource)
- Thoughts of harming others
  - If elicited, note current or past
  - If elicited, conduct full assessment (see Chapter 6, this resource)
- Thought process
  - Quality: linear, goal-directed, logical, incoherent, tangential, circumstantial
  - Unusual features: perseveration, loose associations, flight of ideas, blocking
- Perceptions
  - Illusions
  - Hallucinations (auditory, visual, olfactory, gustatory, tactile, somatic, mood congruent, mood incongruent)
  - Depersonalization (client feels unreal)
  - Derealization (client feels external world is unreal)
- Insight
  - Regarding nature of symptoms: WNL, impaired
  - Regarding cause of symptoms: WNL, impaired
  - Regarding whether symptoms can be treated: WNL, impaired
- Judgment
  - Current: WNL, impaired
  - Past: WNL, impaired

References

American Psychiatric Association. (2006). Psychiatric evaluation of adults: III. Domains of the clinical evaluation. In *American Psychiatric Association practice guidelines for the treatment of psychiatric disorders: Compendium 2006* (2nd ed.). Retrieved from http://www.psychiatryonline.com/content.aspx?aID=137270

Folstein, M. F., Folstein, S., & McHugh, P. R. (1975). Mini-mental state: A practical method for grading the cognitive state of patients for the clinician. *Journal of Psychiatric Research, 12,* 189–198.

Goodman, J. D., & Sours, J. A. (1998). *The child mental status examination: Expanded edition.* Lanham, MD: Rowman & Littlefield.

Paniagua, F. A. (2001). *Diagnosis in a multicultural context.* Thousand Oaks, CA: Sage.

Robinson, D. J. (2008). *The mental status exam explained* (2nd ed.). Port Huron, MI: Rapid Psychler Press.

Sommers-Flanagan, R., & Sommers-Flanagan, J. (2009). *Clinical interviewing* (4th ed.). New York, NY: Wiley.

Trzepacz, P. T., & Baker, R. W. (1993). *The psychiatric mental status examination.* New York, NY: Oxford University Press.

Zuckerman, E. L. (2005). *Clinician's thesaurus, 6th ed: The guide to conducting interviews and writing psychological reports (The clinician's toolbox).* New York, NY: Guilford Press.

Zuckerman, E. L. (2008). *The paper office: Forms, guidelines, and resources to make your practice work ethically, legally, and profitably* (4th ed.). New York, NY: Guilford Press.

CHAPTER 5

Psychological Assessment Measures

An accurate understanding of the assets and impairments in a client's psychological functioning is best derived from several sources of information, including clinical and structured interviews with the client and with others familiar with the client as well as psychological assessment measures. Assessment measures are numerous. Some are comprehensive and evaluate a full spectrum of psychological functioning, and some are disorder or problem specific. Some are clinician administered, and some are client self-report or significant other report. Some have computer administration and/or interpretation programs. Many are standardized, published, and available for commercial purchase, often from more than one publisher. But many are not commercially published. Unpublished measures and relevant information about them usually may be secured directly from the individuals who created them.

The clinician should consider carefully the selection of any psychological measure to assess a client. First, the test should be relevant to the client's presenting problems and the clinician's diagnostic process. It should be valid and reliable and provide the clinician with norms that are developmentally, culturally, and gender appropriate for the client. The format in which the test is presented must be aligned with the client's capabilities (i.e., presented in client's primary language and at an appropriate reading level). And the test should be as efficient as possible—providing the maximum amount of information for time and monetary expense. Additional resources are available to assist clinicians in finding and obtaining appropriate measures for the specific intended purposes of an assessment. For example, the American Psychological Association Science Directorate (2011) has offered guidance regarding a wide variety of published and unpublished psychological tests. The Buros Institute of Mental Measurements provides free information on nearly 4,000 commercially available tests as well as more than 2,000 test reviews that can be purchased and displayed online (available at http://www.unl.edu/buros/bimm/index.html). Maddox (2008) compiled short descriptions of over 2,000 published instruments in psychology, education, and business.

Several common assessment measures are presented in the sections that follow, with brief descriptions of the areas of psychological functioning evaluated; the age range for which the measure is intended; and the measure format, scoring information, and the publisher. Most of the measures chosen for this list are standardized and published. Some unstandardized measures are included because of their common use in assessment of specific issues. This is not intended to be an exhaustive list but to provide the clinician with a starting point in the assessment process.

Cognitive Functioning: Intelligence Measures

- Comprehensive Test of Nonverbal Intelligence, Second Edition (CTONI–2)
  - Ages 6–89 years
  - Clinician administered with stimulus booklet
  - Uses nonverbal formats
  - Provides measure of general intelligence in standard scores, percentile ranks, and age equivalents
  - Available from Psychological Assessment Resources (PAR; http://www4.parinc.com)
    - Examiner oral instructions are available for common languages other than English
- Kaufman Assessment Battery for Children, Second Edition (KABC–II)
  - Ages 3–18 years
  - Clinician administered with stimulus materials and manipulatives

- Minimizes verbal instructions and responses
- Nonverbal Composite Index, Mental Processing/Fluid-Crystallized Index, individual scale scores
- Conormed with Kaufman Test of Educational Achievement, Second Edition
- Available from PsychCorp (http://www.psychcorp.com)
  - ASSIST Scoring and Report Software
- Available from Western Psychological Services (http://www.wpspublish.com)

➢ Leiter International Performance Scale—Revised (Leiter–r)
- Ages 2–20 years, 11 months
- Clinician administered with stimulus books and manipulatives
- Provides a nonverbal measure of intelligence and cognitive abilities with composite IQ score, subtest scaled scores, and percentile and age equivalent scores
  - Two standardized batteries: Visualization and Reasoning (for measuring IQ) and Attention and Memory
- Available from PAR (http://www4.parinc.com)

➢ Reynolds Intellectual Assessment Scales (RIAS)
- Ages 3–94 years
- Clinician-administered with stimulus book
- Verbal Intelligence Index (VIX; two subtests), Nonverbal Intelligence Index (NIX; two subtests), Composite Intelligence Index (CIX; overall general intelligence [g])
- Composite Memory Index (CMX; two supplementary subtests measuring verbal and nonverbal short-term memory)
- Can compare with Wide Range Achievement Test 4 scores to derive discrepancy scores
- Available from PAR (http://www.parinc.com)
  - Scoring, feedback, and interpretive report software available; Discrepancy interpretive report software available
- Available from MHS (http://www.mhs.com); PRO-ED Inc. (http://www.proedinc.com); Western Psychological Services (http://www.wpspublish.com)

➢ Stanford–Binet Intelligence Scales—Fifth Edition (SB–5)
- Ages 2–85+ years

- Clinician administered with stimulus books and manipulatives
- Full-scale IQ ($M = 100$, $SD = 15$), Verbal IQ, Nonverbal IQ, Brief IQ, five factor scores (Fluid Reasoning, Knowledge, Quantitative, Visual–Spatial, Working Memory), subtest standard scores ($M = 10$, $SD = 3$)
- Available from Western Psychological Services (http://www.wpspublish.com)
  - Computer scoring compact disc (CD) available

➢ Universal Nonverbal Intelligence Test (UNIT)
- Ages 5–17 years, 11 months
- Clinician administered with stimulus books and manipulatives
- Uses only hand signals and manipulation of objects
- Full-scale IQ ($M = 100$, $SD = 15$); memory, reasoning, symbolic, and nonsymbolic quotients ($M = 100$, $SD = 15$); scaled subtest scores ($M = 10$, $SD = 3$)
- Available from MHS (http://www.mhs.com), PAR (http://www4.par.com)
  - UNIT Compuscore Software program
- Available from Riverside Publishing (http://www.riverpub.com), Western Psychological Services (http://www.wpspublish.com)

➢ Wechsler Adult Intelligence Scale, Fourth Edition (WAIS–IV)
- Ages 16–90 years, 11 months
- Clinician administered with stimulus books and manipulatives
- Full-scale IQ ($M = 100$, $SD = 15$), four index scores (Verbal Comprehension, Perceptual Reasoning, Working Memory, and Processing Speed), subtest scaled scores ($M = 10$, $SD = 3$)
- Available from PsychCorp (http://www.psychcorp.com)
  - Scoring Assistant software and Report Writer software available

➢ Wechsler Intelligence Scale for Children, Fourth Edition (WISC–IV)
- Ages 6–16, years, 11 months
- Clinician administered with stimulus books and manipulatives

- Full-scale IQ ($M = 100$, $SD = 15$), four index scores (Verbal Comprehension, Perceptual Reasoning, Working Memory, and Processing Speed), subtest scaled scores ($M = 10$, $SD = 3$)
- Available from PsychCorp (http://www.psychcorp.com)
  - Scoring Assistant software and Report Writer software available
  - Available in several languages other than English
➢ Wechsler Intelligence Scale for Children, Fourth Edition Integrated (WISC–IV Integrated)
  - Ages 6–16 years, 11 months
  - Clinician administered with stimulus books and manipulatives
  - Adds more than 25 additional process scores to WISC–IV to help identify strengths and weaknesses
  - Available from PsychCorp (http://www.psychcorp.com)
    - Scoring Assistant software and Report Writer software available
    - Spanish form
➢ Wechsler Nonverbal Scale of Ability (WNV)
  - Ages 4–21 years, 11 months
  - Clinician administered with pictorial directions and stimulus books and manipulatives
  - Four-subtest battery and two-subtest battery assessment of cognitive abilities
  - Full-scale score, norm-referenced composite score, and separate subtest scores
  - Available from PsychCorp (http://www.psychcorp.com)
    - Scoring Assistant software available
➢ Wechsler Preschool and Primary Scale of Intelligence, Third Edition (WPPSI–III)
  - Ages 2 years, 6 months–7 years, 3 months
  - Clinician administered with stimulus books and manipulatives
  - Full-scale IQ ($M = 100$, $SD = 15$), Verbal IQ, Performance IQ, Processing Speed Quotient
  - Available from PsychCorp (http://www.psychcorp.com)
    - Scoring Assistant software and Report Writer software available
    - Available in several languages other than English

Cognitive Functioning: Neuropsychological Measures

- ➤ Halstead–Reitan Battery
  - ■ Ages 15 years and older
  - ■ Highly trained clinician- or technician-administered comprehensive assessment of brain-behavior functioning
  - ■ Eight main battery tests: The Category Test, Speech-Sounds Perception, Seashore Rhythm, Tactual Performance Tests, Finger Oscillation, Trail Making A & B, Aphasia Screening, and Sensory-Perceptual Examination
  - ■ Interpretation of results is based on battery test performance and performance on other measures, history, and behavioral observations
  - ■ Available from http://www.reitanlabs.com
- ➤ Luria–Nebraska Neuropsychological Battery (LNNB)
  - ■ Ages 15 years and older
  - ■ Clinician administered with stimulus books and manipulatives
  - ■ Two equivalent test forms (Form I and Form II)
  - ■ Twelve clinical scales (Motor Functions, Rhythm, Tactile Functions, Visual Functions, Receptive Speech, Expressive Speech, Writing, Reading, Arithmetic, Memory, Intellectual Processes, Intermediate memory [on Form II only]), eight localization scales, five summary scales (Pathognomonic, Left Hemisphere, Right Hemisphere, Profile Elevation, Impairment), 28 factor scales
  - ■ Available from Western Psychological Services (http://www.wpspublish.com)
- ➤ Luria–Nebraska Neuropsychological Battery Children's Revision (LNNB–C)
  - ■ Ages 8–12 years
  - ■ Clinician administered with stimulus books and manipulatives
  - ■ Eleven clinical scales (Motor Functioning, Rhythm, Tactile Functions, Visual Functions, Receptive Speech, Expressive Speech, Writing, Reading, Arithmetic,

Memory, Intellectual Processes), three summary scales (Pathognomonic, Left Sensorimotor, Right Sensorimotor), 11 factor scales
- Available from Western Psychological Services (http://www.wpspublish.com)
> NEPSY, Second Edition (NEPSY–II)
  - Ages 3–16 years, 11 months
  - Clinician administered with stimulus cards and manipulatives
  - Thirty-two stand-alone subtests covering attention and executive functioning, language, memory and learning, sensorimotor functioning, visuospatial processing, and social perception
  - Uses scaled scores, process scores, combined scores, contrast scores, behavioral observations, and percentile rank categories
  - Available from PsychCorp (http://www.psychcorp.com)
    o Scoring Assistant software available
> Wechsler Memory Scale, Fourth Edition (WMS–IV)
  - Ages 16–90 years, 11 months
  - Clinician administered with stimulus books and manipulatives
  - Visual, auditory, immediate, delayed, and visual working memory indices
  - Conormed with WAIS–IV
  - Available from PsychCorp (http://www.psychcorp.com)
    o Scoring Assistant software and Report Writer software available
> Wisconsin Card Sorting Test (WCST)
  - Ages 6.5–89 years
  - Clinician-administered (with cards or on computer screen)
  - Assesses executive functioning (sensitive to frontal lobe impairment)
  - Uses raw scores, percentiles, T scores, and standard scores
  - Available from PAR (http://www4.parinc.com); Western Psychological Services (http://wpspublish.com)
    o Administration, scoring, and interpretive report software available

Achievement Measures

- ➢ Basic Achievement Skills Inventory Comprehensive Version (BASI Comprehensive Version)
  - Ages 8 years–adult
  - Clinician administered or computer administered
  - Six timed subtests (Vocabulary, Spelling, Language Mechanics, Reading Comprehension, Math Computation, Math Application)
  - Uses standard scores, percentile scores, growth scale value scores, equivalent scores, percentage correct, performance classification at the skill composite, subtest, and learning standard levels
  - Available from PsychCorp (http://www.psychcorp.com)
    - ○ Scoring and report software and mail-in services available
- ➢ Kaufman Test of Educational Achievement—Second Edition (KTEA–II) Comprehensive Form
  - Ages 4 years, 6 months–25 years
  - Clinician administered
  - Reading-related subtests, Reading Composite, Math Composite, Written Language Composite, Oral Language Composite, Comprehensive Achievement Composite
  - Uses standard scores ($M = 100$, $SD = 15$), equivalent scores, percentile ranks, normal curve equivalents, stanines, and growth scale value
  - Conormed with KABC–II
  - Available from PsychCorp (http://www.psychcorp.com)
    - ○ ASSIST Scoring and Report software available
- ➢ Weschler Individual Achievement Test—Third Edition (WIAT–III)
  - Ages 4–50 years, 11 months
  - Clinician administered
  - Sixteen subtests, seven composite scores depending on grade level (Oral Language, Total Reading, Basic Reading, Reading Comprehension and Fluency, Written Expression, Mathematics, Math Fluency)
  - Uses standard scores, equivalent scores, percentile ranks, stanines, normal curve equivalents, growth scores
  - Comparable with Wechsler Intelligence Tests

- Available from PsychCorp (http://www.psychcorp.com)
  - Scoring Assistant software—parent, clinician, and skill analysis reports available
- ➤ Wide Range Achievement Test—Fourth Edition (WRAT–4)
  - Ages 5–94 years
  - Clinician administered
  - Two alternate forms available
  - Four subtests (Sentence Comprehension, Word Reading, Spelling, Math Computation)
  - Subtest scores and Reading Composite score in standard scores, percentiles, stanines, normal curve equivalents, grade equivalents, Rasch ability scale scores
  - Available from MHS (http://www.mhs.com), Western Psychological Services (http://www.wpspublish.com)
    - Computer scoring CD available
  - Available from PAR (http://www4.parinc.com)
    - WRAT 4 Scoring Program available
    - WRAT 4 Interpretive Report available

Developmental Measures: General Motor, Behavioral, Emotional, Social

- ➤ Bayley Scales of Infant and Toddler Development, Third Edition (Bayley–III)
  - Ages 1–42 months
  - Clinician-administered
    - Administration software for personal digital assistant available
  - Five subtests (Cognitive, Social–Emotional, Motor, Adaptive Behavior, and Language)
  - Uses standard, age equivalents, percentiles with cutoff scores, and T scores
  - Available from PsychCorp (http://www.psychcorp.com)
    - Scoring Assistant software available
- ➤ Infant–Toddler Social and Emotional Assessment (ITSEA)
  - Ages 12–36 months
  - Parent and child care provider report
  - Four domains (Externalizing, Internalizing, Dysregulation, and Competence)
  - Uses T scores for four domains, 17 percentile ranking subscales, and three item cluster scores

- Available from PsychCorp (http://www.psychcorp.com)
  - Scoring Assistant software available
  - Spanish forms
- Roberts Apperception Test for Children: 2 (Roberts–2)
  - Ages 6–18 years
  - Clinician administered using set of 16 pictures
  - Two theme overview scales, six available resources scales, five problem identification scales, five resolution scales, four emotion scales, four outcome scales, two unusual or atypical responses scales
  - Available from MHS (http://www.mhs.com), PAR (http://www4.parinc.com), Western Psychological Services (http://www.wpspublish.com)
    - Roberts–2 Computer Scoring Program available
- Vineland Adaptive Behavior Scales—Second Edition (Vineland–II)
  - Ages birth–90 years (survey Interview form, Expanded Interview form, and Parent/Caregiver Rating form); 3–21 years, 11 months (Teaching Rating form)
  - Parent, caregiver, and teacher report; paper-and-pencil administration; semistructured interview form
  - Four adaptive domains (Communication, Daily Living Skills, Socialization, Motor Skills) and Adaptive Behavior Composite, 11 subdomains
  - Presents standard scores ($M = 100$, $SD = 15$), percentile ranks, adaptive levels (for adaptive domains), V-scale scores ($M = 15$, $SD = 3$), adaptive levels, and age equivalents (for subdomains)
  - Available from PsychCorp (http://www.psychcorp.com)
    - ASSIST scoring and reports available
    - Spanish forms

Developmental Measures: Asperger's Syndrome, Autism

- Asperger Syndrome Diagnostic Scale (ASDS)
  - Ages 5–18 years
  - Other-report checklist of behaviors characteristic of Asperger's disorder
  - Five subtests scores, total score
  - Uses raw scores, standard scores, and percentiles

- Asperger's syndrome quotient provides likelihood that individual has Asperger's syndrome
- Available from PRO-ED Inc. (http://www.proedinc.com)

> Childhood Autism Rating Scale, Second Edition (CARS2)
- Ages > 2 years
- Two clinician-completed rating scales (standard version and high-functioning version), unscored parent and caregiver questionnaire
- Quantifiable ratings to detect autism spectrum disorders, including Asperger's syndrome
- Presents total raw score, standard score, percentile rank
- Available from PRO-ED Inc. (http://www.proedinc.com), PsychCorp (http://www.psychcorp.com), Western Psychological Services (http://www.wpspublish.com)

> Gillliam Asperger's Disorder Scale (GADS)
- Ages 3–22 years
- Parent- or other-report rating scale
- Four subscale scores (Social Interaction, Restricted Patterns of Behavior, Cognitive Patterns, Pragmatic Skills)
- Uses standard scores and percentiles
- Available from PRO-ED Inc. (http://www.proedinc.com), PsychCorp (http://www.psychcorp.com), Western Psychological Services (http://www.wpspublish.com)

> Gilliam Autism Rating Scale—2 (GARS–2)
- Ages 3–22 years
- Parent-, teacher-, or clinician-completed rating scale
- Three subscale scores (Stereotyped Behaviors, Communication, Social Interaction), total score (Autism index)
- Available from PsychCorp (http://www.psychcorp.com)
- Available from PRO-ED Inc. (http://www.proedinc.com), Western Psychological Services (http://www.wps publish.com)
  - Scoring and report software available

Multiple Axis I and/or Axis II Characteristics and Symptoms Measures

> 16PF Fifth Edition
- Ages 16 years and older
- Client self-report, paper-and-pencil administration
  - Computer administration also available

- Three response style indices, 16 personality factors, five global factors
- Uses sten scores ($M = 5.5$, $SD = 2$)
- Available from PsychCorp (http://www.psychcorp.com)
  - Q Local Scoring and Reporting Software or mail-in scoring and reports (Basic Interpretive, Human Resource Development, Couple's Counseling, Karson Clinical) available

> Behavior Assessment System for Children—Second Edition (BASC–2)
- Ages 2–21 years
- Parent and teacher report and client self-report (6 years and older), paper-and-pencil administration
  - Audio CD and online administration also available
- Evaluates a wide range of behavioral and emotional concerns
- Validity indices; various clinical, adaptive, composite, and content scales depending on reporter and age of client
- Uses T scores and percentiles for general and clinical populations
- Available from PsychCorp (http://www.psychcorp.com)
  - ASSIST software or online scoring and reports available
  - Spanish forms

> Conners Comprehensive Behavior Rating Scales (Conners CBRS)
- Ages 6–18 years (parent- and teacher-rating scales); 8–18 years (self-report)
- Parent and teacher report and client self-report; paper-and-pencil administration
  - Computer administration also available
- Twelve Conners CBRS scales, 14 *Diagnostic and Statistical Manual of Mental Disorders* (4th ed., text revision; American Psychiatric Association, 2000) *DSM–IV–TR* symptom scales, three validity scales, 11 other clinical indicator scales, three impairment item scales, two critical item scales, other concerns, and strengths
- Conormed with Conners 3

- Available from MHS (http://www.mhs.com)
  - Online and software scoring and reports (assessment, progress, and comparative) available
  - Spanish forms
- Available from PAR (http://www4.parinc.com), Psych-Corp (http://www.psychcorp.com), Western Psychological Services (http://www.wpspublish.com)
  - Software scoring and reports (assessment and progress) available
  - Spanish forms
- ➢ Millon Adolescent Clinical Inventory (MACI)
  - Ages 13–19 years
  - Client self-report, paper-and-pencil administration
    - Audio CD or computer administration also available
  - One validity scale, three modifying indices, 12 personality patterns, eight expressed concerns, seven clinical syndromes
  - Uses base-rate (BR) scores: BR = 75–84 indicates *presence* level; $BR \geq 85$ indicates *prominence* level
  - Available from PsychCorp (http://www.psychcorp.com)
    - Q Local Scoring and Reporting Software or mail-in scoring and computer-generated interpretive reports available
- ➢ Millon Pre-Adolescent Clinical Inventory (M–PACI)
  - Ages 9–12 years
  - Client self-report, paper-and-pencil administration
    - Audio CD or computer administration also available
  - Two response validity indicators, seven emerging personality patterns, seven current clinical signs
  - Available from PsychCorp (http://www.psychcorp.com)
    - Q Local Scoring and Reporting Software or mail-in scoring and computer-generated interpretive reports available
- ➢ Millon Clinical Multiaxial Inventory—III (MCMI–III)
  - Ages 18 years and older
  - Client self-report, paper-and-pencil administration
    - Audio CD or computer administration also available
  - One validity index, four modifying indices, 14 personality disorder scales, 10 clinical syndrome scales, Grossman Facet Scales identifying underlying personality processes

- Uses BR scores: $BR = 60$ represents *median* for all patients; $BR \geq 74$ indicates *presence* of clinically significant personality style or syndrome; $BR \geq 84$ indicates *prominence* of personality style or syndrome for client
- Available from PAR (http://www4.parinc.com)
    - MCMI II/III Interpretive System Version 2 computer-generated interpretive report available (no scoring)
- Available from PsychCorp (http://www.psychcorp.com)
    - Q Local Scoring and Reporting Software or mail-in scoring and computer-generated interpretive reports available
    - Spanish forms
➢ Minnesota Multiphasic Personality Inventory—Adolescent (MMPI–A)
    - Ages 14–18 years
    - Client self-report, paper-and-pencil administration
        - Audio CD or computer administration also available
    - Eight validity scales, 10 clinical scales, clinical subscales, content scales, content component scales, supplementary scales
    - Uses T scores: $T > 65$ is cutoff for clinical interpretation; $T = 60–64$ may yield significant descriptors
    - Available from MHS (http://www.mhs.com), PAR (http://www4.parinc.com)
        - MMPI–A Interpretive System Version 3 computer-generated interpretive reports available (no scoring)
    - Available from PsychCorp (http://www.psychcorp.com)
        - Q Local Scoring and Reporting Software or mail-in scoring and computer-generated interpretive reports available for outpatient mental health, inpatient mental health, general medical, school counseling, correctional, and alcohol and drug treatment settings
➢ Minnesota Multiphasic Personality Inventory—2 (MMPI–2)
    - Ages 18 years and older
    - Client self-report, paper-and-pencil administration
        - Audio cassette, CD, or computer administration also available
    - Nine validity scales, 10 clinical scales, nine restructured clinical scales, clinical subscales, content scales, content component scales, and supplementary scales

- Uses T scores: $T > 65$ is cutoff for clinical interpretation
- Available from MHS (http://www.mhs.com), PAR (http://www4.parinc.com)
  - MMPI–2 Adult Interpretive System Version 3 computer-generated interpretive reports (no scoring)
- Available from PsychCorp (http://www.psychcorp.com)
  - Q Local Scoring and Reporting Software or mail-in scoring and computer-generated interpretive reports available for clinical, forensic, correctional, and employment settings

➤ Minnesota Multiphasic Personality Inventory—2—Restructured Form (MMPI–2–RF)
  - Ages 18 years and older
  - Client self-report, paper-and-pencil administration
    - Audio CD or computer administration also available
  - Eight validity scales, 50 new and revised clinical scales
  - Uses T scores: $T > 65$ is cutoff for clinical interpretation
  - Available from PsychCorp (http://www.psychcorp.com)
    - Q Local Scoring and Reporting Software scoring and computer-generated interpretive reports available

➤ NEO Five-Factor Inventory—3 (NEO–FFI–3)
  - Ages 12 years and older
  - Client self-report and observer report, paper-and-pencil administration
    - Computer administration also available
  - Five domains of personality (Neuroticism, Extraversion, Openness to Experience, Agreeableness, Conscientiousness)
  - Uses T scores with separate norms for adolescents and adults
  - Available from PAR (http://www4.parinc.com)
    - NEO Software System scoring and reports available

➤ NEO Personality Inventory—3 (NEO–PI–3)
  - Ages 12 years and older
  - Client self-report and observer report, paper-and-pencil administration
    - Computer administration also available
  - Three validity items, five domains of personality (Neuroticism, Extraversion, Openness to Experience,

Agreeableness, Conscientiousness), six facet scales within each domain
- Uses T scores with separate norms for adolescents and adults
- Available from PAR (http://www4.parinc.com)
  - NEO Software System or mail-in scoring and reports available

> Personality Assessment Inventory (PAI)
- 18 years and older
- Client self-report, paper-and-pencil administration
  - Audio CD and computer administration also available
- Four validity scales, 11 clinical scales, five treatment consideration scales, two interpersonal scales
- Uses T scores
- Available from PAR (http://www4.parinc.com)
  - PAI Software Portfolio or mail-in scoring and interpretive reports available (PAI–SP reports available for a variety of settings)
  - Spanish forms

> Personality Assessment Inventory—Adolescent (PAI–A)
- Ages 12–18 years
- Client self-report, paper-and-pencil administration
- Four validity scales, 11 clinical scales, five treatment consideration scales, two interpersonal scales
- Uses T scores
- Available from PAR (http://www4.parinc.com)
  - PAI–A Software Portfolio or mail-in scoring and interpretive reports available

> Roberts Apperception Test for Children: 2 (Roberts–2)
- Ages 6–18 years
- Clinician administered using set of 16 pictures
- Two theme overview scales, six available resources scales, five problem identification scales, five resolution scales, four emotion scales, four outcome scales, two unusual or atypical responses scales
- Available from MHS (http://www.mhs.com), PAR (http://www4.parinc.com), Western Psychological Services (http://www.wps.com)
  - Roberts–2 Computer Scoring Program available

> Rorschach
  - Ages 5–70 years
  - Clinician administered using 10 stimulus plates
  - Comprehensive scoring and interpretation systems
  - Available from MHS (http://www.mhs.com), Psych-Corp (http://www.psychcorp.com), Western Psychological Services (http://www.wpspublish.com)
  - Available from MHS (http://www.mhs.com), PAR (http://www4.parinc.com)
    o RIAP5: Scoring Program (RIAP5:S) and the Rorschach Interpretation Assistance Program: Version 5 (RIAP5) software available for scoring and interpretive reports

Attention-Deficit Disorder and Attention-Deficit/Hyperactivity Disorder Measures

> Conners' Adult ADHD Rating Scales (CAARS)
  - 18 years and older
  - Client self-report and observer report, paper-and-pencil administration
    o Online and computer software administration also available (MHS)
  - Nine problem scales, three *DSM–IV–TR* attention-deficit/hyperactivity disorder (ADHD) symptom sub-scales, an ADHD index, an inconsistency index to detect random or careless responding
  - Available from MHS (http://www.mhs.com)
    o Online and software scoring and reports available
    o Long and short forms
  - Available from PAR (http://www4.parinc.com), Western Psychological Services (http://www.wpspublish.com)
    o Long and short forms
> Conners' Continuous Performance Test II, Version Five (CPT II Version 5) and Conners' Kiddie Continuous Performance Test (K–CPT)
  - Ages 6 years and older for CPT–II, 4–5 years for K–CPT
  - Computer-administered attention task
  - Standard T scores and percentile ranks regarding performance on task

- Available from MHS (http://www.mhs.com), PAR (http://www4.parinc.com), PsychCorp (http://www.psychcorp.com), Western Psychological Services (http://www.wpspublish.com)
  - Computer scoring and reports available
- ➤ Conners Third Edition (Conners 3)
  - Ages 6–18 years (parent and teacher rating scales), 8–18 years (self-report)
  - Parent and teacher report and client self-report, paper-and-pencil administration
    - Online administration available (MHS, PsychCorp)
  - Six empirical scales, one rational scale, five *DSM–IV–TR* symptom scales as differentials for ADHD, three validity scales, two global indices (Global Index and ADHD Index), and several red-flag items
  - Available from MHS (http://www.mhs.com)
    - Online and software scoring and reports available
    - Spanish forms
  - Available from PAR (http://www4.parinc.com), PsychCorp (http://www.psychcorp.com)
    - Software scoring and reports available
    - Long and short forms
    - Spanish forms
  - Available from Western Psychological Services (http://www.wpspublish.com)
    - Software scoring available
    - Long and short forms
- ➤ Test of Variables of Attention (visual; T.O.V.A.), Test of Variables of Attention (auditory; T.O.V.A.–A.)
  - Ages 4–80 years
  - Computer-administered continuous performance tasks
  - Standard scores and standard deviations for four areas of performance (impulse control or commissions, inattention or omissions, response time, and response time variability), an ADHD score
  - Available from PAR (http://www4.parinc.com), Western Psychological Services (http://www.wpspublish.com)
    - Computer scoring and reports available

➢ Wender Utah Rating Scale
- Ages 18 years and older
- Client self-report, paper-and-pencil administration
- Sixty-one items, 25 items associated with ADHD (scored 0–4), score of 46 or more on 25 ADHD questions is significant
- Available from http://www.neurotransmitter.net/Wender_Utah.doc

Conduct Disorder and Oppositional Defiant Disorder

➢ Conners Third Edition (Conners 3)
- Ages 6–18 years (parent and teacher rating scales), 8–18 years (self-report)
- Parent and teacher report and client self-report, paper-and-pencil administration
  ○ Online administration available (MHS, PsychCorp)
- Six empirical scales, one rational scale, five *DSM–IV–TR* symptom scales (including Conduct Disorder and Oppositional Defiant Disorder), three validity scales, two global indices (Global Index and ADHD Index), and several red-flag items
- Available from MHS (http://www.mhs.com)
  ○ Online and software scoring and reports available
  ○ Spanish forms
- Available from PAR (http://www4.parinc.com), PsychCorp (http://www.psychcorp.com)
  ○ Software scoring and reports available
  ○ Long and short forms
  ○ Spanish forms
- Available from Western Psychological Services (http://www.wpspublish.com)
  ○ Software scoring available
  ○ Long and short forms

Eating Disorders Measures

➢ Eating Disorder Inventory—3 (EDI–3)
- Ages 13–53 (females only)
- Client self-report, paper-and-pencil administration

- Twelve primary scales (three eating-disorder-specific scales and nine general symptom scales relevant to eating disorders), six composite scores (Eating Disorder Risk, Ineffectiveness, Interpersonal Problems, Affective Problems, Overcontrol, General Psychological Maladjustment)
- Uses T scores and percentiles
- Available from PAR (http://www4.parinc.com)
  - EDI Scoring Program available
- Available from Western Psychological Services (http://www.wpspublish.com)

Pain Measures

➢ Chronic Pain Coping Inventory (CPCI)
  - Ages 20–80 years
  - Client self-report, paper-and-pencil administration
  - Two domains (illness-focused coping and wellness-focused coping), nine scales (Guarding, Resting, Asking for Assistance, Exercise/Stretch, Relaxation, Task Persistence, Coping Self-Statements, Pacing, Seeking Social Support)
  - Available from PAR (http://www4.parinc.com)
    - CPCI/SOPA Scoring Program available for scoring and reports (see the description of the Survey of Pain Attitudes)
➢ Pain Patient Profile (P–3)
  - Ages 17–76 years
  - Client self-report, paper-and-pencil administration
    - Computer administration also available
  - Three scales (Depression, Anxiety, Somatization)
  - Uses T scores
  - Available from PsychCorp (http://www.psychcorp.com)
    - Q Local Scoring and Reporting Software available
➢ Survey of Pain Attitudes (SOPA)
  - Ages 20–80 years
  - Client self-report, paper-and-pencil administration
  - Validity scale (inconsistency score), two domains (adaptive beliefs domain and maladaptive beliefs domain), seven scales (Control, Emotion, Disability, Harm, Medication, Solicitude, Medical Cure)

- Uses percentiles and T scores
- Available from PAR (http://www4.parinc.com)
  - CPCI/SOPA Scoring Program available for scoring and reports (see description of CPCI)

Posttraumatic Stress Disorder and Trauma Symptom Measures

> Detailed Assessment of Posttraumatic Stress (DAPS)
  - Ages 18 years and older
  - Client self-report, paper-and-pencil administration
    - Computer administration also available
  - Two validity scales, three posttraumatic stress disorder (PTSD) symptom clusters (reexperiencing, avoidance, hyperarousal), three associated features of PTSD (trauma-specific dissociation, suicidality, substance abuse)
  - Generates a tentative *DSM–IV–TR* diagnosis of PTSD or acute stress disorder
  - Available from PAR (http://www4.parinc.com)
    - DAPS Interpretive Report software for scoring and reports available
> Dissociative Experiences Scale (DES)
  - Late adolescence through adult
  - Client self-report, paper-and-pencil administration
  - Taps a range of dissociative symptoms
  - Comes in two forms, DES and DES–II; both have the same items but differ in their response formats
  - Available from Eve Bernstein Carlson, PhD, Department of Psychology, Beloit College, Beloit, WI; also http://cps.nova.edu/~cpphelp/DES.html; see Bernstein and Putnam (1986)
  - An adolescent version is also available (A–DES) from http://www.icpsr.umich.edu/icpsrweb/PHDCN/descriptions/ades-w3.jsp
> Impact of Events Scale—Revised (IES–R)
  - Adult
  - Client self-report, paper-and-pencil administration
  - Assesses three domains of *DSM–IV–TR* criteria for PTSD (intrusive, avoidant, and hyperarousal symptoms)

- Available from Daniel Weiss, PhD, Department of Psychiatry, University of California, San Francisco, Box F-0984, San Francisco, CA 94143-0984; see Weiss and Marmar (1996)
- Los Angeles Symptom Checklist (LASC)
  - Adult and adolescent (two versions)
  - Client self-report, paper-and-pencil administration
  - Seventeen items that tap *DSM–IV–TR* symptoms of PTSD are embedded in a 43-item measure; other items tap general distress
  - Available from David Foy, PhD (dfoy@pepperdine. edu); see King, King, Leskin, and Foy (1995)
- Trauma and Attachment Belief Scale (TABS)
  - Ages 9 years and older
  - Client self-report, paper-and-pencil administration
  - Five dimensions of beliefs (about self and others) related to safety, trust, esteem, intimacy, control
  - Available from Western Psychological Services (http://www.wpspublish.com)
- Trauma Symptom Checklist for Children (TSCC)
  - Ages 8–16 years
  - Client self-report, paper-and-pencil administration
  - Two validity scales, six clinical scales (Anxiety, Depression, Anger, Posttraumatic Stress, Dissociation, Sexual Concerns), eight critical items
  - Uses T scores
  - Available from PAR (http://www4.parinc.com)
    - Trauma Symptom Checklist Software Portfolio software for scoring and reports available
  - Available from Western Psychological Services (http://www.wpspublish.com)
- Trauma Symptom Checklist for Children—Alternate (TSCC–A)
  - Ages 8–16 years
  - Client self-report, paper-and-pencil administration
  - Identical to TSCC but has no reference to sexual issues
  - Two validity scales, five clinical scales (no Sexual Concerns scale), seven critical items

- Available from PAR (http://www4.parinc.com)
  - Trauma Symptom Checklist Software Portfolio software for scoring and reports available
- Trauma Symptom Checklist for Young Children (TSCYC)
  - Ages 3–12 years
  - Caretaker report, paper-and-pencil administration
  - Eight clinical scales (Anxiety, Depression, Anger/ Aggression, Posttraumatic Stress-Intrusion, Posttraumatic Stress-Arousal, Dissociation, Sexual Concerns), a Summary Posttraumatic Stress scale
  - Uses T scores
  - Available from PAR (http://www4.parinc.com)
    - Trauma Symptom Checklist Software Portfolio software for scoring and reports available
  - Available from Western Psychological Services (http:// www.wpspublish.com)
- Trauma Symptom Inventory—2 (TSI–2)
  - Ages 18 years and older
  - Client self-report, paper-and-pencil administration
  - Validity scales; clinical scales reflecting PTSD symptoms, dissociation, somatization, insecure attachment styles, impaired self-capacities, and dysfunctional behaviors; critical items
  - Uses T scores
  - Available from PAR (http://www4.parinc.com)
    - Trauma Symptom Inventory—2 Scoring Program software for a score summary report and change score report available
- Trauma Symptom Inventory—2—Alternate (TSI–2–A)
  - Ages 18 years and older
  - Client self-report, paper-and-pencil administration
  - Identical to the TSI–2 but does not contain any sexual symptom items
  - Validity scales, clinical scales (no Sexual Concerns or Dysfunctional Sexual Behavior scales), critical items
  - Uses T scores
  - Available from PAR (http://www4.parinc.com)
    - Trauma Symptom Inventory—2 Scoring Program software for a score summary report and change score report available

Substance Abuse and Dependence Measures

> Alcohol Use Inventory (AUI)
  - Ages 16 years and older
  - Client self-report, paper-and-pencil administration
    ○ Computer administration also available
  - Seventeen primary scales, six second-order factor scales, one General Alcohol Involvement scale
  - Available from PsychCorp (http://www.psychcorp.com)
    ○ Q Local Scoring and Reporting Software or mail-in scoring and reports available
    ○ Spanish forms

References

American Psychiatric Association. (2000). *Diagnostic and statistical manual of mental disorders* (4th ed., text revision). Washington, DC: Author.

American Psychological Association. (2011). *FAQ/Finding information about psychological tests.* Retrieved from http://www.apa.org/science/programs/testing/find-tests.aspx

Bernstein, E. M., & Putnam, F. W. (1986). Development, reliability, and validity of a dissociation scale. *Journal of Nervous and Mental Disease, 174,* 727–735. doi:10.1097/00005053-198612000-00004

King, L. A., King, D. W., Leskin, G. A., & Foy, D. W. (1995). The Los Angeles Symptom Checklist: A self-report measure of posttraumatic stress disorder. *Assessment, 2,* 1–17. doi:10.1177/1073191195002001001

Maddox, T. (2008). *Tests: A comprehensive reference for assessments in psychology, education, and business* (6th ed.). Austin, TX: PRO-ED Inc.

Weiss, D. S., & Marmar, C. R. (1996). The Impact of Event Scale—Revised. In J. P. Wilson & T. Keane (Eds.), *Assessing psychological trauma and PTSD: A handbook for practitioners* (pp. 399–411). New York, NY: Guilford Press.

CHAPTER 6

Clinical Assessment of Self-Harm and Interpersonally Violent Thoughts and Behaviors

When a client reports present or past thoughts or acts of self-harm (nonsuicidal self-injury [NSSI] or suicide) or harm to others in a session or the clinician suspects such a concern given the client's presentation or receives information from another source to that effect, the clinician should conduct a full clinical assessment. The assessment typically involves further interviewing of the client, focused on fully exploring past or current thoughts or acts of self-harm or other harm. Collateral information from family members or others closely associated with the client is often very valuable. In addition, the clinical assessment may include paper-and-pencil measures designed specifically to elicit further information about ideation and behavior from the client.

These clinical assessments provide some critical information for the clinician's completion of a risk evaluation of a client for whom self-harm or other harm is a concern (see Chapter 7, this resource) to ensure appropriate intervention. Gathering the information described in the sections that follow is only one step in the process of safeguarding the client's or others' welfare. Informed by the client's answers to specific interview questions about past or potential harm, other psychosocial history reported by the client, direct observations of the client, collateral input, results from test measures, and diagnostic impressions, the clinician then should determine the degree of risk the client poses to him- or herself or to another by methodically evaluating risk and protective factors. And, if necessary on the basis of that evaluation, the clinician should develop an appropriate treatment plan to contain the risk.

Self-Harm

The client's thoughts and behaviors about self-harm may be subdivided into two categories: NSSI and suicidal self-injury. The two categories are distinct. They differ in the intent of the act; the types of methods engaged; the degree of physical damage typically incurred; the attendant feelings of psychological pain, hopelessness, and helplessness; and the emotional experience following the self-harming act. Clients should be assessed for both NSSI and suicidal thoughts and behaviors.

This chapter contains the clinician interview guidelines (including some structured interview formats when available). The outlines for clinical interview assessments presented in the sections that follow represent integrations of those offered by others. The guidelines for NSSI assessment are derived from the work of Klonsky and Glenn (2009), Klonsky and Muehlenkamp (2007), Nock (2009), Nock and Prinstein (2004), and Walsh (2006, 2007). The guidelines for suicidal self-injury assessment reflect the elements discussed by Ash (2006); Bennett et al. (2006); Berman, Jobes, and Silverman (2006); Bongar (2002); Chiles and Strosahl (2005); Conwell and Heisel (2006); Jobes (2006); Simon (2006); and Sommers-Flanagan and Sommers-Flanagan (2009). Examples of paper-and-pencil measures for the clinical assessment of the two types of self-harm (NSSI and suicidal self-injury) are included. Clinicians are reminded, however, that research indicates that self-injury (particularly suicide) assessment scales have low positive predictive values. As such, the measures should be used as sources of collateral information about a client and not as a substitute for a careful clinical interview in evaluation of self-injury risk (American Psychiatric Association, 2003).

As with any intervention, the clinician should carefully consider the most appropriate nature, timing, and pace of these follow-up inquiries for a particular client. Chiles and Strosahl (2005) and Jobes (2006) promoted strategies for suicide assessment (and intervention) that are based on the perspective that suicidal thoughts and behaviors represent a client's efforts to cope with life stressors, and they emphasized a collaborative approach with the client. Sommers-Flanagan and Sommers-Flanagan (2009) encouraged clinicians to engage in the assessment with a non-judgmental and validating attitude. Their suggestions are equally applicable to the assessment of NSSI. Furthermore, the clinician is advised to maintain sensitivity to relevant cultural considerations in the assessment of a client's self-harm thoughts or behaviors; the reader is referred to Wendler and Matthews (2006) for a discussion of cultural competence in suicide assessment.

> Clinical interview assessment of NSSI thoughts and behaviors
  - Current NSSI thoughts
    - Passive (general thoughts, thoughts of other's self-injury) versus active (thoughts about inflicting injury on self)
      - If active, has there been a recent shift from passive to active?
      - If active, when thoughts began
      - If active, frequency and intensity of the thoughts
      - If active, potential plan and method(s)
        - If a plan and method, type(s) of injury considered, the dangerousness of the method(s), and the access to planned method(s)
      - If active, any specific situational stressors that trigger the client's thoughts
  - Current NSSI behavior
    - NSSI behavior within past 2 months
      - If yes, body area involved (Note: Injuries to face, eyes, breasts in women, and genitals in either gender are unusual and denote potentially severe psychological disturbance.)
      - If yes, method(s) used, the number of wounds, any pattern to the wounds, and whether the wounds depict any words or symbols
      - If yes, duration and frequency of NSSI episode(s)
      - If yes, time of day of NSSI episode(s), the location, and the social context (i.e., was the client alone or with someone else?)
      - If yes, degree of physical damage (e.g., length and width of cut, need for suture, degree of burn) and whether medical attention was required or obtained

- ◆ If yes, significant precipitating or contributing factors at time of episode(s)
    - · Interpersonal stress (e.g., parental or peer conflict)
    - · Physiological influence (e.g., fatigue, substance intoxication)
    - · Emotional stress (e.g., sadness, anger, frustration, body dissatisfaction or hatred)
  - ◆ If yes, function of current NSSI (e.g., emotion regulation, self-punishment, interpersonal influence, emotion generation, suicide resistance, sensation seeking, marking interpersonal boundaries)
  - ◆ If yes, consequences of NSSI (e.g., physical, emotional, responses from others)
- ■ Chronological history of NSSI
  - ○ Age of onset
  - ○ Context of onset (precipitating factors)
  - ○ Body areas injured over time
  - ○ Type(s) of methods used over time
  - ○ Number of wounds per episode
  - ○ Duration and frequency of episodes (including whether there were periods of abstinence)
  - ○ Degree of physical damage
  - ○ Client's reported level of physical pain
  - ○ Note: In a sample of adolescents, those who acknowledged NSSI in the past year and attempted suicide engaged in a greater frequency of moderate to severe NSSI, used more methods of NSSI, and endorsed a greater number of reasons for NSSI than those who engaged in NSSI but did not attempt suicide (Lloyd-Richardson, Perrine, Dierker, & Kelley, 2007).
- ➤ Structured interviews for assessment of NSSI thoughts and behaviors
  - ■ Self-Injurious Thoughts and Behaviors Interview
    - ○ Adolescent and older
    - ○ Clinician administered
    - ○ Assesses several aspects of thoughts and acts of NSSI (and suicidal ideation and behavior)

- ○ Short form and parent report are also available
- ○ Available in Nock, Holmberg, Photos, and Michel (2007)
- Suicide Attempt Self-Injury Interview (SASII)
  - ○ Ages as appropriate
  - ○ Clinician administered
  - ○ Elicits a full description of each act of self-injury, including the intention
  - ○ A short form and a computerized-scoring version are also available
  - ○ Available in Linehan, Comtois, Brown, and Heard (2006)
- ➢ Paper-and-pencil measures for assessment of NSSI
  - Note: Only a few NSSI measures have been developed to date, and empirical evidence of their validity and reliability is just beginning to emerge. In addition, many of the measures were initially developed for research purposes and may prove cumbersome in a clinical setting. However, they do provide the clinician with a structured review of factors critical to assess with a client for whom NSSI is a concern.
  - Deliberate Self-Harm Inventory (DSHI)
    - ○ Ages as appropriate
    - ○ Client self-report, paper-and-pencil administration
    - ○ Assesses the history of 16 specific NSSI behaviors
    - ○ Available in Gratz (2001)
  - Functional Assessment of Self-Mutilation (FASM)
    - ○ Adolescent and older
    - ○ Client self-report, paper-and-pencil administration
    - ○ Assesses the history, age of onset, frequency, and methods of various common NSSI acts, and 22 possible reasons for the behaviors
    - ○ Available from E. E. Lloyd-Richardson (erichardson@umassd.edu)
  - Inventory of Statements About Self-Injury (ISAS)
    - ○ Ages college and older
    - ○ Client self-report, paper-and-pencil administration
    - ○ Assesses the presence and strength of different motivations for clients known to be engaged in NSSI

- Available from E. David Klonsky (edklonsky@gmail.com)
- Clinical interview assessment of suicidal thoughts and behavior
  - Current thoughts of suicide
    - Passive (e.g., the client wishes he or she could go to sleep and not wake up) versus active (e.g., the client has thoughts of ending his or her own life)
      - If active, was there a recent shift from passive to active ideation?
      - If active, when thoughts began
      - If active, frequency and intensity of the thoughts
      - If active, potential plan and method
        - If plan and method, potential lethality of that plan and method (both the actual potential lethality and the client's belief regarding the lethality)
        - If plan and method, access to the potential method
        - If plan and method, any behavioral preparation to execute the plan (e.g., *acts of closure* such as writing a note, settling affairs, actual practice of the plan)
        - If plan and method, degree of intent the client has to execute the plan and client's sense of control over any impulse to act out the plan
  - Current suicidal behaviors
    - Any recent attempt(s) to commit suicide
      - If yes, was or were attempt(s) impulsive or planned and intentional?
        - If impulsive, any contextual triggers
        - If impulsive, was client intoxicated at the time?
      - If yes, was or were attempt(s) private or concealed?
      - If yes, what was resolution of the attempt(s) (e.g., Was the client interrupted? Did the client change his or her mind? Did the method not work?)?

- ◆ If yes, client's thoughts or feelings about the unsuccessful attempt
- ■ Chronological history of past suicidal thoughts and/or behaviors
  - ○ If thoughts, passive or active
  - ○ If thoughts, dates and context
  - ○ If attempts,
    - ◆ Dates of all prior attempt(s)
    - ◆ Method(s) used
    - ◆ Lethality of the method(s)
    - ◆ Was or were attempt(s) impulsive or planned and intentional?
    - ◆ Any substance use or abuse involved at the time of the attempt(s)
    - ◆ Strength of client's desire to die
    - ◆ Circumstances of attempt(s)
    - ◆ Resolution of the attempt(s)
    - ◆ Client's thoughts and feelings about the attempt(s)
    - ◆ Any treatment client received following attempt(s)
- ➢ Paper-and-pencil measures for assessment of suicidal thoughts and behaviors
  - ■ Adult Suicidal Ideation Questionnaire (ASIQ)
    - ○ Ages 18 years and older
    - ○ Client self-report, paper-and-pencil administration
    - ○ Screens for suicidal ideation
    - ○ Available from Psychological Assessment Resources (PAR; http://www4.parinc.com)
  - ■ Beck Hopelessness Scale
    - ○ Ages 17 years and older
    - ○ Client self-report, paper-and-pencil administration
      - ◆ Computer administration also available
    - ○ Assesses three major aspects of hopelessness: feelings about the future, loss of motivation, and expectations
    - ○ Available from PsychCorp (http://www.psych corp.com)
      - ◆ Q Local Scoring and Reporting Software available
      - ◆ Spanish form

- Beck Scale for Suicide Ideation (BSS)
  - Ages 17 years and older
  - Client self-report, paper-and-pencil administration
    - Computer administration also available
  - Assesses passive and active suicidal ideation, suicide plan, expectations regarding an attempt, preparations for an attempt, past suicide attempts, and various protective factors
  - Available from PsychCorp (http://www.psych corp.com)
    - Q Local Scoring and Reporting Software available
    - Spanish form
- Cornell Scale for Depression in Dementia (CSDD)
  - Elderly clients with cognitive deficits
  - Clinician-administered measure that uses information from client and a caregiver
  - Available in Alexopoulos, Abrams, Young, and Shamoian (1988)
- Geriatric Depression Scale (GDS)
  - Elderly clients who are cognitively intact and without visual impairment
  - Client self-report, paper-and-pencil administration
  - Assesses symptoms of depression in a yes–no format
  - Available from http://www.stanford/edu/~yesavage
    - Available in several languages
- Firestone Assessment for Self-Destructive Thoughts (FAST)
  - Ages 16–70 years
  - Client self-report, paper-and-pencil administration
  - Assesses 11 levels of self-destructive thoughts; five composite scores (Self-Defeating, Addictions, Self-Annihilating, Suicide Intent, Total Score)
  - Available from PAR (http://www4.parinc.com)
- Hopelessness Scale for Children (HPLS)
  - Children reading at first- to second-grade level
  - Client self-report, paper-and-pencil administration
  - Modification of the Beck Hopelessness Scale and assesses negative expectations about the future
  - Available in Kazdin, Rogers, and Colbus (1986)

- Positive and Negative Suicide Ideation Inventory (PANSI)
  - High school adolescents
  - Client self-report, paper-and-pencil administration
  - Assesses both risk and protective factors for suicide
  - Available from Augustine Osman, PhD, Department of Psychology, University of Northern Iowa, 334 Baker Hall, Cedar Falls, IA 50614-0505
- Reasons for Living Inventory for Adolescents (RFL–A)
  - High school adolescents
  - Client self-report, paper-and-pencil administration
  - Assesses potential reasons for not committing suicide
  - Available in Osman et al. (1998)
- Reasons for Living Inventory (RFL–48)
  - Adult
  - Client self-report, paper-and-pencil administration
  - Assesses protective factors against suicide: survival and coping beliefs, responsibility to family, child-related concerns, fear of suicide, fear of social disapproval, and moral objections to suicide
  - Available in Linehan, Goodstein, Nielsen, and Chiles (1983)
- Suicidal Ideation Questionnaire (SIQ), (SIQ–JR)
  - 10th–12th graders (SIQ), 7th–9th graders (SIQ–JR)
  - Client self-report, paper-and-pencil administration
  - Assesses frequency of suicidal ideation
  - Available from PAR (http://www4.parinc.com)

Other Harm

During an initial clinical assessment or subsequent session, the client may reveal current or past thoughts of physically injuring another or actually having engaged in behaviors that injure others (or are likely to). At such times, a more in-depth assessment should be conducted. Interview guidelines and a selection of paper-and-pencil measures for the clinical assessment of other-harm ideations and behaviors are presented in the outline that follows. The guidelines reflect an integration of elements noted by Benjamin, Kent, and Sirikantraporn (2009); Monahan and colleagues (2001); and Pagani and Pinard (2001).

> ➢ Clinical interview assessment of other harm thoughts and behaviors
>> ▪ Currents thoughts of other harm
>>> ○ Passive (e.g., general thoughts of physical violence) versus active (thoughts of perpetrating violence on another person)
>>>> ◆ If active, was there a recent shift from passive to active?
>>>> ◆ If active, when thoughts began
>>>> ◆ If active, frequency and intensity
>>>> ◆ If active, have thoughts increased or decreased in seriousness since onset?
>>>> ◆ If active, is a specific person the target?
>>>>> · If yes, identify the person (name, age, psychological condition)
>>>>> · If yes, do thoughts occur in presence of person?
>>>> ◆ If active, potential plan and method
>>>>> · If plan and method, access to potential method
>>>>> · If plan and method, any behavioral preparation to execute plan
>>>>> · If plan and method, degree of client's intent to carry out plan
>>>>> · If plan and method, client's sense of control over impulse to carry out plan
>> ▪ Recent threats of or acts that physically injured another person (including forcible sexual contact)
>>> ○ If yes, were threats and/or act(s) impulsive or planned and intentional?
>>>> ◆ If impulsive, any contextual triggers
>>>> ◆ If impulsive, any substance intoxication at the time
>>> ○ If yes, identity and age of the intended or actual victim
>>> ○ If yes, outcome (e.g., target's reaction to threats, any injuries to the target)

- o If yes, client's thoughts or feelings now about the threats or acts
- ■ Chronological history of past thoughts, threats, or behaviors
  - o If thoughts, active or passive
  - o If thoughts, dates, identity and age of target, and context
  - o If threats or behaviors,
    - ◆ Dates
    - ◆ Identity and age of target
    - ◆ Method(s) intended or used
    - ◆ Lethality of the method(s)
    - ◆ Was or were threat(s) or act(s) impulsive or planned and intentional?
    - ◆ Was any substance use or abuse involved?
    - ◆ Strength of the client's desire to physically harm or control the other
    - ◆ Circumstances surrounding (or triggers for) threat(s) or act(s
    - ◆ Outcome of the threat(s) or act(s)
    - ◆ Client's thoughts and feelings about the threat(s) or act(s)
    - ◆ Consequences of the threat(s) or act(s), including treatment or incarceration
- ➢ Paper-and-pencil measures for assessment of other harm
  - ■ Aggression Questionnaire (AQ)
    - o Ages 9–88 years
    - o Client self-report, paper-and-pencil administration
      - ◆ Computer administration also available
    - o Assesses physical, verbal, and indirect aggression tendencies
    - o Inconsistent Responding Index
    - o Available from Western Psychological Services (http://www.wpspublish.com)
      - ◆ Scoring software available
  - ■ Anger Disorders Scale (ADS) and Anger Disorders Scale: Short Form (ADS:S)
    - o Ages 18–76 years
    - o Client self-report, paper-and-pencil administration
      - ◆ Computer administration also available

- ○ Assesses dysfunctional anger across five domains (Provocations, Arousal, Cognitions, Motives, and Behaviors), 18 subscales
- ○ Available from MHS (http://www.mhs.com)
  - ◆ ADS VS.5 software for scoring and reports available
- ■ Child Abuse Potential Inventory (CAP)
  - ○ Parents or primary caregivers
  - ○ Client self-report, paper-and-pencil administration
  - ○ Screening measure for detection of physical child abuse in a parent or caregiver suspected of such behavior
  - ○ Three validity scales (Lie, Random Response, Inconsistency), 10 scales
  - ○ Primary scale (Abuse) divided into six factor scales (Distress, Rigidity, Unhappiness, Problems With Child and Self, Problems With Family, Problems With Others)
  - ○ Available from PAR (http://www4.parinc.com)
- ■ Children's Aggression Scale (CAS)
  - ○ Ages 5–18 years
  - ○ Parent or teacher report, paper-and-pencil administration
  - ○ Evaluates frequency and severity of aggression
  - ○ Available from PAR (http://www4.parinc.com)
    - ◆ CAS Scoring Program software for scoring and reports available
- ■ Conflict Tactics Scale: Parent–Child Version (CTSPC)
  - ○ Adults
  - ○ Client self-report or interview measure, paper-and-pencil administration
  - ○ Assesses respondent's behavior with own child and parent's experiences as a child in six areas (Nonviolent Discipline, Weekly Discipline, Psychological Aggression, Neglect, Physical Assault, Sexual Abuse)
  - ○ Available from Western Psychological Services (http://www.wpspublish.com)
- ■ Firestone Assessment of Violent Thoughts (FAVT)
  - ○ Ages 18–75 years
  - ○ Client self-report, paper-and-pencil administration

- Two validity scales (Inconsistency and Negativity Scales), five domains (Paranoid/ Suspicious, Persecuted Misfit, Self-Depreciating/ Pseudo-Independent, Overtly Aggressive, Self-Aggrandizing), two theoretical subscales (Instrumental/ Proactive Violence, Hostile/ Reactive Violence)
- Available from PAR (http://www4.parinc.com)
- Firestone Assessment of Violent Thoughts—Adolescent (FAVT–A)
  - Ages 11–18 years
  - Client self-report, paper-and-pencil administration
  - Two validity scales (Inconsistency and Negativity Scales), four domains (Paranoid/ Suspicious, Persecuted Misfit, Self-Depreciating/ Pseudo-Independent, Overtly Aggressive), two theoretical subscales (Instrumental/ Proactive Violence, Hostile/ Reactive Violence)
  - Available from PAR (http://www4.parinc.com)
- Novaco Anger Scale and Provocation Inventory (NAS–PI)
  - Ages 9–84 years
  - Client self-report, paper-and-pencil administration
  - Assesses anger reactivity and regulation and nature of provocations
  - Validity index to identify inconsistent responding
  - Available from Western Psychological Services (http://www.wpspublish.com)
    - Scoring software available
- Revised Conflict Tactics Scale (CTS–2)
  - Adult
  - Client self-report or interview measure, paper-and-pencil administration
  - Assesses various partner violent behaviors (Psychological Aggression, Physical Assault, Sexual Coercion, and Injury)
  - Half of the items refer to respondent's behavior and half to partner's behavior
  - Available from Western Psychological Services (http://www.wpspublish.com)
- State–Trait Anger Expression Inventory—2 (STAXI–2)
  - Ages 16 years and older

- ○ Client self-report, paper-and-pencil administration
- ○ Includes State Anger scale (three subscales), Trait Anger scale (two subscales), Anger Expression scale (two subscales), and Anger Control scale (two subscales)
- ○ Uses T scores and percentile conversions for all scales and subscales by gender
- ○ Available from PAR (http://www4.parinc.com)
  - ◆ Scoring and report software available
- State–Trait Anger Expression Inventory—2 Child and Adolescent (STAXI-2 C/A)
  - ○ Ages 9–18 years
  - ○ Client self-report, paper-and-pencil administration
  - ○ Includes State Anger scale (two subscales), Trait Anger scale (two subscales), Anger Expression scale (two subscales), and Anger Control scale (one subscale); sensitive to developmental aspects of anger
  - ○ Uses T scores and percentile conversions for scales and subscales for the total normative sample and six normative age-by-gender groups
  - ○ Available from PAR (http://www4.parinc.com)

References

Alexopoulos, G. A., Abrams, R. C., Young, R. C., & Shamoian, C. A. (1988). Cornell scale for depression in dementia. *Biological Psychiatry, 23*, 271–284. (Also available from http://www.qualitynet.org; go to Medqic tab and search for measure)

American Psychiatric Association. (2003). Practice guideline for the assessment and treatment of patients with suicidal behaviors. *American Journal of Psychiatry, 160* (Suppl. 11), 1–60.

Ash, P. (2006). Children and adolescents. In R. I. Simon & R. E. Hales (Eds.), *The textbook of suicide assessment and management* (pp. 35–55). Washington, DC: American Psychiatric Publishing.

Benjamin, G. A. H., Kent, L., & Sirikantraporn, S. (2009). A review of duty-to-protect statutes, cases, and procedures for positive practice. In J. L. Werth, E. R. Welfel, & G. A. H. Benjamin (Eds.), *The duty to protect: Ethical, legal, and professional considerations for mental health professionals* (pp. 9–28). Washington, DC: American Psychological Association. doi:10.1037/11866-002

Bennett, B. E., Bricklin, P. M., Harris, E., Knapp, S., VandeCreek, L., & Younggren, J. N. (2006). *Assessing and managing risk in psychological practice: An individualized approach.* Rockville, MD: The Trust.

Berman, A. L., Jobes, D. A., & Silverman, M. M. (2006). *Adolescent suicide: Assessment and intervention* (2nd ed.). Washington, DC: American Psychological Association. doi:10.1037/11285-000

Bongar, B. (2002). *The suicidal patient: Clinical and legal standards of care* (2nd ed.). Washington, DC: American Psychological Association. doi:10.1037/10424-000

Chiles, J. A., & Strosahl, K. D. (2005). *Clinical manual for assessment and treatment of suicidal patients.* Washington, DC: American Psychiatric Publishing.

Conwell, Y., & Heisel, M. J. (2006). The elderly. In R. I. Simon & R. E. Hales (Eds.), *The textbook of suicide assessment and management* (pp. 57–76). Washington, DC: American Psychiatric Publishing.

Gratz, K. L. (2001). Measurement of deliberate self-harm: Preliminary data on the Deliberate Self-Harm Inventory. *Journal of Psychopathology and Behavioral Assessment, 23,* 253–263.

Jobes, D. A. (2006). *Managing suicidal risk: A collaborative approach.* New York, NY: Guilford Press.

Kazdin, A., Rogers, A., & Colbus, D. (1986). The hopelessness scale for children: Psychometric characteristics and concurrent validity. *Journal of Consulting and Clinical Psychology, 54,* 241–245.

Klonsky, E. D., & Glenn, C. R. (2009). Assessing the functions of non-suicidal self-injury: Psychometric properties of the Inventory of Statements About Self-injury (ISAS). *Journal of Psychopathology and Behavioral Assessment, 31,* 215–219. doi:10.1007/s10862-008-9107-z

Klonsky, E. D., & Muehlenkamp, J. J. (2007). Self-injury: A research review for the practitioner. *Journal of Clinical Psychology: In Session, 63,* 1045–1056.

Linehan, M. M., Comtois, K. A., Brown, M. Z., Heard, H. L., & Wagner, A. (2006). Suicide attempt self-injury interview (SASII): Development, reliability, and validity of a scale to assess suicide attempts and intentional self-injury. *Psychological Assessment, 18,* 302–312.

Linehan, M., Goodstein, J., Nielsen, S., & Chiles, J. (1983). Reasons for staying alive when you are thinking of killing yourself: The Reasons for Living Inventory. *Journal of Consulting and Clinical Psychology, 51,* 276–286.

Lloyd-Richardson, E. E., Perrine, N., Dierker, L., & Kelley, M. L. (2007). Characteristics and functions of non-suicidal self-injury in a community sample of adolescents. *Psychological Medicine: A Journal of Research in Psychiatry and Allied Sciences, 37,* 1183–1192. doi:10.1017/S003329170700027X

Monahan, J., Steadman, H. J., Silver, E., Appelbaum, P. S., Robbins, P. C., Mulvey, E. P., . . . Banks, S. (2001). *Rethinking risk assessment: The MacArthur study of mental disorder and violence.* New York, NY: Oxford University Press.

Nock, M. K. (Ed.). (2009). *Understanding nonsuicidal self-injury: Origins, assessment, and treatment.* Washington, DC: American Psychological Association. doi:10.1037/11875-000

Nock, M. K., Holmberg, E. B., Photos, V.I., & Michel, B. D. (2007). The self-injurious thoughts and behaviors interview: Development, reliability, and validity in an adolescent sample measure. *Psychological Assessment, 19,* 309–317.

Nock, M. K., & Prinstein, M. J. (2004). A functional approach to the assessment of self-multilative behavior. *Journal of Consulting and Clinical Psychology, 72,* 885–890. doi:10.1037/0022-006X.72.5.885

Osman, A., Downs, W. R., Kopper, B. A., Barrios, F. X., Baker, M. T., Osman, J. R., . . . Linehan, M.. M. (1998). The Reasons for Living Inventory for Adolescents (RFL-A): Development and psychometric properties. *Journal of Clinical Psychology, 54,* 1063–1078.

Pagani, L., & Pinard, G.-F. (2001). Clinical assessment of dangerousness: An overview of the literature. In G.-F. Pinard &

L. Pagani (Eds.), *Clinical assessment of dangerousness: Empirical contributions* (pp. 1–22). New York, NY: Cambridge University Press.

Simon, R. (2006). Suicide risk: Assessing the unpredictable. In R. I. Simon & R. E. Hales (Eds.), *The textbook of suicide assessment and management* (pp. 1–32). Washington, DC: American Psychiatric Publishing.

Sommers-Flanagan, J., & Sommers-Flanagan, R. (2009). *Clinical interviewing* (4th ed.). Hoboken, NJ: Wiley.

Walsh, B. (2007). Clinical assessment of self-injury: A practical guide. *Journal of Clinical Psychology: In Session, 63,* 1057–1068.

Walsh, B. W. (2006). *Treating self-injury: A practical guide.* New York, NY: Guilford Press.

Wendler, S., & Matthews, D. (2006). Cultural competence in suicide risk assessment. In R. I. Simon & R. E. Hales (Eds.), *The textbook of suicide assessment and management* (pp. 159–176). Washington, DC: American Psychiatric Publishing.

CHAPTER 7

Risk Evaluation and Management of Self-Harm and Interpersonal Violence

In the course of their practices, most mental health professionals encounter clients who acknowledge past or current thoughts of self-injury or suicide or of harming another person. And many clinicians hear reports from clients that they have acted or intend to act on those ideations. Furthermore, therapists may also receive such information from clients' significant others. Such disclosures can evoke significant stress for practitioners because they are challenged to help their clients and prevent serious injury or even death. That stress response is natural. The assessments and decisions that clinicians make regarding clients who experience thoughts or engage in acts of self-harm or other harm have very serious implications—for the client, for others who may be injured, for other third parties, and for the clinician. At times, unfortunately, practitioners may attempt to alleviate that stress by foreclosing the assessment and decision-making processes (Wingate, Joiner, Walker, Rudd, & Jobes, 2004). Some assume that any mention by a client of such thoughts or acts requires the most cautious intervention; some too quickly dismiss the disclosures through inattention or rationalization. Neither approach is clinically, ethically, or legally appropriate.

This chapter contains a step-by-step outline for the evaluation and management of clients for whom the issues of self- or other harm ideation, intentions, or acts have been raised. The clinician is encouraged to seek consultation as necessary at each step to ensure competent practice within the standards of care.

First, the clinician should conduct a structured evaluation of the risk for harm that the client presents. Second, he or she should determine the estimated level of risk on the basis of the information gathered in the evaluation. Third, on the basis of the estimation of risk of harm to the client or another person, the clinician should decide whether immediate actions are necessary to reduce any acute danger of harm, including changing the level of intervention and fulfilling possible legal responsibilities to warn another person of potential injury by the client. Fourth, if the level of risk is not so high as to necessitate a transfer of the client from the clinician's care, or when the client returns to the clinician's care following an acute intervention, the clinician should create a treatment plan that targets individual and contextual risk factors that may be treated or reduced and protective factors that may be created or enhanced. Fifth, the clinician should carefully document the risk evaluation process and findings (including an estimate of risk level), the plan for any immediate intervention, the longer term treatment plan, the client's response to the intervention plans, contacts with significant others, and any consultation.

Steps 1 and 2: Conduct a Structured Risk Evaluation and Determine an Estimated Level of Risk

A *structured risk evaluation* determines the presence of individual and contextual factors identified by empirical research as contributing to self- or other-injurious behavior (risk factors) and of those identified as mitigating the potential for the behavior (protective factors). The evaluation results in an estimate of risk that the client may engage in harmful behavior (e.g., low, moderate, high). Two approaches to risk evaluation have evolved: clinical and actuarial. For a *clinical* risk evaluation, the practitioner gathers and synthesizes information about the client from several possible sources, including information obtained in the initial (or subsequent) interview, results of assessment measures, previous treatment records, and collateral reports. Then the practitioner engages in a reasoning process and makes a subjective judgment regarding the level of risk (a *structured professional judgment*). For an *actuarial* risk evaluation, the clinician gathers specific information according to an empirically derived protocol and, through a computational analysis, derives a probability estimate of risk (Pagani & Pinard, 2001). Each method has advantages and disadvantages. Major debates have transpired over which is best (Litwack & Schlesinger, 1999).

This chapter contains outlines of risk and protective factors for potential self-harm and other harm: one for nonsuicidal self-injury (NSSI), three for suicidal self-harm (separate outlines for child and adolescent, adult, and elderly clients), and one for interpersonal violence. In addition, references to some published structured clinical interview guidelines are included for the risk assessment of interpersonal violence. Examples of some actuarial measures for the assessment of potential suicide in child or adolescent clients and interpersonal violence follow those clinical evaluation outlines. At the conclusion of the risk evaluation section for each type of potential harm, there is a list to aid the clinician's analysis of the client's risk level. The lists provide some anchor points for the assignment of low risk, moderate risk, or high risk. It is worth noting that others have developed systematic schemas for the estimation of risk level based on 5-point scales (e.g., see Jobes, 2006; Rudd & Joiner, 1999; Rudd, Joiner, & Rajab, 2001, for suicide risk evaluation).

The outlines of factors to be considered for the risk evaluation of NSSI were derived from the work of Klonsky and Muehlenkamp (2007), Nock (2009), Nock and Prinstein (2004), and Walsh (2006). Those factors for the assessment of suicidal self-injury represent an integration of the elements discussed by the American Psychiatric Association (2003); Ash (2006); Bennett and colleagues (2006); Berman, Jobes, and Silverman (2006); Bongar (2002); Chiles and Strosahl (2005); Conwell and Heisel (2006); Jobes (2006); Rudd and Joiner (1999); Rudd, Joiner, and Rajab (2001); Simon (2006); and Sommers-Flanagan and Sommers-Flanagan (2009). The factors identified for the estimation of risk for interpersonal violence reflect those noted by Benjamin, Kent, and Sirikantraporn (2009), Monahan (2001), Monahan et al. (2001), Pagani and Pinard (2001), and Tardiff (2001). In addition, the references included at the end of the chapter provide the clinician with important principles that should guide the process of the risk evaluations (e.g., Granello, 2010; Jobes, 2006; Pope & Vasquez, 2010; Sommers-Flanagan & Sommers-Flanagan, 2009; Walsh, 2006).

Five important caveats to the risk evaluations are crucial to consider. First, the goal of a risk evaluation is not to predict whether a client will engage in self-injury, commit suicide, or harm another person. Researchers have repeatedly demonstrated that such rare events cannot be accurately predicted. Instead, the primary goal is to identify risk and protective factors that may be treated or modified. Armed with that information, the clinician may then develop an appropriate intervention plan to safeguard each client and other potential targets of harm. Second, the understanding of risk and protective factors evolves with ongoing research; the lists provided in the sections that follow are not intended to be timeless or comprehensive. Third, research has not yet clarified how each identified factor (or combination of factors) may be weighted in terms of its contribution to risk. It is likely that weights vary from client to client and within each client from time to time. The clinician is encouraged to attend to individual and contextual considerations in judging the importance of each risk or protective factor. Fourth, the lists of factors presented in the sections that follow are intended to aid the clinician's reasoned and careful decision making; the lists are not intended to be followed in cookbook style, supplanting clinical judgment. And the clinician's judgments are often strengthened by consultation with other professionals. Fifth, risk is not a static concept; it is dynamic and can increase or decrease as factors in the client's experience fluctuate. For example, a client judged to be at low risk at a time when external stressors are relatively manageable may be at a higher risk when an unexpected or significant negative event occurs. As such, estimations of risk level should be framed as short-term (i.e., a few days to a week) and contextual (i.e., this client in this context). Furthermore, risk evaluations should be repeated as the client's psychological or situational status changes.

Risk Evaluation of Nonsuicidal Self-Injury

> Clinical risk evaluation of NSSI
>> ■ Note: Research investigating the possible risk and protective factors for NSSI lags behind that for suicide. The risk evaluation guidelines for NSSI presented here are based on existing research findings and multiple-factor models of NSSI (e.g., Nock, 2009; Walsh, 2006).

- Risk factors
  - Current passive thoughts of NSSI
  - Current active thoughts of NSSI
    - Recent shift from passive to active thoughts
    - Active thoughts are intense
    - Active thoughts are frequent
    - Active thoughts include plan and method
      - Method is dangerous
      - Client has access to method
    - Presence of situational stressors that trigger thoughts
  - Current NSSI acts
    - Acts target atypical body part (face, eyes, breasts [in women], genitals)
    - Longer duration of episodes of acts
    - High frequency of episodes of acts
    - Serious physical damage caused by acts (required medical attention)
    - Client experienced physical pain
    - Presence of situational stressors that trigger acts
  - History of previous NSSI acts
    - Early age of onset
    - Acts within past 12 months
    - Atypical body part (face, eyes, breasts [for women], genitals) injured by act
    - Longer duration of episodes of acts
    - High frequency of episodes of acts
    - Serious physical damaged caused by acts (required medical attention)
    - Client's experience of physical pain
  - Frequent and/or intense negative emotionality in response to daily life
  - Difficulty identifying or expressing (negative) emotions
  - Difficulty regulating (negative) emotions
  - Self-derogation
  - Presence of profoundly negative body image
  - Poor social problem-solving skills (particularly when distressed)
  - Motivation to reduce or regulate negative thoughts and emotions with NSSI

- o Motivation to generate feelings (e.g., excitement, any feeling that lifts numbness or dissociative experience) with NSSI
- o Motivation to self-punish with NSSI
- o Motivation to communicate with or influence others with NSSI (e.g., elicit a response or escape a demand)
- o Having friends or family members who engage in NSSI
- o Recent interpersonal stressors (loss, conflict)
- Protective factors
  - o Family (or significant others) involvement and support
  - o Positive peer social network
  - o Religious and spiritual beliefs and institutional supports
  - o History of coping skills
  - o Recreational activities and interests
  - o Rapport with clinician and compliance with efforts to help
- ➢ Analysis of risk potential for NSSI
  - Low risk (e.g., no history of NSSI acts within past 12 months, no current NSSI thoughts or acts, presence of protective factors)
  - Moderate risk (e.g., no history of NSSI acts within past 12 months, current active ideation without clear idea of method, presence of some ability to cope with negative affect, some interpersonal stressors, presence of protective factors)
  - High risk (e.g., history of NSSI within past 12 months, current active ideation with clear idea of and access to method, current NSSI behavior, current psychological impairment, low number of protective factors)

Risk Evaluation of Suicide

- ➢ Clinical risk evaluation of suicide in child and adolescent clients
  - Risk factors
    - o History of previous suicide attempts (strongest predictor, especially for boys)

- In past 12 months
- Lethal method(s)
- Intent to die
- Required medical intervention
○ Current passive thoughts
○ Current active thoughts
  - Resolved plan and preparation factors
    · Plan is realistic
    · Method is lethal
    · Method is accessible (firearm in the home)
    · Current intent to die or inability to control impulse
○ Axis I risk factors
  - Major depressive disorder
    · With severe hopelessness
  - Bipolar disorder
  - Conduct disorder (for boys)
  - Substance abuse or dependence (particularly when comorbid with mood disorders)
  - Psychosis
    · With self-injury or suicide command hallucinations
○ Axis II trait risk factors (Apter, 2000; Brent et al., 1994)
  - Narcissistic perfectionist
  - Impulsive aggressive
  - Avoidant dependent
○ Learning disability (for girls)
○ Sexual orientation issues
○ NSSI history
  - High frequency of moderate to severe NSSI
  - Several types of NSSI
  - Several reasons for NSSI
  - Several functions served by NSSI (e.g., regulate emotional state, influence others)
○ Demographic risk factors
  - Male
  - Native American, Alaskan Native
○ Psychosocial risk factors
  - Childhood history of physical and/or sexual abuse or neglect

- ◆ Recent legal or discipline problem (incarceration, physical fights)
- ◆ Interpersonal loss or conflict
- ○ Family history and developmental trauma risk factors
  - ◆ Family member suicide attempts or completions
  - ◆ Family history of depression and/or substance abuse
  - ◆ Family history of violence
- ○ Personal contact with or media exposure to suicide
- Protective factors
  - ○ Family (or significant others) involvement and support
  - ○ Concern for loved ones
  - ○ Ability to see and/or have hope for future
  - ○ History of coping skills
  - ○ Religious and spiritual beliefs and institutional supports
  - ○ Access to mental health and medical treatment
  - ○ Rapport with clinician and compliance with efforts to help
- ➢ Actuarial measures of suicide risk for child and adolescent clients
  - Suicide Probability Scale (SPS)
    - ○ Ages 13 years and older
    - ○ Client self-report, paper-and-pencil administration
    - ○ Provides three summary scores (a total weighted score, a normalized T score, and a suicide probability score), four subscales (Hopelessness, Suicide Ideation, Negative Self-Evaluation, Hostility)
    - ○ Available from Western Psychological Services (http://www.wpspublish.com)
  - Adolescent & Child Urgent Threat Evaluation (ACUTE)
    - ○ Ages 8–18 years
    - ○ Clinician completed, paper-and-pencil administration
    - ○ Structured assessment based on information from client interview, collateral interview, and table review

- o Provides an overall threat classification, five cluster scores (e.g., precipitating factors, predisposing factors), and the ACUTE total score
- o Available from Psychological Assessment Resources (PAR; http://www4.parinc.com)
- ➢ Analysis of risk potential for child or adolescent client suicide
  - Low risk (e.g., no history of attempts within past 12 months, no current ideation, high number of protective factors, low-risk score on actuarial measure)
  - Moderate risk (e.g., no history of attempts within past 12 months, current active ideation without plan or intent, moderate number of protective factors, moderate-risk score on actuarial measure)
  - High risk (e.g., history of attempt within past 12 months, current active ideation with intent and/or plan, low number of protective factors, high-risk score on actuarial measure)
- ➢ Clinical risk evaluation of suicide in adult clients (older than 65 years)
  - Risk factors
    - o History of previous suicide attempts
      - ◆ In past 12 months
      - ◆ Lethal method(s)
      - ◆ Intent to die
      - ◆ Required medical intervention
    - o Current passive thoughts
    - o Current active thoughts
      - ◆ Resolved plan and preparation factors
        - · Plan is realistic
        - · Method is lethal
        - · Method is accessible
        - · Current intent to die or inability to control impulse
    - o Axis I risk factors
      - ◆ Major depressive disorder
        - · With severe hopelessness
        - · With generalized anxiety disorder or panic disorder

- - - Bipolar disorder
    - Chronic alcohol abuse dependence
    - Other substance abuse
    - Eating disorders, anorexia nervosa
    - Schizophrenia, psychosis
      - With self-injury or suicide command hallucinations
  - Axis II risk factors
    - Borderline personality disorder
    - Antisocial personality disorder
  - Impulsivity, aggression
  - NSSI history
  - Sleep disruption
  - Physical impairment (e.g., chronic illness, recent injury)
  - Demographic risk factors
    - Male
    - American Indian, Alaskan Native, or non-Hispanic White
  - Psychosocial risk factors
    - History of trauma or victimization (including combat exposure, sexual abuse, physical abuse)
    - Divorce
    - Death of a loved one
    - Other interpersonal loss or conflict
      - Coworker conflict
    - Recent financial disruption
    - Recent discharge from psychiatric hospital (within 3 months)
  - Family history risk factors
    - Family member suicide
    - Family history of mood disorders, substance abuse, schizophrenia, Cluster B personality disorders
- Protective factors
  - Commitment to family members
    - Custodial parent to child younger than 18 years
    - Pregnant
  - Family (or significant other) involvement and support

- History of coping skills
- Ability to see and have hope for future
- Religious and spiritual beliefs and institutional supports
- Access to mental health and medical treatment
- Rapport with clinician and compliance with efforts to help

> Analysis of risk potential for adult (less than 65 years) client suicide

- Low risk (e.g., no history of attempts within past 12 months, no current ideation, high number of protective factors)
- Moderate risk (e.g., no history of attempts within past 12 months, current active ideation without plan or intent, moderate number of protective factors)
- High risk (e.g., history of attempt within past 12 months, current active ideation with intent and/or plan, low number of protective factors)

> Clinical risk evaluation of suicide in elderly adult clients (65 years and older)

- Note: Older adults have the highest rate of suicide of any age group in the United States, and they have a significantly lower attempt:completion ratio than younger adults. This outline includes some of the special considerations in the evaluations of elderly clients (Bongar, 2002; Conwell & Heisel, 2006)
- Risk factors
    - History of previous suicide attempts
        - In past 12 months
        - Lethal method(s)
        - Intent to die
        - Required medical intervention
    - Current passive thoughts
    - Current active thoughts
        - Resolved plan and preparation factors
            - Plan is realistic
            - Method is lethal
            - Method is accessible (handgun in the home)
            - Current intent to die or inability to control impulse

- Axis I risk factors
  - Major depressive disorder (Note: Psychological disorder in the elderly is often undiagnosed; symptoms may be masked by the reluctance of older clients to disclose emotional difficulty and by comorbid medical illness and/or cognitive impairment.)
    - With severe hopelessness
  - Substance abuse or dependence, particularly alcohol
- NSSI history
- Physical impairment or change in physical functioning (particularly with comorbid depression)
  - Insomnia
  - Intractable pain
  - Loss of motor function
  - Central nervous system impairment (delirium, confusion)
  - Other changes that contribute to perceived loss of autonomy or dignity
- Demographic risk factors
  - Male
  - Over 65 years old, particularly over 80
  - Non-Hispanic White
- Psychosocial risk factors
  - Interpersonal loss or conflict
  - Recent major life transition
  - Recent discharge from psychiatric hospital (within 3 months)
- Protective factors
  - Family (or significant other) involvement and support
  - Concern for loved ones
  - Aspects of life over which client feels some control or sense of accomplishment
  - Access to a confidant
  - Access to mental health and medical treatment
  - Rapport with clinician and compliance with efforts to help
  - Religious and spiritual beliefs and institutional supports

➢ Analysis of risk potential for elderly adult client suicide
- Low risk (e.g., no history of attempts within past 12 months, no current ideation, high number of protective factors)
- Moderate risk (e.g., no history of attempts within past 12 months, current active ideation without plan or intent, moderate number of protective factors)
- High risk (e.g., history of attempt within past 12 months, current active ideation with intent and/or plan, low number of protective factors)

Risk Evaluation of Interpersonal Violence

Several structured clinical guidelines and actuarial measures are available for those clinicians working with violent offenders but not included in this chapter. For examples, see Webster (2004).

➢ Clinical risk evaluation of interpersonal violence
- Risk factors
  - History of sadistic fantasies
  - History of making threats of assault
    - In past 12 months
  - History of acts of aggression
    - In past 12 months
    - Lethal methods
    - Result of long-range planning or impulsive
    - Intoxicated at the time
    - Target injured
  - Current thoughts or fantasies of violence
    - Intense thoughts or sadistic fantasies
    - Thoughts increasing in seriousness of injury to target
    - Specific target
      - Available target
      - Child, elderly, or disabled target
      - Thoughts or fantasies in presence of target
    - Resolved plan and preparation factors
      - Plan is realistic
      - Method is injurious
      - Method is accessible
      - Current intent to execute plan or inability to control impulse

- Axis I risk factors
  - ◆ Active psychotic symptoms (especially paranoid schizophrenia)
    - · Command hallucinations
    - · Delusions of threat or control by outside forces (persecutory)
  - ◆ Substance abuse (particularly alcohol, PCP, cocaine, amphetamines, anabolic steroids and particularly when comorbid with a major mental disorder)
  - ◆ Major depressive disorder
  - ◆ Bipolar disorder
  - ◆ Paranoid symptoms
  - ◆ Depression symptoms and/or despair
- Axis II risk factors
  - ◆ Cluster B personality disorders (antisocial, borderline, narcissistic)
  - ◆ Paranoid personality disorder
  - ◆ Psychopathy
- Brain injury associated with increased aggressiveness and/or impulsivity
- Central nervous system impairment (clouded sensorium)
- Demographic risk factors
  - ◆ Males older than 20 years, females older than 34 years
- Psychosocial risk factors
  - ◆ Childhood history of fire setting, enuresis, and cruelty to animals (triad of all three)
  - ◆ Experience of serious child abuse
  - ◆ Prior convictions for violence
  - ◆ Pattern of unstable, highly conflicted interpersonal relationships
  - ◆ Dangerous or criminal social networks (e.g., gang membership)
- Protective factors
  - Family (or significant others) involvement and support
  - Positive peer social contact/support
  - Access to mental health and medical treatment

- o Rapport with clinician and compliance with efforts to help
- ➤ Structured clinical guidelines for risk evaluation of interpersonal violence
  - ■ Chronic Violent Behavior Risk and Needs Assessment (CARE–2)
    - o Ages 6–19 years
    - o Clinician completed, paper-and-pencil administration
    - o Screening measure for risk and protective factors associated with violent behavior
    - o Available from MHS (http://www.mhs.com)
  - ■ HCR-20, Assessing Risk for Violence (Version 2)
    - o Adults
    - o Clinician completed, paper-and-pencil administration
    - o Structured assessment of 20 risk factors (10 historical items, five clinical items, five risk management items)
    - o HCR-20 Violence Risk Management Companion Guide provides brief descriptions of violence intervention strategies
    - o Available from PAR (http://www4.parinc.com)
  - ■ Structured Assessment of Violence Risk in Youth (SAVRY)
    - o Ages 12–18 years
    - o Clinician completed, paper-and-pencil administration
    - o Structured assessment of three risk domains (historical risk factors, social/contextual risk factors, individual/clinical factors) and protective factors
    - o Available from PAR (http://www4.parinc.com)
  - ■ Spousal Assault Risk Assessment (SARA)
    - o Ages 18 years and older
    - o Males only
    - o Clinician completed, paper-and-pencil administration
    - o Checklist to ensure assessment of risk factors associated with perpetration of spousal abuse
    - o Available from MHS (http://www.mhs.com)

> Actuarial Measures of Interpersonal Violence Risk
>   - Adolescent & Child Urgent Threat Evaluation (ACUTE)
>   - Ages 8–18 years
>   - Clinician completed, paper-and-pencil administration
>   - Structured assessment based on information from client interview, collateral interview, and table review
>   - Provides an overall threat classification, five cluster scores (e.g., precipitating factors, predisposing factors), and the ACUTE total score
>   - Available from PAR (http://www4.parinc.com)
>   - Classification of Violence Risk (COVR)
>   - Software program classification system
>   - Involves 10-min interview with client and a record review for specific clinical information (e.g., diagnosis, seriousness of prior arrests)
>   - Provides an actuarial determination of low to high risk for near-future (within several months) violence for psychiatric inpatients released into the community
>   - Available from PAR (http://www4.parinc.com)
>   - Psychosocial Evaluation & Threat Risk Assessment (PETRA)
>   - Ages 11–18 years
>   - Client self-report questionnaire for adolescents who have already exhibited threatening behavior primarily in school, paper-and-pencil administration
>   - Four domain scores (psychosocial, resiliency problems, ecological, total), eight cluster scores (e.g., depressed mood, alienation), two response style indicators, and eight critical items (threat risk factors)
>   - Uses T scores and percentiles; provides an estimation of risk (low, medium, high) based on threat itself
>   - Available from PAR (http://www4.parinc.com)
> Analysis of risk potential for interpersonal violence
>   - Low risk (e.g., no history of physical violence threats or acts, no current ideation, presence of protective factors; low-risk score on actuarial measure)

- Moderate risk (e.g., no history of physical violence threats or acts within past 12 months, current active ideation without plan or intent, presence of protective factors, moderate-risk score on actuarial measure)
- High risk (e.g., history of physical threats or acts within past 12 months, current active ideation with intent and/or plan, high impulsivity or substance abuse, low number of protective factors, high-risk score on actuarial measure)

Step 3: On the Basis of the Risk Evaluation, Determine Whether Immediate Actions Are Necessary to Safeguard Client or Others

> Seek consultation as necessary with other professionals (including those who also may be treating the client) regarding specific risk evaluation findings, intervention strategies and resources, and the clinician's legal responsibilities (e.g., duty to protect or warn a potential victim) with the consent of client or within legally permissive standards.
> Consider increasing level of care of client (e.g., inpatient hospitalization, partial hospitalization), including involuntary restraint if client is unwilling or unable to comply with treatment recommendations.
> Fulfill legally mandated duties (e.g., Tarasoff warning).
> Involve significant others (particularly parents or guardians if the client is a child or adolescent, or caretaker or guardian if the client is an elderly person, with consent of client or within legally permissive standards).

Step 4: Create and Implement a Treatment Plan That Targets Treatable or Modifiable Risk and Protective Factors

> List significant risk and protective factors identified in the risk evaluation for the client.
> Seek consultation as necessary with other professionals (including those who also may be treating the client) regarding intervention strategies and resources.
> Develop a treatment plan by identifying specific interventions to target each significant factor, reducing the risk factors and creating or enhancing the protective factors

(e.g., removal of available weapons by a third party, medication evaluation for serious psychological symptoms, involvement in Alcoholics Anonymous or Narcotics Anonymous to address substance abuse issues, exploration of community resources to increase social contact, family therapy to improve family communication and problem solving, increased frequency of therapeutic contacts with the clinician).

➤ Discuss the treatment plan with the client, soliciting his or her input and commitment.

Step 5: Document, Document, Document

➤ As always, document dates and substance of face-to-face sessions with client as well as dates and substance of telephone calls, notes, or other communications from the client.
➤ Outline the factors considered in the risk evaluation and the level of risk assigned.
➤ Describe the decision-making process regarding immediate actions considered and taken (including options weighed, rationales for choices and client's response).
➤ Document the longer term treatment plan (including options weighed, rationales for choices, and client's response).
➤ Record the date and substance of consultations.
➤ Document any contacts with family members or significant others during the implementation of the treatment plan.

References

American Psychiatric Association. (2003). Practice guideline for the assessment and treatment of patients with suicidal behaviors. *American Journal of Psychiatry, 16*(Suppl. 11), 1–60.

Apter, A. (2000). Personality constellations in suicidal behavior. In *Proceedings of the Fifth Annual Conference, Irish Association of Suicidology* (pp. 14–25). Castlebar, County Mayo, Ireland: Irish Association of Suicidology.

Ash, P. (2006). Children and adolescents. In R. I. Simon & R. E. Hales (Eds.), *The textbook of suicide assessment and management* (pp. 35–55). Washington, DC: American Psychiatric Publishing.

Benjamin, G. A. H., Kent, L., & Sirikantraporn, S. (2009). A review of duty-to-protect statutes, cases, and procedures for positive practice. In J. L. Werth, E. R. Welfel, & G. A. H. Benjamin (Eds.), *The duty to protect: Ethical, legal, and professional considerations for mental health professionals* (pp. 9–28). Washington, DC: American Psychological Association. doi:10.1037/11866-002

Bennett, B. E., Bricklin, P. M., Harris, E., Knapp, S., VandeCreek, L., & Younggren, J. N. (2006). *Assessing and managing risk in psychological practice: An individualized approach.* Rockville, MD: The Trust.

Berman, A. L., Jobes, D. A., & Silverman, M. M. (2006). *Adolescent suicide: Assessment and intervention* (2nd ed.). Washington, DC: American Psychological Association. doi:10.1037/11285-000

Bongar, B. (2002). *The suicidal patient: Clinical and legal standards of care* (2nd ed.). Washington, DC: American Psychological Association. doi:10.1037/10424-000

Brent, D. A., Johnson, B. A., Perper, J., Connolly, J., Bridge, J., Bartle, S., & Rather, C. (1994). Personality disorder, personality traits, impulsive violence, and completed suicide in adolescents. *Journal of the American Academy of Child and Adolescent Psychiatry, 33,* 1080–1086.

Chiles, J. A., & Strosahl, K. D. (2005). *Clinical manual for assessment and treatment of suicidal patients.* Washington, DC: American Psychiatric Publishing.

Conwell, Y., & Heisel, M. J. (2006). The elderly. In R. I. Simon & R. E. Hales (Eds.), *The textbook of suicide assessment and management* (pp. 57–76). Washington, DC: American Psychiatric Publishing.

Granello, D. H. (2010). The process of suicide risk assessment: Twelve core principles. *Journal of Counseling & Development, 88,* 363–371.

Jobes, D. A. (2006). *Managing suicidal risk: A collaborative approach.* New York, NY: Guilford Press.

Klonsky, E. D., & Muehlenkamp, J. J. (2007). Self-injury: A research review for the practitioner. *Journal of Clinical Psychology: In session, 63,* 1045–1056.

Litwack, T. R., & Schlesinger, L. B. (1999). Dangerousness risk assessments: Research, legal, and clinical considerations. In A. K. Hess & I. B. Weiner (Eds.), *The handbook of forensic psychology* (2nd ed., pp. 171–217). New York, NY: Wiley.

Monahan, J. (2001). Major mental disorder and violence: Epidemiology and risk assessment. In G.-F. Pinard & L. Pagani (Eds.), *Clinical assessments of dangerousness: Empirical contributions* (pp. 89–102). Cambridge, England: Cambridge University Press.

Monahan, J., Steadman, H. J., Silver, E., Appelbaum, P. S., Robbins, P. C., Mulvey, E. P., . . . Banks, S. (2001). *Rethinking risk assessment: The MacArthur Study of Mental Disorder and Violence.* New York, NY: Oxford University Press.

Nock, M. K. (Ed.). (2009). *Understanding nonsuicidal self-injury: Origins, assessment, and treatment.* Washington, DC: American Psychological Association. doi:10.1037/11875-000

Nock, M. K., & Prinstein, M. J. (2004). A functional approach to the assessment of self-mutilative behavior. *Journal of Consulting and Clinical Psychology, 72,* 885–890. doi:10.1037/0022-006X.72.5.885

Pagani, L., & Pinard, G.-F. (2001). Clinical assessment of dangerousness: An overview of the literature. In G.-F. Pinard & L. Pagani (Eds.), *Clinical assessments of dangerousness: Empirical contributions* (pp. 1–22). New York, NY: Cambridge University Press.

Pope, K. S., & Vasquez, M. J. T. (2010). *Ethics in psychotherapy and counseling: A practical guide* (4th ed.). San Francisco, CA: Wiley.

Rudd, M. D., & Joiner, T. E. (1999). Assessment of suicidality in outpatient practice. In L. VandeCreek & T. Jackson (Eds.), *Innovations in clinical practice: A sourcebook* (Vol. 17, pp. 101–117). Sarasota, FL: Professional Resource Press.

Rudd, M. D., Joiner, T. E., & Rajab, H. (2001). *Treating suicidal behavior: An effective time-limited approach.* New York, NY: Guilford Press.

Simon, R. (2006). Suicide risk: Assessing the unpredictable. In R. I. Simon & R. E. Hales (Eds.), *The textbook of suicide assessment and management* (pp. 1–32). Washington, DC: American Psychiatric Publishing.

Sommers-Flanagan, J., & Sommers-Flanagan, R. (2009). *Clinical interviewing* (4th ed.). Hoboken, NJ: Wiley.

Tardiff, K. (2001). Axis II disorders and dangerousness. In G.-F. Pinard & L. Pagani (Eds.), *Clinical assessments of dangerousness: Empirical contributions* (pp. 103–120). Cambridge, England: Cambridge University Press.

Walsh, B. W. (2006). *Treating self-injury: A practical guide.* New York, NY: Guilford Press.

Webster, C. D. (2004). *Risk assessment: Actuarial instruments & structured clinical guides.* Retrieved from http://www.violence-risk.com/risk/instruments.htm

Wingate, L. R., Joiner, T. E., Walker, R. L., Rudd, M. D., & Jobes, D. A. (2004). Empirically informed approaches to topics in suicide risk assessment. *Behavioral Sciences & the Law, 22,* 651–665. doi:10.1002/bsl.612

CHAPTER 8

Child Abuse Reporting

Mandatory reporting of child abuse and neglect by health professionals did not appear in U.S. state laws until the 1960s, although social concern for child welfare arose as a national issue nearly a century before (Barnett, Miller-Perrin, & Perrin, 2005). As a result of early clinical reports from medical professionals regarding children who were physically abused (e.g., the introduction of *battered child syndrome* as a new medical diagnosis; Kempe, Silverman, Steele, Droegemueller, & Silver, 1962), model reporting statutes were proposed by the Children's Bureau of the National Center on Child Abuse and Neglect in 1963 and the American Medical Association and the Program of State Governments in 1965. Within 1 year, all states (except Hawaii) wrote and adopted laws mandating physicians to report suspected physical abuse of a child. Over the next 3 decades the definitions of child abuse were expanded by federal and, subsequently, state legislators to include emotional abuse (or psychological maltreatment), sexual abuse or exploitation, and negligent treatment. The range of professionals mandated to report such maltreatment was also expanded to include mental health professionals, teachers, and others. Legislation enacted by Congress (i.e., the Child Abuse Prevention and Treatment Act of 1974 and a subsequent amendment, the Child Abuse Prevention, Adoption, and Family Services Act of 1988) made federal funds available to help states develop child protection programs (see Kalichman, 1999, for information on this legislation).

Currently, all 50 states and the District of Columbia have laws specifying a system for reporting, investigating, and responding to child abuse. The laws vary from state to state. Laws differ in the definitions of the subtypes of child abuse and neglect, the threshold for reporting (e.g., "reasonable suspicion," "having knowledge through observation"), the designation of mandated reporters (e.g., any person who suspects child abuse or neglect, professionals [including mental health professionals] in the performance of their work duties), and the requirements for reporting (e.g., oral vs. oral and written, time limits).

Psychologists and other mental health professionals may be required at some point in their careers to report a case of child abuse or neglect. They should be aware of and able to access for review the specific elements of their state laws to ensure their compliance with the law and, most important, the protection of the child. Table 8.1 is intended to provide an initial resource for therapists. The table lists national Internet resources, citations for state child abuse reporting statutes, reporting contacts, child abuse hotline telephone numbers, and additional Internet resources (some containing official reporting forms, e.g., Connecticut, Maryland, Nevada). Although all attempts were made at the time of the creation of Table 8.1 to ensure that the information was current and correct, it is important to keep in mind that state laws continually undergo revision and that telephone contacts and Internet links are subject to change at any time. It is also noteworthy that in some states the clinician may need to research more than one law. Several states have specific statutes that articulate the definitions of child abuse and different statues regarding the reporting requirements. The U.S. Department of Health and Human Services provides a website offering up-to-date information on a variety of child welfare topics, including abuse and neglect, and a state statutes database of the state laws and regulations related to child protection (Child Welfare Information Gateway, 2009). Therapists are advised to study all relevant child abuse statutes in their practice state as well as consult with other professionals (including attorneys knowledgeable about mental health law), if necessary, as they determine how best to deal with suspected child maltreatment.

TABLE 8.1
Child Abuse: National Resources and Reporting Information by State

National resources	Child Welfare Information Gateway at http://www.childwelfare.gov is the successor to the National Clearinghouse on Child Abuse and Neglect Information. It includes a database of state-specific statutes, searchable by topic. National Child Abuse Hotline: 1-800-4-A-CHILD (1-800-422-4453) Prevent Child Abuse America at http://www.preventchildabuse.org/about_us/index.shtml provides general information to raise awareness and provide education as well as state-specific links for 47 states.
State	**State law regarding reporting abuse, report contact numbers, and additional web resources**
Alabama	Law: Alabama Code 26-14-1 et seq. Call: local county Department of Human Resources or law enforcement agency or 1-334-242-9500 Additional web resources: Child Protective Services at http://www.dhr.alabama.gov/services/Child_Protective_Services/Child_Protective_Services.aspx
Alaska	Law: Alaska Stat. 47.17.010 et seq. Call: local Health and Social Services agency or law enforcement (if cannot reach social services and child is in imminent danger) or 1-800-478-4444 Additional web resources: Office of Children's Services at http://www.hss.state.ak.us/ocs/
Arizona	Law: Arizona Rev. Stat. 13-3620 Call: local law enforcement or Child Protective Services agency (in Department of Economic Security) or 1-888-SOS-CHILD (1-888-767-2443) Additional web resources: Child Protective Services at http://www.azdes.gov/dcyf/cps

(continued)

TABLE 8.1 (*Continued*)
**Child Abuse: National Resources and
Reporting Information by State**

Arkansas	Law: Arkansas Code Ann. 12-12-507 Call: 1-800-482-5964 Additional web resources: Reporting Child Abuse & Neglect in Arkansas at http://www.arkansas.gov/reportARchildabuse/
California	Law: California Penal Code 11165 et seq.; 11166 et seq. Call: local Child Protective Services or law enforcement agency or 1-800-4-A-CHILD for assistance Additional web resources: Child Protective Services at http://www.dss.cahwnet.gov/cdssweb/PG93.htm The Child Abuse & Neglect Reporting Law in California at http://www.cdss.ca.gov/cdssweb/entres/forms/English/PUB132.pdf
Colorado	Law: Colorado Rev. Stat. 19-3-304 et seq. Call: local Department of Human Services or law enforcement agency or 1-800-4-A-CHILD for assistance Additional web resources: Listings of county departments of human services offices at http://www.cdhs.state.co.us/childwelfare/FAQ.htm
Connecticut	Law: Connecticut Gen. Stat. 17a-101a et seq. Call: local Department of Children and Families or law enforcement agency or 1-800-842-2288 Additional web resources: Department of Children and Families' Q & A About Reporting Child Abuse and Neglect at http://www.ct.gov/dcf/cwp/view.asp?a=2556&q=314388
Delaware	Law: Delaware Code Ann. Title 16, 901 et seq. Call: 1-800-292-9582, 1-302-577-6550 Additional web resources: Delaware State Child Abuse Intervention at http://kids.delaware.gov/fs/fs_cai.shtml

TABLE 8.1 (*Continued*)
Child Abuse: National Resources and
Reporting Information by State

District of Columbia	Law: D.C. Code Ann. 4-1321.01 et seq. Call: 1-202-671-7233, 1-877-671-SAFE (1-877-671-7233), or local police department Additional resources: Child and Family Services Agency Reporting and Investigations at http://cfsa.dc.gov/DC/CFSA
Florida	Law: Florida Stat. Ann. 39.201 et seq. Call: 1-800-96-ABUSE (1-800-962-2873) Additional web resources: Department of Children and Families Abuse Hotline at http://www.dcf.state.fl.us/programs/abuse/
Georgia	Law: Georgia Code Ann. 19-7-5; 16-12-100 Call: local child welfare agency (Division of Family and Children Services) or law enforcement (if child welfare agency is unavailable or child is in imminent danger) or 1-800-4-A-CHILD for assistance Additional web resources: Child Protection Services at http://dfcs.dhr.georgia.gov/portal/site/DHS-DFCS/menuitem.5d32235bb09bde9a50c8798dd03036a0/?vgnextoid=213a2b48d9a4ff00VgnVCM100000bf01010aRCRD
Hawaii	Law: Hawaii Rev. Stat. 350-1 et seq. Call: 1-800-832-5300 (Oahu), 1-800-4-A-CHILD (1-800-422-4453 for other callers), or local law enforcement Additional web resources: Child Welfare Services at http://hawaii.gov/dhs/protection/social_services/child_welfare/
Idaho	Law: Idaho Code 16-1605 et seq. Contact: local Department of Health and Welfare or law enforcement agency or 1-800-926-2588 Additional web resources: Child Protection Services at http://www.healthandwelfare.idaho.gov/?TabId=74

(*continued*)

TABLE 8.1 (*Continued*)
**Child Abuse: National Resources and
Reporting Information by State**

Illinois	Law: Illinois Cons. Stat. Ch. 325, 5/2; 5/3; 5/4; 5/7; 5/9; Ch. 720, 5/11-20.2 Call: 1-800-252-2873, 1-217-785-4020, 1-217-782-6533 (after hours) Additional web resources: Department of Child and Family Services Child Abuse and Neglect at http://www.state.il.us/dcfs/FAQ/faq_faq_can.shtml
Indiana	Law: Indiana Code Ann. 31-33-5-1 et seq. Call: local Department of child services; law enforcement agency or 1-800-800-5556, 1-317-542-7002 Additional web resources: Child Protective Services http://www.in.gov/dcs/2362.htm
Iowa	Law: Iowa Ann. Stat. 232.68-70 Call: local Department of Human Services agency (and local law enforcement if immediate protection is required) or 1-800-362-2178, 1-515-281-3240 Additional web resources: Prevent Child Abuse Iowa at http://www.pcaiowa.org/
Kansas	Law: Kansas Stat. Ann. 38-2223; 22a-242 Call: local Department of Social and Rehabilitation Services agency or law enforcement agency (if the department is not open) or 1-800-922-5330, 1-785-296-0044 Additional web resources: Child Protective Services at http://www.srs.ks.gov/agency/cfs/pages/childprotectiveservices.aspx
Kentucky	Law: Kentucky Rev. Stat. 620.030 Call: local Cabinet for Health and Family Services or law enforcement agency; commonwealth attorney; county attorney; or 1-800-752-6200, 1-502-595-4550 Additional web resources: Cabinet for Health and Family Services Child Safety Branch at http://chfs.ky.gov/dcbs/dpp/childsafety.htm

TABLE 8.1 (*Continued*)
Child Abuse: National Resources and Reporting Information by State

Louisiana	Law: Louisiana Children's Code Art. 603(13); 609-611 Call: local Child Protection Unit in Department of Social Services or 1-225-342-6832 Additional web resources: Department of Social Services Reporting Child Abuse or Neglect at http://dss.louisiana.gov/index.cfm?md=pagebuilder&tmp=home&pid=109
Maine	Law: Maine Rev. Stat. Ann. Title 22, 4011-A; 4011-B; 4012; 4014 Call: local Department of Human Services or 1-800-452-1999, 1-207-287-2983 Additional web resources: Child and Family Services Child Welfare and Child Protection at http://www.maine.gov/dhhs/ocfs/cw/abuse.shtml
Maryland	Law: Maryland Code Ann., Family Law 5-701 et seq. Call: local Department of Social Services or law enforcement agency or 1-800-322-6347 Additional web resources: Child Protective Services at http://www.dhr.state.md.us/cps/address.php
Massachusetts	Law: Massachusetts Gen. Laws Ch. 119, 51A Call: 1-800-792-5200, 1-617-232-4882 Additional web resources: Department of Children and Families at http://www.mass.gov/?pageID=eohhs2subtopic&L=4&L0=Home&L1=Consumer&L2=Family+Services&L3=Child+Abuse+and+Neglect&sid=Eeohhs2
Michigan	Law: Michigan Comp. Laws 722.621 et seq. Call: local Family Independence Agency or 1-800-942-4357, 1-517-373-3572 Additional web resources: Child Protective Services at http://www.michigan.gov/dhs/0,1607,7-124-5452_7119—-,00.html

(continued)

TABLE 8.1 (*Continued*)
Child Abuse: National Resources and Reporting Information by State

Minnesota	Law: Minnesota Stat. Ann. 626.556 (subd. 3, 7, 9); 626.5561 et seq. Call: local welfare or law enforcement agency or 1-651-291-0211 Additional web resources: Child Protection at http://www.dhs.state.mn.us/main/idcplg?Idc Service=GET_DYNAMIC_CONVERSION& RevisionSelectionMethod=LatestReleased&dD ocName=id_000152
Mississippi	Law: Mississippi Code Ann. 43-21-353 Call: local Department of Human Services agency or 1-800-222-8000, 1-601-359-4991 Additional web resources: Child Protective Services at http://www.mdhs.state.ms.us/fcs_ prot.html
Missouri	Law: Missouri Ann. Stat. 210.110; 210.115; 210.130; 210.135; 568.110 Call: local Children's Division of the Department of Social Services or 1-800-392-3738, 1-573-751-3448 Additional web resources: Department of Social Services Reporting Child Abuse and Neglect at http://www.dss.mo.gov/cd/rptcan.htm
Montana	Law: Montana Code Ann. 41-3-101 & 102; 41-3-201 et seq. Call: local Department of Public Health and Human Services agency or 1-866-820-KIDS, 1-406-444-5900 Additional web resources: Child & Family Services Division at http://www.dphhs.mt. gov/cfsd/index.shtml
Nebraska	Law: Nebraska Rev. Stat. 28-710 & 711 Call: local Department of Health and Human Services agency or 1-800-652-1999, 1-402-595-1324 Additional web resources: Department of Health and Human Services, Child Abuse at http:// www.hhs.state.ne.us/cha/chaindex.htm

TABLE 8.1 (*Continued*)
**Child Abuse: National Resources and
Reporting Information by State**

Nevada	Law: Nevada Rev. Stat. 432B.010 et seq.; 432B.220 through 250 Call: local child welfare services or law enforcement agency or 1-800-992-5757, 1-775-684-4400 Additional web resources: Child Protective Services at http://www.dcfs.state.nv.us/DCFS_ChildProtectiveSvcs.htm
New Hampshire	Law: New Hampshire Rev. Stat. Ann. 169-C:3 & 29-32 Call: local Department of Health and Human Services agency or 1-800-894-5533, 1-800-852-3388 (after hours), 1-603-271-6556 Additional web resources: Department of Health and Human Services, Division for Children, Youth, and Families Child Protective Services at http://www.dhhs.nh.us/dcyf/cps/index.htm
New Jersey	Law: New Jersey Stat. Ann. 9:6-8.9 et seq. Call: local Division of Youth and Family Services agency or 1-800-792-8610 Additional web resources: How and When to Report Child Abuse or Neglect at http://www.state.nj.us/dcf/abuse/how/index.html
New Mexico	Law: New Mexico Stat. Ann. 32A-4-3 Call: local Children, Youth, and Families Department; law enforcement; tribal law enforcement or social services agency; or 1-800-797-3260, 1-505-841-6100 Additional web resources: Child Abuse & Neglect at http://www.cyfd.org/node/26
New York	Law: New York Soc. Serv. Law. 412-413; 415-416; 418-420 Call: 1-800-342-3720, 1-518-474-8740 Additional web resources: Office of Children and Family Services, Child Abuse Prevention at http://www.ocfs.state.ny.us/main/prevention/

(*continued*)

TABLE 8.1 (*Continued*)
**Child Abuse: National Resources and
Reporting Information by State**

North Carolina	Law: North Carolina Gen. Stat. 7B-101; 7B-301; 8-53.3 Call: local Department of Social Services agency or 1-800-4-A-CHILD for assistance Additional web resources: Child Protective Services at http://www.dhhs.state.nc.us/dss/cps/index.htm
North Dakota	Law: North Dakota Cent. Code 50-25.1-01 et seq. Call: local Department of Human Services agency or 1-800-245-3736, 1-701-328-2316 Additional web resources: Child Protection Program at http://www.nd.gov/dhs/services/childfamily/cps/
Ohio	Law: Ohio Rev. Stat. 2151.01 through .05; 2151.421 et seq. Call: local Public Children Services or law enforcement agency or 1-800-4-A-CHILD for assistance. Additional web resources: Child Protective Services at http://jfs.ohio.gov/ocf/childprotectiveservices.stm
Oklahoma	Law: Oklahoma Stat. Ann. Title 10, 7101 et seq. Call: local Department of Human Services agency or 1-800-522-3511 Additional web resources: Child Protective Services at http://www.okdhs.org/programsandservices/cps/default.htm
Oregon	Law: Oregon Rev. Stat. 419B.005-.015 Call: local Department of Human Services or law enforcement agency or 1-800-854-3508, ext. 2402; 1-503-378-6704 Additional web resources: Child Abuse & Neglect at http://www.oregon.gov/DHS/children/abuse/

TABLE 8.1 (*Continued*)
**Child Abuse: National Resources and
Reporting Information by State**

Pennsylvania	Law: Pennsylvania Cons. Stat. Title 23, 6301-6303; 6311 et seq. Call: local Department of Public Welfare agency or 1-800-932-0313, 1-717-783-8744 Additional web resources: Child Welfare Services at http://www.dpw.state.pa.us/forchildren/childwelfareservices/index.htm
Rhode Island	Law: Rhode Island Gen. Laws 40-11-3; 40-11-6; 40-11-11 Call: 1-800-RI-CHILD (1-800-742-4453) Additional web resources: Child Protective Services at http://www.dcyf.ri.gov/child_welfare/index.php
South Carolina	Law: South Carolina Code Ann. 63-7-10; 63-7-310; 63-7-360; 63-7-390 Call: local Department of Social Services or law enforcement agency or 1-803-898-7318 Additional web resources: Child Protective Services at http://dss.sc.gov/content/customers/protection/cps/index.aspx
South Dakota	Law: South Dakota Ann. Laws 26-8A-1 et seq. Call: local Department of Social Services or law enforcement agency, the state's attorney, or 1-605-773-3227 Additional web resources: Child Protection Services at http://dss.sd.gov/cps/protective/reporting.asp
Tennessee	Law: Tennessee Code Ann. 37-1-401 et seq.; 37-1-605 Call: local Department of Children's Services or law enforcement agency, juvenile court judge, or 1-877-237-0004 Additional web resources: Department of Children's Services Child Safety at at http://state.tn.us/youth/childsafety.htm

(*continued*)

TABLE 8.1 (*Continued*)
**Child Abuse: National Resources and
Reporting Information by State**

Texas	Law: Texas Fam. Code 261.001 et seq. Call: local Department of Family and Protective Services or law enforcement agency or 1-800-252-5400 Additional web resources: Department of Family and Protective Services at http://www.dfps.state.tx.us
Utah	Law: Utah Code Ann. 62A-4a-401 et seq. Call: local Division of Child and Family Services or law enforcement agency or 1-800-678-9399 Additional web resources: Child and Family Services, Child Abuse and Neglect Investigation at http://dcfs.utah.gov/can_investigation.htm
Vermont	Law: Vermont Stat. Ann. Title 33, 4911 et seq. Call: 1-800-649-5285, 1-802-863-7533 (after hours) Additional web resources: Reporting Child Abuse at http://dcf.vermont.gov/fsd/reporting_child_abuse
Virginia	Law: Virginia Code Ann. 63.2-1501 et seq. Call: local Department of Social Services agency or 1-800-552-7096, 1-804-786-8536 Additional web resources: Child Protective Services at http://www.dss.virginia.gov/family/cps/index.html
Washington	Law: Washington Rev. Code 26.44.020 et seq. Call: local Department of Social and Health Services or law enforcement agency or 1-866-END-HARM (1-866-363-4276) Additional web resources: Child Safety and Protection, Report Abuse at http://www.dshs.wa.gov/ca/safety/abuseReport.asp?2

TABLE 8.1 (*Continued*)
Child Abuse: National Resources and
Reporting Information by State

West Virginia	Law: West Virginia Code Ann. 49-6A-1 et seq. Call: local Child Protective Services in the Department of Health and Human Resources or law enforcement if the child has suffered serious physical or sexual abuse or 1-800-352-6513 Additional web resources: Child Protective Services at http://www.wvdhhr.org/bcf/children_adult/cps/report.asp
Wisconsin	Law: Wisconsin Stat. Ann. 48.981 Call: local Department of Children and Families or law enforcement agency or 1-608-266-3036 Additional web resources: Child Protective Services at http://dcf.wisconsin.gov/children/CPS/index.htm
Wyoming	Law: Wyoming Stat. Ann. 14-3-201 et seq. Call: local Department of Family Services Child Protection or law enforcement agency or 1-800-457-3659 Additional web resources: Child Protective Services at http://dfsweb.state.wy.us/protective-services/cps/index.html

References

Barnett, O., Miller-Perrin, C. L., & Perrin, R. D. (2005). *Family violence across the lifespan: An introduction* (2nd ed.). Thousand Oaks, CA: Sage.

Child Welfare Information Gateway. (2009). State statutes retrieved from http://www.childwelfare.gov/systemwide/laws_policies/state/

Kalichman, S. C. (1999). *Mandated reporting of suspected child abuse: Ethics, law, and policy* (2nd ed.). Washington, DC: American Psychological Association. doi:10.1037/10337-000

Kempe, C. H., Silverman, F. N., Steele, B. F., Droegemueller, W., & Silver, H. K. (1962). The battered child syndrome. *JAMA, 181,* 17–24.

CHAPTER 9

Reporting Abuse of Elderly and Dependent, Vulnerable, or Disabled Adults

The federal Older Americans Act was enacted in 1965 to ensure and enhance the welfare of older adult citizens in the United States through community-based services systems organized at the state level. The act established the Administration on Aging within the Department of Health and Human Services and initiated federal funding for state agencies on aging (Administration on Aging, 2009). Over the next decade, elder abuse was identified as a social problem of increasing concern by governmental agencies and community and professional organizations (Barnett, Miller-Perrin, & Perrin, 2005). Legislative responses followed. Some type of adult protection program had been established in every state by 1985 (Quinn, 1985), and in 1988 the Administration on Aging founded the National Center on Elder Abuse. By 1989, 42 states had established mandatory elder abuse reporting laws (Wolf & Pillemer, 1989). Funding from the 1992 Vulnerable Elder Rights Protection Title (Title VII, an amendment to the Older Americans Act) and other programs supported further state legislation for and coordination of the mechanisms for reporting and responding to complaints of elder abuse, neglect, or exploitation (Administration on Aging, 2009). In March 2010, President Barack Obama signed the Elder Justice Act and the Patient Safety and Abuse Prevention Act into law as part of health care reform legislation, creating federal oversight of elder abuse prevention efforts for the first time (International Federation on Ageing, 2010).

Currently, all 50 states and the District of Columbia have laws authorizing the establishment of adult protective services agencies, specifying a system for reporting and investigating elder abuse, and providing services to those abused. The laws vary from state to state (National Center on Elder Abuse, 2010). Most state adult protective services laws (but not all) also provide protection for adults (18 and older) who are dependent, vulnerable, or disabled as a result of physical or mental disability or incapacitation that restricts the individual's ability to perform normal activities of daily living. Some states have adult protective services laws that include provisions only for endangered adults living in the community and have separate laws for those adults who live in long-term care facilities and/or medical or mental health hospitals or institutions (including state developmental centers), whereas some states cover adults living in either location. State laws also vary regarding the age at which a patient is considered an elder adult (60 or 65 years or older); the definitions of what constitutes abuse, neglect, or exploitation (e.g., whether neglect includes self-neglect); whether reporting is mandated by any individual or by specific professionals (as in the majority of states) or is permissive for all; the threshold for reporting (e.g., substantial cause to believe, reasonable cause to suspect, observation, report from the individual); whether there are any exceptions to the reporting mandate; and the requirements for reporting (e.g., oral vs. oral and written, time limits).

Typically, the laws specify that reports of in-home abuse are made to local adult protective services agencies (and/or, in some states, to law enforcement). Alternatively, reports of abuse occurring in long-term care facilities, hospitals, or institutions must be made to other state or local agencies (e.g., long-term care ombudsmen), in some cases directly by the person who first receives the information and in some cases by the person in charge of the institution. In some states (e.g., Alaska), all reports of fraud or financial exploitation are made to other specific agencies (e.g., the Office of Elder Fraud & Assistance), regardless of where the individual is living.

Because psychologists and other mental health professionals may encounter a case in which they are required or permitted to report abuse, neglect, or exploitation of an elderly or vulnerable client, they should be aware of the specific elements of the laws of the state in which they work. Table 9.1 is intended as an initial resource to assist therapists in assessing reporting requirements for vulnerable adults who reside in the community. The table lists national Internet resources and adult protective services statutes, contact information for filing reports of in-home abuse, and additional Internet resources by state. It is worth

TABLE 9.1
Elder and Dependent, Vulnerable, or Disabled Adult Abuse: National Resources and Reporting Information by State

National resources	The Clearinghouse on Abuse and Neglect of the Elderly presents the nation's most extensive database of annotated references for elder abuse literature at http://www.cane.udel.edu
	The website Elder Abuse includes a directory of links to state-specific reporting hotlines, laws and regulations, and other resources regarding elder and dependent, vulnerable, or disabled adult abuse occurring in home or out of home at http://www.elder-abuseca.com.
	ElderCare Locator offers information and referrals at 1-800-677-1116
	ElderWeb contains information on a range of topics regarding the welfare of elderly adults, including fraud and abuse as well as day-to-day living concerns (e.g., Medicare coverage, assisted living arrangements, Alzheimer's care) at http://www.elderweb.com
	National Center on Elder Abuse includes a directory of state-specific reporting hotlines, government agencies, laws and regulations (with links to many of the statutes), and other resources regarding elder and dependent, vulnerable, or disabled adult abuse occurring in home or out of home at http://www.ncea.aoa.gov
State	**State law regarding in-home abuse, report contact numbers, and additional web resources**

(continued)

TABLE 9.1 (*Continued*)
Elder and Dependent, Vulnerable, or Disabled Adult Abuse: National Resources and Reporting Information by State

Alabama	Law: Alabama Code 38-9-1 et seq. Call: local Department of Human Resources or law enforcement agency or 1-800-458-7214 Additional web resources: Adult Protective Services at http://www.dhr.alabama.gov/directory/adult_prot_svcs.aspx
Alaska	Law: Alaska Stat. 47.24.010 et seq Call: 1-800-478-9996 (in-state caller) or 1-907-269-3666 (out-of-state caller) Additional web resources: Adult Protective Services at http://www.hss.state.ak.us/dsds/aps.htm
Arizona	Law: Arizona Rev. Stat. Ann. 46-451 et seq. Call: local law enforcement or protective services agency or 1-877-767-2385, 1-602-674-4200 Additional web resources: Adult Protective Services at http://www.azdes.gov/common.aspx?menu=620&menuc=100&id=1708
Arkansas	Law: Arkansas Code Ann. 12-12-1701 et seq. Call: 1-800-332-4443 (in-state caller) or 1-800-482-8049 (out-of-state caller) Additional web resources: Adult Protective Services at http://www.aradultprotection.com/
California	Law: California Welf. & Inst. Code 15630-15634 Call: local Adult Protective Services or law enforcement agency or 1-888-436-3600 (toll-free in state) Additional web resources: Adult Protective Services at http://www.cdss.ca.gov/agedblinddisabled/PG1298.htm
Colorado	Law: Colorado Rev. Stat. Ann 26-3.1-101 et seq. Call: local Department of Protective Services for Adults or (during nonbusiness hours) law enforcement agency or 1-800-773-1366 Additional web resources: Adult Protective Services at http://www.colorado.gov/cs/SatelliteCDHS-SelfSuff/CBON/125182068463

TABLE 9.1 (*Continued*)
**Elder and Dependent, Vulnerable, or Disabled Adult Abuse:
National Resources and Reporting Information by State**

Connecticut	Law: Connecticut Gen. Stat. Ann 17b-450 et seq. Call: 1-888-385-4225 (in-state caller), 1-860-424-5241 (out-of-state caller), or 211 (in-state caller after hours) Additional web resources: Protective Services at http://www.ct.gov/dss/cwp/ view.asp?a=2353&q=305232
Delaware	Law: Delaware Code Ann. Title 31, 3901 et seq. Call: 1-800-223-9074 Additional web resources: Adult Division of Services for Aging and Adults With Physical Disabilities at http://dhss.delaware.gov/ dsaapd/index.html
District of Columbia	Law: D.C. Code Ann. 7-1901 et seq. Call: 1-202-541-3950 Additional web resources: Adult Protective Services at http://www.dhs.dc.gov/dhs/cwp/ view,a,3,q,492691,dhsNav,30980.asp
Florida	Law: Florida Stat. Ann. 415.101 et seq.; Florida Stat. Ann. 825.101 et seq. Call: 1-800-962-2873 Additional web resources: Adult Protective Services at http://www.dcf.state.fl.us/ programs/aps, Department of Children & Families Abuse Hotline at http://www.dcf.state. fl.us/programs/abuse/
Georgia	Law: Georgia Code Ann. 30-5-1 et seq. Call: 1-888-774-0152 or 1-404-657-5250 (metropolitan Atlanta area) Additional web resources: Adult Protective Services at http://aging.dhr.georgia.gov/portal/ site/DHR-DAS/menuitem.9e91405d0e424e248 e738510da1010a0/?vgnextoid=018267b27e db0010VgnVCM100000bf01010aRCRD

(continued)

TABLE 9.1 (*Continued*)
**Elder and Dependent, Vulnerable, or Disabled Adult Abuse:
National Resources and Reporting Information by State**

Hawaii	Law: Hawaii Rev. Stat. 346-221 et seq., including Part X (Act 154, SLH 2008) Call: 1-808-832-5115 (Oahu), 1-808-243-5151 (Maui, Molokai, and Lanai), 1-808-241-3432 (Kauai), 1-808-933-8820 (Hilo, Hamakua, and Puna), or 1-808-327-6280 (Kau, Kona, Kohala, and Kamuela) Additional web resources: Adult and Community Care Services at http://hawaii.gov/dhs/protection/social_services/adult_services/
Idaho	Law: Idaho Code 39-5301 et seq. Call: local area agency of Adult Protection Services or (if abuse has resulted in death or serious injury) law enforcement agency or 1-877-471-2777 Additional web resources: Idaho Adult Protection at http://www.idahoaging.com/IdahoCommissiononAging/ICOAProgramsandServices/AdultProtection/tabid/135/Default.aspx
Illinois	Law: 320 Illinois Comp. Stat. 20/1 et seq. Call: local Department on Aging agency or 1-866-800-1409 (in-state caller), 1-217-524-6911 (out-of-state caller), 1-800-279-0400 (after hours hotline) Additional web resources: Adult Protective Services at http://www.state.il.us/aging/1abuselegal/abuse.htm
Indiana	Law: Indiana Code Ann. 12-10-3-1 et seq.; 35-46-1-12 et seq.; 35-46-7-1 Call: local Adult Protective Services or law enforcement agency or 1-800-992-6978 (in-state caller); 1-800-545-7763, ext. 20135 (out-of-state caller) Additional web resources: Adult Protective Services at http://www.in.gov/fssa/da/3479.htm

TABLE 9.1 (*Continued*)
Elder and Dependent, Vulnerable, or Disabled Adult Abuse: National Resources and Reporting Information by State

Iowa	Law: Iowa Code Ann. 235B.1 et seq. Call: 1-800-362-2178 Additional web resources: Department of Human Services Dependent Adult Abuse at http://www.dhs.state.ia.us/Consumers/Safety_and_Protection/Abuse_Reporting/DependentAdultAbuse.html
Kansas	Law: Kansas Stat. Ann. 39-1430 et seq. Call: 1-800-922-5330 (in-state caller) or 1-785-296-0044 (out-of-state caller) or local law enforcement agency when Department of Social and Rehabilitation Services is not in operation Additional web resources: Adult Protective Services at http://www.srs.ks.gov/agency/fingertipfacts/pages/cfs/aps.aspx
Kentucky	Law: Kentucky Rev. Stat. Ann. 209.005 et seq. Call: 1-800-752-6200 Additional web resources: Adult Protective Services at http://www.chfs.ky.gov/dcbs/dpp/adult+protective+and+general+adult+services.htm
Louisiana	Law: Louisiana Rev. Stat. Ann 14:403.2; Louisiana Rev. Stat. Ann 15:1501 et seq. Call: any adult protective or local or state law enforcement agency or 1-800-259-4990 (Elder Abuse, in-state caller), 1-225-342-9722 (Elder Abuse, out-of-state caller), 1-800-898-4910 (Disabled Adult Abuse, in-state caller), 1-225-342-9057 (Disabled Adult Abuse, out-of-state caller) Additional web resources: Elderly Protective Services at http://goea.louisiana.gov/index.cfm?md=pagebuilder&tmp=home&pid=5&pnid=2&nid=16

(*continued*)

TABLE 9.1 (*Continued*)
**Elder and Dependent, Vulnerable, or Disabled Adult Abuse:
National Resources and Reporting Information by State**

Maine	Law: Maine Rev. Stat. Ann. Title 22, 3470 et seq. Call: 1-800-624-8404 (in-state caller), 1-207-532-5047 (out-of-state caller), 1-207-287-6083 (after hours) Additional web resources: Adult Protective Services at http://www.maine.gov/dhhs/oes/aps/index.shtml
Maryland	Law: Maryland Code Ann., Family Law 14-101 et seq. Call: local Department of Human Resources agency or 1-800-917-7383 (in-state caller), 1-800-677-1116 (ElderCare Locator, out-of-state caller) Additional web resources: Adult Protective Services at http://www.dhr.state.md.us/oas/protect.php
Massachusetts	Law: Massachusetts Gen. Laws Ann. 19A, 14 et seq.; Massachusetts Gen. Laws 19C, 1 Call: local Department of Elder Affairs agency or 1-800-922-2275 (in-state caller), 1-800-243-4636 (out-of-state caller) Additional web resources: Adult Protective Services at http://www.massresources.org/elder-protective-services.html
Michigan	Law: Michigan Comp. Laws Ann. 400.11 et seq. Call: local Department of Social Services agency or 1-800-996-6228 Additional web resources: Adult Protective Services at http//www.michigan.gov/dhs/0,1607,7-124-5452_7119-15663—,00.html

TABLE 9.1 (*Continued*)
**Elder and Dependent, Vulnerable, or Disabled Adult Abuse:
National Resources and Reporting Information by State**

Minnesota	Law: Minnesota Stat. Ann. 626.557 et seq. Call: 1-800-333-2433 (connects to the Senior Linkage Line, an information and referral line, which directs callers to appropriate reporting agencies) Additional web resources: Adult Protective Services at http://www.dhs.state.mn.us/main/idcplg?IdcService=GET_DYNAMIC_CONVERSION&RevisionSelectionMethod=LatestReleased&dDocName=id_005710
Mississippi	Law: Mississippi Code Ann. 43-47-1 et seq. Call: local Department of Human Services agency or 1-800-222-8000 (in-state caller), 1-601-359-4991 (out-of-state caller) Additional web resources: Adult Protective Services at http://www.mdhs.state.ms.us/fcs_aps.html
Missouri	Law: Missouri Ann. Stat. 660.250 et seq. & 660.300 et seq. Call: 1-800-392-0210 Additional web resources: Health and Senior Services at http://www.dhss.mo.gov/safety/abuse/index.php
Montana	Law: Montana Code Ann. 52-3-801 et seq. Call: local Department of Public Health and Human Services agency or the county attorney or 1-800-551-3191 (in-state caller), 1-406-444-4077 (out-of-state caller) Additional web resources: Adult Protective Services at http://www.dphhs.mt.gov/sltc/services/APS/index.shtml

(*continued*)

TABLE 9.1 (*Continued*)
Elder and Dependent, Vulnerable, or Disabled Adult Abuse: National Resources and Reporting Information by State

Nebraska	Law: Nebraska Rev. Stat. 28-348 et seq. Call: local Department of Health and Human Services or law enforcement agency or 1-800-652-1999 (in-state caller), 1-402-595-1324 (out-of-state caller) Additional web resources: Adult Protective Services at http://www.hhs.state.ne.us/nea/aps/apsindex.htm
Nevada	Law: Nevada Rev. Stat. Ann. 200.5091 et seq. Call: local office of the Aging and Disability Services Division of the Department of Health and Human Services or law enforcement agency or 1-800-992-5757 (in-state caller or after hours), 1-775-687-4210 (Carson City area), 1-775-688-2964 (Reno area), 1-775-738-1966 (Elko area), 1-702-486-3545 (Las Vegas area) Additional web resources: Adult Protective Services at http://www.nvaging.net/protective_svc.htm
New Hampshire	Law: New Hampshire Rev. Stat. Ann. 161-F:42 et seq. Call: local Commissioner of Health and Human Services representative or (if outside of working hours) law enforcement agency or 1-800-949-0470 (in-state caller), 1-603-271-7014 (out-of-state caller) Additional web resources: Adult Protection Program at http://www.dhhs.nh.gov/dcbcs/beas/adultprotection.htm
New Jersey	Law: New Jersey Stat. Ann. 52:27D-406 et seq. Call: local Adult Protective Services agency or 1-800-792-8820 (in-state caller), 1-609-943-3473 (out-of-state caller) Additional web resources: Adult Protective Services at http://www.state.nj.us/health/senior/aps.shtml

TABLE 9.1 (*Continued*)
**Elder and Dependent, Vulnerable, or Disabled Adult Abuse:
National Resources and Reporting Information by State**

New Mexico	Law: New Mexico Stat. Ann 27-7-14 et seq. Call: 1-866-654-3219 (in-state caller) or 1-505-476-4912 (out-of-state caller) Additional web resources: Adult Protective Services at http://www.nmaging.state.nm.us/Adult_Protective_Services_Division.html
New York	Law: New York Soc. Serv. Law Chapter 381 (Kathy's Law), Article 260.30; New York Soc. Serv. Law Chapter 473 The laws define types of abuse of impaired adults and designate elder abuse as a criminal offense but do not address reporting requirements. Call: 1-800-342-3009 (in-state caller) Additional web resources: Protective Services for Adults at http://www.ocfs.state.ny.us/main/psa/
North Carolina	Law: North Carolina Gen. Stat. 14-112.2; 108A-99 et seq. Call: local Director of Department of Social Services or 1-800-662-7030 Additional web resources: Adult Protective Services at http://www.dhhs.state.nc.us/aging/adultsvcs/afs_aps.htm
North Dakota	Law: North Dakota Cent. Code 50-25.2-01 et seq. Call: local Department of Human Services or law enforcement agency or 1-800-451-8693 Additional web resources: Vulnerable Adult Protective Services at http://www.nd.gov/dhs/services/adultsaging/vulnerable.html
Ohio	Law: Ohio Rev. Code Ann. 5101.60 et seq. Call: local Department of Job and Family Services (for suspected abuse, neglect, and exploitation of adults age 60 and older) or 1-866-635-3748 (in-state caller), 1-800-677-1116 (ElderCare Locator, out-of-state caller) Additional web resources: Adult Protective Services at http://jfs.ohio.gov/families/protective_services/index.stm

(*continued*)

TABLE 9.1 (*Continued*)
**Elder and Dependent, Vulnerable, or Disabled Adult Abuse:
National Resources and Reporting Information by State**

Oklahoma	Law: Oklahoma Stat. Ann. Title 21, 843.1 et seq.; Title 43A, 10-101 et seq. Call: local Department of Human Services or law enforcement agency or 1-800-522-3511 Additional web resources: Adult Protective Services at http://www.okdhs.org/programsandservices/aps/apsdefault.htm
Oregon	Law: Oregon Rev. Stat. 124.050-124.095 (for adults 65 and older), Oregon Rev. Stat. 430.735 et seq. (for mentally or developmentally disabled persons 18 and older who receive services from a community program or facility) Call: local Department of Human Services or law enforcement agency or 1-800-232-3020 (in-state caller) or 1-503-945-5832 (out-of-state caller) Additional web resources: Adult Protective Services at http://www.oregon.gov/DHS/dd/abuse/protective_services.shtml
Pennsylvania	Law: 35 Pennsylvania Cons. Stat. Ann 10225.101 et seq. Contact: local Area Agency on Aging provider of protective services or 1-800-490-8505 Additional web resources: Department of Aging, Abuse or Crime at http://www.portal.state.pa.us/portal/server.pt/community/abuse_or_crime/17992
Rhode Island	Law: Rhode Island Gen. Laws 42-66-4.1 et seq. Call: 401-462-0555 Additional web resources: Protective Services at http://www.dea.ri.gov/programs/protective_services.php

TABLE 9.1 (*Continued*)
**Elder and Dependent, Vulnerable, or Disabled Adult Abuse:
National Resources and Reporting Information by State**

South Carolina	Law: South Carolina Code Ann. 43-35-5 et seq. Call: local Adult Protective Services Program or law enforcement agency (law enforcement must be contacted in cases of an emergency, serious injury, or suspected sexual assault) or 1-803-898-7318 Additional web resources: Adult Protective Services Program at http://dss.sc.gov/content/customers/protection/aps/index.aspx
South Dakota	Law: South Dakota Codified Laws Ann. 22-46-1 et seq. Call: local state attorney, Adult Services and Aging office in the Department of Social Services or law enforcement agency or 1-866-854-5465 (in-state caller), 1-605-773-3656 (out-of-state caller) Additional web resources: Adult Protective Services at http://dss.sd.gov/elderlyservices/services/adultprotective.asp
Tennessee	Law: Tennessee Code Ann. 71-6-101 et seq. Call: 1-865-594-5685 (Knoxville), 1-423-634-6624 (Chattanooga), 1-615-532-3492 (Nashville), 1-901-320-7220 (Memphis), 1-888-APS-TENN (1-888-277-8366, outside of these areas) Additional web resources: Adult Protective Services at http://www.state.tn.us/humanserv/adfam/afs_aps.html
Texas	Law: Texas Hum. Res. Code Ann. 48.001 et seq. Call: 1-800-252-5400 Additional web resources: Department of Family and Protective Services, Adult Protective Services at http://www.dfps.state.tx.us/Adult_Protection/About_Adult_Protective_Services/

(*continued*)

Table 9.1 (*Continued*)
Elder and Dependent, Vulnerable, or Disabled Adult Abuse:
National Resources and Reporting Information by State

Utah	Law: Utah Code Ann. 62A-3-301 et seq. Call: local Adult Protective Services or law enforcement agency or 1-800-371-7897 (for all counties other than Salt Lake County) and 1-801-264-7669 (within Salt Lake County) Additional web resources: Adult Protective Services at http://www.hsdaas.utah.gov/ap_purpose.htm
Vermont	Law: Vermont Stat. Ann. Title 33, 6901 et seq. Call: local law enforcement agency or 1-800-564-1612 (in-state caller) or 1-802-241-3918 (out-of-state caller) Additional web resources: Adult Protective Services at http://www.dlp.vermont.gov/protection Raising Awareness: A Guide to Recognizing and Reporting Abuse, Neglect, and Exploitation of Vulnerable Adults at http://www.dlp.vermont.gov/raising-awareness-handbook
Virginia	Law: Virginia Code Ann. 63.2-1603 et seq. Call: local Department of Social Services agency or 1-888-832-3858, 1-804-371-0896 (Richmond area) Additional web resources: Adult Protective Services at http://www.dss.virginia.gov/family/as/aps.cgi
Washington	Law: Washington Rev. Code Ann. 74.34.005 et seq. Call: 1-866-363-4276 (statewide referral line, which connects reporters to appropriate regional investigation agency) Additional web resources: Adult Protective Services at http://www.aasa.dshs.wa.gov/APS/

TABLE 9.1 (*Continued*)
**Elder and Dependent, Vulnerable, or Disabled Adult Abuse:
National Resources and Reporting Information by State**

West Virginia	Law: West Virginia Code 9-6-1 et seq. Call: local Department of Health and Human Resources Adult Protective Services agency or 1-800-352-6513 Additional web resources: Adult Protective Services at http://www.wvdhhr.org/bcf/children_adult/aps/
Wisconsin	Law: Wisconsin Stat. Ann. 46.90 (for persons 60 or older or who are subject to infirmities of aging), Wisconsin Stat. Ann. 55.001 et seq. (for adults with disabilities) Call: local Department of Social Services and Health Services agency or elder-at-risk or adult-at-risk agency or state or local law enforcement or 1-608-266-2536 Additional web resources: Adult Protective Services at http://dhs.wisconsin.gov/aps/index.htm
Wyoming	Law: Wyoming Stat. Ann. 35-20-101 et seq. Call: local Department of Family Services or law enforcement agency or 1-800-457-3659 (in-state caller, 8 a.m.–5 p.m.), 1-307-777-3602 (out-of-state caller) Additional web resources: Adult Protective Services at http://dfsweb.state.wy.us/protective-services/aps/index.html

noting that although some of the information offered by the national resources listed at the beginning of the table is relevant for all elderly or vulnerable clients regardless of where they are residing, therapists working in long-term care facilities or medical or mental hospitals or institutions are advised to check state laws regarding their elder or vulnerable adult reporting responsibilities. Readers are also advised that despite all attempts made at the time Table 9.1 was created to ensure that the information was current, state laws continually undergo revision, and telephone contacts and Internet links are subject to change at any time. The U.S. Administration on Aging National Center on Elder Abuse website offers an extensive directory of help lines and hotlines, analyses of state laws, and other resources for elder abuse prevention (National Center on Elder Abuse, 2010). The American Bar Association Commission on Law and Aging website presents several valuable documents pertaining to state and federal adult protective laws (American Bar Association, 2011).

References

Administration on Aging. (2009). *Historical evolution of programs for older Americans*. Retrieved from http://www.aoa.gov/AoA Root/AoA_Programs/OAA/resources/History.aspx

American Bar Association. (2011). *Elder abuse*. Retrieved from http://www.americanbar.org/groups/law_aging/resources/elder_abuse.html

Barnett, O. W., Miller-Perrin, C. L., & Perrin, R. D. (2005). *Family violence across the lifespan* (2nd ed.). Thousand Oaks, CA: Sage.

Elder Justice Act and the Patient Safety and Abuse Prevention Act, 111 Pub. L. No. 148, 124 Stat. 119 (2010).

International Federation on Ageing. (2010). *President Obama signs elder justice bill into law*. Retrieved from http://www.ifa-fiv.org/index.php?option=com_content&view=article&id=463&catid=84&Itemid=251

National Center on Elder Abuse. (2010). *State directory of helplines, hotlines, and elder abuse prevention resources*. Retrieved from http://www.ncea.aoa.gov/NCEAroot/Main_Site/Find_Help/State_Resources.aspx

Older Americans Act of 1965, 42 U.S.C.A § 3021 (1965).

Quinn, M. J. (1985). Elder abuse and neglect. *Generations, 10,* 22–25.

Vulnerable Elder Rights Protection Title, 42 U.S.C.A § 3021(1992).

Wolf, R. S., & Pillemer, K. A. (1989). *Helping elderly victims: The reality of elder abuse*. New York, NY: Columbia University Press.

CHAPTER 10

Duty to Protect: Reporting Client Threat of Harm to Another

The duty of mental health professionals to protect a potential third party victim from a client's violence has been recognized (and often hotly debated) in U.S. legal systems and professional organizations since the initial *Tarasoff v. The Regents of the University of California* decision by the California Supreme Court in 1976 (Tarasoff II). Nearly all states (and the District of Columbia) have some legal standard regarding the duty to protect triggered by a communication of a client's potential danger to another within the context of the professional relationship. However, the standards vary considerably. Some standards are set in statutes; some have evolved through case law. In some, the duty arises only when specific features of the threat are present (e.g., there is an actual threat of physical violence, the danger is considered imminent, there is an identifiable victim). In others, the duty is triggered by a more general threat of harm. Some legal standards mandate report of the threat of danger, and some permit the reports as an exception to the confidentiality of therapist–client communications. Some standards require that the mental health professional communicate the threat to law enforcement only; some require that the intended victim also be notified. And some standards require or present as an option that the professional offer specific measures to prevent the violence (e.g., hospitalizing the client [Arizona, Tennessee]). Finally, in some state standards the duty to protect extends to individuals who threaten harm to themselves (e.g., Massachusetts), whereas in other state statutes and/or case law (e.g., New Hampshire) the duty is specifically restricted to third parties. Werth, Welfel, and Benjamin (2009) recently edited a book that offers a wealth of information on this topic and an online appendix with detailed analyses of state laws regarding mental health professionals' duty to protect.

Clearly, practitioners should be aware of and compliant with the legal standards regarding the duty to protect of the state in which they practice. Many state statutes and case decisions can be accessed online. Table 10.1 provides an initial resource for clinicians confronted with issues around their professional duty to protect. The table, derived from the work of Benjamin, Kent, and Sirikantraporn (2009) and Edwards (2010), lists state-by-state citations for legal standards (statutes, case law), whether the report (given that the threat meets statutory criteria, some of which are highly specific) is mandatory or permissive, and to whom the professional must or may present the report. Although at the time Table 10.1 was created all attempts were made to ensure that the information was current and correct, it is important for the reader to keep in mind that state and case laws continually change.

In addition, clinicians should be familiar with how to conduct a risk evaluation of potential harm to others or self to determine imminence and/or seriousness of the threat and should perform (and document) an evaluation when indicated (see Chapter 7, this resource). And professionals should consider consultation with clinical colleagues and with a mental health attorney when a client makes an apparent threat of harm to another or to self. Some state legal standards have highly specific circumstances that must be evident before any duty arises. Clinicians who disclose otherwise confidential information to a third party without understanding the complexities of their state laws risk compromising the welfare of the client as well as professional or legal sanctions. Finally, the practitioner should complete careful documentation in the client's chart of the decision-making process regarding whether to report, any action taken, and the rationale for the action. Notes reflecting the clinician's consultations should be included in the records (Benjamin et al., 2009).

TABLE 10.1
Duty to Protect: Legal Guidelines by State

State	State statutes and case laws regarding duty to protect, mandatory versus permissive warning
Alabama	Legal standard: *Donohoo v. State,* 479 So. 2d 1188; *Morton v. Prescott,* 564 So. 2d 913 (Supreme Court of Alabama) Warning: no duty in statutes; duty is implied in case law To whom: not specified
Alaska	Legal standard: Alaska Stat. 08.86.200 Warning: permissive To whom: not specified
Arizona	Legal standard: Arizona Rev. Stat. 36-517.02 Warning: mandatory To whom: all clearly identified or identifiable potential victims and law enforcement and taking additional precautions (e.g., hospitalizing the client)
Arkansas	Legal standard: none Warning: N/A To whom: N/A
California	Legal standard: California Civil Code 43.92 Warning: mandatory To whom: reasonably identifiable victim(s); law enforcement
Colorado	Legal standard: Colorado Rev. Stat. Ann. 13-21-117 Warning: mandatory To whom: person specifically threatened (extended to general public in *Perreira v. State,* 768 P.2d 1198 [1989]) and law enforcement or taking appropriate action (e.g., hospitalizing the client)
Connecticut	Legal standard: Connecticut General Statute 52-146c; 52-146f, 52-146p, 52-146q; *Fraser v. United States,* 674 A.2d 811; *Almonte v. New York Medical College,* 851 F.Supp. 34, 40-41 (U.S. District Court for Connecticut) Warning: permissive in statute; duty is narrowly specified in case law To whom: not specified

(*continued*)

TABLE 10.1 (*Continued*)
Duty to Protect: Legal Guidelines by State

State	State statutes and case laws regarding duty to protect, mandatory versus permissive warning
Delaware	Legal standard: 16 Delaware Code 5402; *Naidu v. Laird*, 539 A.2d 1064 (Supreme Court of Delaware) Warning: mandatory To whom: clearly identified victim(s) and law enforcement and attempt to immediately hospitalize the client
District of Columbia	Legal standard: D.C. Code 6-2023(a); 7-1203.03(a) Warning: permissive To whom: client's spouse, parent, legal guardian, officer or agent of the District of Columbia in charge of public health; Department of Mental Health officer in the District of Columbia authorized to make arrests; or intended victim
Florida	Legal standard: Florida Stat. 491.0147(3) Warning: permissive To whom: identifiable potential victim(s), appropriate family member, or law enforcement or other appropriate authorities
Georgia	Legal standard: *Bradley Center, Inc. v. Wessner*, 296 S.E.2d 693 (Supreme Court of Georgia); *Jacobs et al. v. Taylor et al.*, 190 Ga. App. 520, 379 S.E.2d 593 (Supreme Court of Georgia) Warning: no duty in statutes; duty is implied in specific situations in case law decisions To whom: not specified
Hawaii	Legal standard: Hawaii Rev. Stat. 626-504.1 Warning: permissive To whom: not specified
Idaho	Legal standard: Idaho Code 6-1902 Warning: mandatory To whom: clearly identified or identifiable potential victim(s), parents or legal guardian of minor potential victim(s), and local law enforcement

TABLE 10.1 (*Continued*)
Duty to Protect: Legal Guidelines by State

State	State statutes and case laws regarding duty to protect, mandatory versus permissive warning
Illinois	Legal standard: 405 Illinois Comp. Stat. Ann. 5/6-103(b-c); 740 Illinois Comp. Stat. Ann. 110/11(vii) Warning: mandatory To whom: reasonably identifiable victim(s) and law enforcement or initiating or continuing steps for hospitalization or commitment of client
Indiana	Legal standard: Indiana Code Ann. 34-30-16-1 et seq. Warning: mandatory To whom: reasonably identifiable victim(s) or law enforcement or seek civil commitment of client
Iowa	Legal standard: *Anthony v. State,* 374 N.W.2d 662 (Iowa Supreme Court); Iowa Supreme Court has previously decided not to adopt Tarasoff Warning: no duty in statutes; duty in limited situations is specified in case law To whom: not specified
Kansas	Legal standard: *Beck v. Kansas Adult Auth.,* 735 P.2d 222; *Boulanger v. Pol,* 900 P.2d 86; Mahomes-Vinson v. U.S., 751 F. Supp 913 Warning: no duty in statutes; duty in limited situations is specified in case law To whom: not specified
Kentucky	Legal standard: Kentucky Rev. Stat. 202A.400 Warning: mandatory To whom: identifiable victim(s) and law enforcement or seek civil commitment of client
Louisiana	Legal standard: Louisiana Rev. Stat. 9:2800.2A Warning: mandatory To whom: clearly identified victim(s) and local law enforcement
Maine	Legal standard: no law Warning: N/A To whom: N/A

(*continued*)

TABLE 10.1 (*Continued*)
Duty to Protect: Legal Guidelines by State

State	State statutes and case laws regarding duty to protect, mandatory versus permissive warning
Maryland	Legal standard: Maryland Code Ann. Courts and Judicial Proceedings 5-609(b) Warning: mandatory To whom: law enforcement and, if feasible, the specified victim(s) or make efforts to commit the client or engage a treatment plan designed to eliminate the risk of the threat
Massachusetts	Legal standard: Massachusetts Gen. Laws Ch. 123, 36B(1); Ch. 233, 20B (psychiatrists); Ch. 112, 129A (psychologists); Ch. 112, 135A (social workers); Ch. 112, 172 Warning: mandatory To whom: local law enforcement and/or reasonably identifiable victim(s) and/or arrange for voluntary or involuntary hospitalization of client
Michigan	Legal standard: Michigan Comp. Laws 330.1946(1) Warning: mandatory To whom: reasonably identifiable victim (and parents or guardian or Department of Social Services if victim is a minor or incompetent) and local police or arrange for hospitalization of client
Minnesota	Legal standard: Minnesota Stat. 148.975 Warning: mandatory To whom: specific identified or identifiable victim(s) or, if the victim(s) cannot be contacted, to local law enforcement
Mississippi	Legal standard: Mississippi Code Ann. 41-21-97 Warning: permissive To whom: clearly identified or reasonably identifiable potential victim(s), law enforcement, or the parent or guardian of a minor who is identified as a potential victim
Missouri	Legal standard: *Bradley v. Ray*, 904 S.W.2d 302, 312 Warning: no duty in statutes; duty is specified in case law To whom: readily identifiable victim(s) or those likely to notify victim(s) (e.g., law enforcement)

TABLE 10.1 (*Continued*)
Duty to Protect: Legal Guidelines by State

State	State statutes and case laws regarding duty to protect, mandatory versus permissive warning
Montana	Legal standard: Montana Code Ann. 27-1-1102 Warning: mandatory To whom: identified or reasonably identifiable victim and local law enforcement
Nebraska	Legal standard: Nebraska Rev. Stat. 38-3132 Warning: mandatory To whom: reasonably identifiable victim(s) and law enforcement
Nevada	Legal standard: no law Warning: N/A To whom: N/A
New Hampshire	Legal standard: New Hampshire Rev. Stat. Ann. 329:31 Warning: mandatory To whom: clearly identified or reasonably identifiable victim(s) and police department or by obtaining civil commitment for client
New Jersey	Legal standard: New Jersey Stat. 2A:62A-16 Warning: mandatory To whom: local law enforcement, readily identifiable intended victim, or parent or guardian of a potential victim or suicidal client who is a minor or by arranging voluntary or involuntary hospitalization of client
New Mexico	Legal standard: New Mexico Code R. 16.22.2.12 (administrative code for psychologists); 16.27.18.17 (administrative code for counselors and therapists); New Mexico Stat. Ann. 61.31.24 (administrative code for social workers); *Wilschinsky v. Medina,* 775 P.2d 713, 714-15 Warning: permissive in general; duty is specified in specific circumstances addressed in case law To whom: not specified
New York	Legal standard: New York Mental Hygiene Law 33.13 (c) 6 Warning: permissive To whom: potential victim(s) and law enforcement

(*continued*)

TABLE 10.1 (*Continued*)
Duty to Protect: Legal Guidelines by State

State	State statutes and case laws regarding duty to protect, mandatory versus permissive warning
North Carolina	Legal standard: North Carolina Gen. Stat. 122C-55; *Gregory v. Kelbride*, 565 S.E.2d 685, 610, 691 (North Carolina Court of Appeals); *Davis v. North Carolina Department of Human Resources*, 465 S.E.2d 2 (North Carolina Court of Appeals) Warning: permissive, unless highly specific circumstances exist To whom: not specified
North Dakota	Legal standard: North Dakota Cent. Code 43-53-11-02 (marriage and family therapists only) Warning: mandatory for marriage and family therapists only at this time To whom: reasonably identifiable victim(s) and law enforcement
Ohio	Legal standard: Ohio Rev. Code Ann. 2305.51(B) Warning: mandatory To whom: law enforcement, obtaining hospitalization of the client, or creating and enacting a treatment plan designed to remove the danger threat and obtaining a second opinion about that plan and warning all clearly identifiable potential victim(s) if feasible
Oklahoma	Legal standard: Oklahoma Stat. Ann. Title 59, 1376 (3)(a) Warning: mandatory To whom: reasonably identified person or law enforcement or arranging for voluntary or involuntary hospitalization of client
Oregon	Legal standard: Oregon Rev. Stat. 179.505(12) Warning: permissive To whom: appropriate authority

TABLE 10.1 (*Continued*)
Duty to Protect: Legal Guidelines by State

State	State statutes and case laws regarding duty to protect, mandatory versus permissive warning
Pennsylvania	Legal standard: 42 PA. Cons. Stat. Ann. 5928; *Emerich v. Philadelphia Center for Human Development,* 720 A.2d 1031 (Supreme Court of Pennsylvania) Warning: permissive in statute; duty is specified in case law To whom: identifiable potential victim
Rhode Island	Legal standard: Rhode Island Gen. Laws 5-37.3-4(b)(4) Warning: permissive To whom: appropriate law enforcement or the endangered person(s)
South Carolina	Legal standard: South Carolina Code Ann. 19-11-95(c); *Bishop v. South Carolina Department of Mental Health,* 502 S.E.2d 78, 82 (Supreme Court of South Carolina) Warning: permissive in statute; duty is specified in case law To whom: intended victim(s) or others likely to notify the victim(s) of the danger and/or law enforcement and/or whatever other reasonable actions are necessary
South Dakota	Legal standard: South Dakota Codified Laws 19-2-12 (physician); 36-26-30 (social workers); 36-33-29 et seq. (marriage and family therapists); 36-32-27 (licensed professional counselor) Warning: permissive To whom: qualified mental health professional to secure involuntary hospitalization
Tennessee	Legal standard: Tennessee Code Ann. 33-3-206(1)-209 Warning: mandatory To whom: clearly identified victim(s) or arranging for voluntary or involuntary hospitalization of the client or acting consistently with current professional standards to protect potential victim(s)

(*continued*)

TABLE 10.1 (*Continued*)
Duty to Protect: Legal Guidelines by State

State	State statutes and case laws regarding duty to protect, mandatory versus permissive warning
Texas	Legal standard: Texas Health and Safety Code 611.004(a)(2); *Thapar v. Zezulka*, 994 S.W.2d 635, 639 (Supreme Court of Texas; disclosure to law enforcement was allowed but not required) Warning: permissive To whom: law enforcement or medical personnel
Utah	Legal standard: Utah Code Ann. 78-14d-10; 78-14a-102(1) Warning: mandatory To whom: reasonably identifiable victim(s) and law enforcement
Vermont	Legal standard: *Peck v. Counseling Service of Addison County, Inc.*, 499 A.2d. 422 (Supreme Court of Vermont) Warning: no duty in statutes; duty is specified in case law To whom: not specified
Virginia	Legal standard: Virginia Code Ann. 54.1-2400.1(b) Warning: mandatory To whom: identifiable or readily identifiable victim(s) (or the victim's parents if the victim is a minor) and/or law enforcement or counseling the client at the time of the threat until the threat is no longer imminent
Washington	Legal standard: Washington Rev. Code 71.05.120(2) Warning: mandatory To whom: reasonably identifiable victim(s) and law enforcement
West Virginia	Legal standard: West Virginia Code 27-3-1(b)(5) Warning: permissive To whom: not specified

TABLE 10.1 (*Continued*)
Duty to Protect: Legal Guidelines by State

State	State statutes and case laws regarding duty to protect, mandatory versus permissive warning
Wisconsin	Legal standard: *Schuster v. Altenberg,* 424 N.W.2d 159, 164, 166 (Supreme Court of Wisconsin) Warning: no duty in statutes; duty is specified in case law To whom: third party (potential victim), initiating detention or commitment hearings
Wyoming	Legal standard: Wyoming Stat. 33-27-123(a)(iv); 33-38-113(a)(iv) Warning: permissive To whom: not specified

Note. Data from "A Review of Duty-to-Protect Statutes, Cases, and Procedures for Positive Practice," by G. A. H. Benjamin, L. Kent, and S. Sirikantraporn (2009). In J. L. Werth, E. R. Welfel, and G. A. H. Benjamin (Eds.), *The Duty to Protect: Ethical, Legal, and Professional Considerations for Mental Health Professionals.* Copyright 2009 by the American Psychological Association; and *Database of State Tarasoff Laws* by G. S. Edwards. Copyright 2011 by Social Science Electronic Publishing. Retrieved from http://ssrn.com/abstract=1551505.

References

Benjamin, G. A. H., Kent, L., & Sirikantraporn, S. (2009). A review of duty-to-protect statutes, cases, and procedures for positive practice. In J. L. Werth, E. R. Welfel, & G. A. H. Benjamin (Eds.), *The duty to protect: Ethical, legal, and professional considerations for mental health professionals.* Washington, DC: American Psychological Association.

Edwards, G. S. (2010). *Database of state Tarasoff laws.* Retrieved from http://ssrn.com/abstract=1551505

Tarasoff v. The Regents of the University of California, 551, P.2d 334 (Cal. 1976).

Werth, J. L., Welfel, E. R., & Benjamin, G. A. H. (Eds.). (2009). *The duty to protect: Ethical, legal, and professional considerations for mental health professionals.* Washington, DC: American Psychological Association. doi:10.1037/11866-000

CHAPTER 11

Diagnosis

There are two systems of classification of psychiatric disorders used worldwide: the *International Classification of Diseases* (Mental and Behavioural disorders; ICD–10; World Health Organization, 2007) and the *Diagnostic and Statistical Manual of Mental Disorders* (4th ed., text revision; *DSM–IV–TR;* American Psychiatric Association, 2000). The *DSM–IV–TR* is the system most widely used by mental health clinicians and researchers in the United States. It contains explicit diagnostic criteria for a broad spectrum of mental disorders. (Note: The *DSM–IV–TR* is published in print form; diagnostic criteria also may be accessed online at http//www.psychiatryonline.com.)

The *DSM–IV–TR* presents a format for diagnoses organized on five axes:

> ➢ Axis I contains the clinician's report of all of the clinical disorders defined in the *DSM–IV–TR* (except for those listed on Axis II) and any other conditions that may be the focus of clinical attention.

> ➢ Axis II contains diagnoses of personality disorders and mental retardation.

> ➢ Axis III contains indications of general medical conditions that are related to the presented psychological symptoms (i.e., a direct physiological cause of the symptom, a condition to which the client reacts with a psychological symptom, or a condition that is relevant because of its prognostic or treatment implications).

> Axis IV includes descriptions of psychosocial and environmental stressors that are relevant to the clinician's understanding of the onset, exacerbation, course, or consequence of the client's psychological symptoms.
> Axis V indicates a numerical assessment of the client's global functioning (severity of symptoms and/or the extent to which symptoms impair social, occupational, or school functioning) on a scale of 1–100 (0 = *inadequate information*).

The determination of an accurate diagnosis given a client's presenting symptoms and signs is crucial to the development of a beneficial treatment plan. However, the diagnostic process can be a complicated one. From the outset of the initial interview, the clinician begins generating and evaluating several hypotheses about the client's psychological condition and possible diagnoses, always keeping in mind the cultural factors that may bear on the client's presentation and/or the clinician's expectations and perceptions (Paniagua, 2001). Then the clinician rigorously sorts through the information gathered to differentiate the diagnosis that best fits the individual client; it may be that more than one diagnosis is appropriate.

Differential diagnosis decision trees can be helpful in the determination of an accurate diagnosis. The *DSM–IV–TR* presents decision trees for mental disorders due to a general medical condition, substance-induced disorders, psychotic disorders, mood disorders, anxiety disorders, and somatoform disorders in Appendix A of the manual. Two additional resources for differential diagnoses provide the clinician with assistance. The DSM–IV–TR *Handbook of Differential Diagnosis* (First, Frances, & Pincus, 2002) is available both in print and for personal digital assistants. The book contains 27 decision trees that proceed from the most common presenting symptoms to a final diagnosis as well as 62 differential diagnosis tables comparing a specific disorder with other competing diagnoses. *Diagnosis Made Easier: Principles and Techniques for Mental Health Clinicians* (Morrison, 2007) explains the basic process of developing differential diagnoses according to a hierarchy of safety concerns for the client. It contains six decision trees that proceed from common general presenting symptoms to specific diagnoses.

This chapter includes an outline of three basic steps to determine a diagnosis of a client who seeks help with mental health problems. References to possible *DSM–IV–TR* diagnoses given specific presenting symptoms are provided, including page numbers in the *DSM* associated with each diagnosis. The information provided is derived from the works of Blaney and Millon (2009), First et al. (2002), Kay and Tasman (2000), Kupfer et al. (2008), and Morrison (1997, 2007).

Step 1: Differential Diagnoses of Psychological Symptoms Due to the Physiological Effects of a General Medical Condition

The first step in establishing an accurate diagnosis is to differentiate symptoms due to a mental disorder from those that are the direct physiological effects of a general medical condition. A key to determining whether psychological symptoms are linked to a general medical condition is to assess for a temporal association (onset, exacerbation, remission) between the symptoms and the condition. Information regarding a client's physical health may be obtained as part of the initial interview clinical assessment. When symptoms result from a general medical condition, a *DSM–IV–TR* diagnosis indicating that association is rendered on Axis I and the medical condition is noted on Axis III. Examples of medical conditions known to be associated with specific psychological symptoms are listed in the next section, with the corresponding potential *DMS–IV–TR* diagnoses (and *DSM–IV–TR* page numbers in parentheses).

Psychotic Symptoms
Medical Conditions Associated With Psychotic Symptoms

Antidiuretic excess
Brain infection
Brain tumor
Cerebrovascular disease
Chronic obstructive lung disease
Congestive heart failure
Cushing's disease
Electrolyte imbalance

Epilepsy
Head trauma
HIV/AIDS
Hypo- and hyperparathyroidism
Hypo- and hyperthryroidism
Kidney failure
Lupus

Lyme disease
Pernicious anemia
Postoperative states

Rheumatoid arthritis
Sleep apnea
Uremia

> *DSM–IV–TR* diagnoses on Axis I for psychotic symptoms associated with medical conditions
  - Psychotic disorder due to . . . (334)
    o With delusions
    o With hallucinations
  - Catatonic disorder due to . . . (185)

Depression Symptoms

Medical Conditions Associated With Depression Symptoms

Brain tumor
Cancer
Cardiac bypass surgery
Cerebrovascular disease
Chronic obstructive lung
  disease
Congestive heart failure
Cushing's disease
Diabetes
Epilepsy
Fibromyalgia
Head trauma
Hepatitis
HIV/AIDS
Hypo- and
  hyperparathyroidism
Hypo- and
  hyperthyroidism
Hypoglycemia
Influenza
Iron deficiency

Kidney failure
Leukemia
Liver failure
Lupus
Lyme disease
Lymphomas
Meniere's disease
Menstrual syndromes
Migraine
Mononucleosis
Multiple sclerosis
Ovarian or testicular
  failure
Parkinson's disease
Pernicious anemia
Post-heart-attack
Rheumatoid arthritis
Sickle cell disease
Sleep apnea
Systemic infection
Vitamin B deficiencies

> *DSM–IV–TR* diagnoses on Axis I for depression symptoms associated with medical conditions
  - Mood disorder due to . . . (401)
    o With depressive features
    o With major depressive-like features

Manic and Hypomanic Symptoms

Medical Conditions Associated With Manic and Hypomanic Symptoms

B12 deficiency
Brain tumor
Cerebral vascular disease
Chronic obstructive lung
  disease
Cushing's disease
Epilepsy (especially
  complex partial)
Head trauma
HIV/AIDS

Huntington's disease
Hyperglycemia
Influenza
Mononucleosis
Multiple sclerosis
Pernicious anemia
Rheumatoid arthritis
Stroke (especially right
  sided)

> ➢ *DSM–IV–TR* diagnoses on Axis I for manic and hypomanic
  symptoms associated with medical conditions
>   ■ Mood disorder due to . . . (401)
>   ○ With manic features
>   ○ With mixed features

Anxiety Symptoms

Medical Conditions Associated With Anxiety Symptoms

Angina
Brain tumor
Cancer
Cardiac arrhythmia
Cerebrovascular disease
Chronic obstructive
  pulmonary disease
Congestive heart failure
Cushing's disease
Diabetes
Epilepsy
Fibromyalgia
Head trauma
HIV/AIDS
Hyperthyroidism

Hypo- and
  hyperparathyroidism
Hypoglycemia
Lyme disease
Meniere's disease
Menstrual syndromes
Mitral valve prolapse
Myasthenia gravis
Parkinson's disease
Pneumonia
Postoperative states
Pulmonary
  thromboembolism
Sleep apnea
Stroke
Thiamine deficiency

> *DSM–IV–TR* diagnoses on Axis I for anxiety symptoms associated with medical conditions
  - Anxiety disorder due to . . . (476)
    - ○ With generalized anxiety
    - ○ With panic attacks
    - ○ With obsessive–compulsive symptoms

Personality Change Symptoms

Medical Conditions Associated With Personality Change Symptoms

Adrenal disease	Huntington's disease
Antidiuretic excess	Hypo- and hyperparathyroidism
Cerebrovascular disease	
Chronic obstructive lung disease	Hypo- and hyperthyroidism
Cushing's disease	Hypoglycemia
Dementia	Liver failure
Epilepsy	Lupus
Frontal lobe, temporal lobe, or right hemispheric lesions and tumors	Menstrual syndromes
	Migraine
	Multiple sclerosis
	Pernicious anemia
Head trauma	Sleep apnea
HIV/AIDS	Thiamine deficiency

> *DSM–IV–TR* diagnoses on Axis I for personality change symptoms associated with medical condition
  - Personality change due to . . . (187)
    - ○ Labile type
    - ○ Disinhibited type
    - ○ Aggressive type
    - ○ Apathetic type
    - ○ Paranoid type
    - ○ Other type
    - ○ Combined type
    - ○ Unspecified type

Delirium, Dementia, and Amnestic Symptoms

Medical Conditions Associated With Delirium, Dementia, and Amnestic Symptoms

Delirium

Anemia
Brain tumor
Congestive heart failure
Dehydration
Electrolyte imbalance
Head trauma
Heart arrhythmia
Heart attack
Hypoglycemia
Hypoxia
Ictal and postictal states
Infection
Postoperative state
Renal or hepatic disease
Respiratory failure
Sensory deprivation
Severe trauma
Shock
Stroke
Thiamine deficiency

Dementia

Alzheimer's disease
Brain tumor
Cerebrovascular insult (stroke)
Creutzfeldt-Jakob disease
Head trauma (subdural hematoma)
HIV
Huntington's disease
Hypercalcemia
Hypoglycemia
Hypothyroidism
Normal pressure hydrocephalus
Parkinson's disease
Pick's disease
Renal or hepatic malfunction
Systemic lupus erythematosus
Vitamin B12 deficiency

Amnestic Symptoms

Closed head trauma
Herpes simplex encephalitis
Hypoxia
Infarction affecting posterior cerebral artery
Metabolic conditions (transient amnesia)
Seizures (transient amnesia)

> *DSM–IV–TR* diagnoses on Axis I for delirium, dementia, and amnestic symptoms associated with medical condition
>   - Delirium due to . . . (141)
>   - Dementia of the Alzheimer's type (154)
>   - Vascular dementia (158)

- Dementia due to HIV disease (163)
- Dementia due to Creutzfeldt-Jakob Disease (166)
- Dementia due to head trauma (164)
- Dementia due to Huntington's disease (165)
- Dementia due to Parkinson's disease (164)
- Dementia due to Pick's disease (165)
- Dementia due to . . . (167)
- Amnestic disorder due to . . . (175)

Sexual Dysfunction

Medical Conditions Associated With Sexual Dysfunction Symptoms

Cystitis
Diabetes mellitus
Endometriosis
Genital injury or infection
Hypogonadal states
Hypothyroidism
Multiple sclerosis
Neuropathy
Pelvic infections
Pituitary dysfunction
Postprostatectomy complications
Postsurgical (obstetric or gynecological) complications
Shortened vagina
Side effects of cancer treatments
Spinal cord lesions
Temporal lobe lesions
Testicular disease
Urethral infections
Uterine prolapse

> DSM–IV–TR diagnoses on Axis I for sexual dysfunction symptoms associated with medical condition
  - Female hypoactive sexual desire disorder due to . . . (558)
  - Male hypoactive sexual desire disorder due to . . . (558)
  - Male erectile disorder due to . . . (558)
  - Female dyspareunia due to . . . (558)
  - Male dyspareunia due to . . . (558)
  - Other female sexual dysfunction due to . . . (558)
  - Other male sexual dysfunction due to . . . (558)

Sleep Disorder

Medical Conditions Associated With Sleep Disorder Symptoms

Cerebrovascular disease (e.g., vascular lesions to the upper brain stem)
Coughing related to pulmonary disease
Huntington's disease

Hypo- or hyperadrenocorticism	Pain from disease (e.g., fibromyalgia)
Hypo- or hyperthyroidism	Parkinson's disease
	Viral or bacterial infections

> *DSM–IV–TR* diagnoses on Axis I for sleep disorder symptoms associated with medical condition
  - Sleep disorder due to . . . (651)
    - Insomnia type
    - Hypersomnia type
    - Parasomnia type
    - Mixed type

Step 2: Differential Diagnoses of Psychological Symptoms Due to Substance Intoxication and/or Withdrawal

The second step in establishing an accurate diagnosis is to differentiate symptoms due to a mental disorder from those that are the result of substance intoxication and/or withdrawal (recreational drug, medication, or toxin). A key to determining whether a client's presenting symptoms are associated with substance use is the assessment of the immediate temporal association between the symptoms and the ingestion of a substance (with signs of intoxication) or between the symptoms and the long-term use of and/or withdrawal from a substance. When symptoms result from substance use or withdrawal, a specific *DSM–IV–TR* diagnosis capturing that association is rendered on Axis I. Examples of substance use or withdrawal associated with specific psychological symptoms are listed in the outline that follows, with the corresponding *DSM–IV–TR* diagnoses (and *DSM–IV–TR* page numbers in parentheses).

Psychotic Symptoms
Drugs, Medications, and Toxins Associated With Psychotic Symptoms

Drugs (I = intoxication, W = withdrawal)

Alcohol (I/W)	Inhalants (I)
Cannabis (I)	Hallucinogens (I)

Opioids (I)
Phencyclidine (I)
Sedatives, hypnotics,
    anxiolytics (I/W)

Stimulants/
    amphetamines (I)
Stimulants/cocaine (I)

Medications
Analgesics
Anesthetics
Antabuse
Anticholinergics
Anticonvulsants
Antidepressants
Antihypertensives
Antimicrobials

Chemotherapies
Interferon
L-dopa
Muscle relaxants
Nonsteroidal anti-
    inflammatory drugs,
    steroids
Stimulants

Toxins
Heavy metals

Organophosphates (e.g.,
    insecticides)

➢ *DSM–IV–TR* diagnoses on Axis I for psychotic symptoms
  associated with drugs and other substances
  ▪ Alcohol-induced psychotic disorder (338)
  ▪ Amphetamine-induced psychotic disorder (338)
  ▪ Cannabis-induced psychotic disorder (338)
  ▪ Cocaine-induced psychotic disorder (338)
  ▪ Inhalant-induced psychotic disorder (338)
  ▪ Hallucinogen-induced psychotic disorder (338)
  ▪ Opioid-induced psychotic disorder (338)
  ▪ Phencyclidine-induced psychotic disorder (338)
  ▪ Sedative-, hypnotic-, or anxiolytic-induced psychotic
    disorder (338)
  ▪ Other (or unknown) substance-induced psychotic dis-
    order (338)

Depression Symptoms
Drugs, Medications, and Toxins Associated With
Depression Symptoms

Drugs (I = intoxication, W = withdrawal)
Alcohol (I/W)

Hallucinogens (e.g.,
    ecstasy; I)

Inhalants (I)
Opioids (I)
Phencyclidine (I)
Sedatives, hypnotic,
   anxiolytics (I/W)

Stimulants (I/W)
Cannabis (I) (potential)
Caffeine (I/W) (potential)

Medications

Analgesics especially
   narcotics
Anesthetics
Antabuse
Antianxiety agents
Anticholinergics
Anticonvulsants,
   especially barbiturates
Antihypertensives
Antimicrobials
Benzodiazepines

Chemotherapies
Cimetidine (Tagamet)
Estrogen and
   progesterone
Interferon
L-dopa
Muscle relaxants
Oral contraceptive pills
Statins
Steroids

> *DSM–IV–TR* diagnoses on Axis I for depression symptoms
  associated with substances
  - Alcohol-induced mood disorder (405)
  - Amphetamine-induced mood disorder (405)
  - Cocaine-induced mood disorder (405)
  - Hallucinogen-induced mood disorder (405)
  - Inhalant-induced mood disorder (405)
  - Opioid-induced mood disorder (405)
  - Phencyclidine-induced mood disorder (405)
  - Sedative-, hypnotic-, or anxiolytic-induced mood dis-
    order (405)
  - Other (or unknown) substance-induced mood disor-
    der (405)

Manic and Hypomanic Symptoms

Drugs, Medications, and Toxins Associated With Manic and Hypomanic Symptoms

Drugs (I = intoxication, W = withdrawal)
Stimulants/
   amphetamines (I)

Stimulants/cocaine (I)

Medications

Antidepressants
Chemotherapies
Cimetidine (Tagamet)
Isoniazid (tuberculosis
  medication)

L-dopa
Levothyroxine (e.g.,
  Synthroid)
Steroids
Yohimbine

> ➢ *DSM–IV–TR* diagnoses on Axis I for manic and hypomanic
>   symptoms associated with substances
>   - Amphetamine-induced mood disorder (405)
>   - Cocaine-induced mood disorder (405)
>   - Other (or unknown) substance-induced mood disor-
>   der (405)

Anxiety Symptoms

Drugs, Medications, and Toxins Associated With Anxiety Symptoms

Drugs (I = intoxication, W = withdrawal)

Alcohol (I/W)
Cannabis (I)
Hallucinogens (I)
Inhalants (I)
Phencyclidine (I)

Sedative, hypnotics,
  anxiolytics (W)
Stimulants/
  amphetamines (I)
Stimulants/caffeine (I)
Stimulants/cocaine (I/W)

Medications

Analgesics
Anesthetics
Antiarrhythmics
Anticholinergics
Anticonvulsants
Antidepressants
Antihistamines
Antihypertensives
Antipsychotics
Bronchodilators (e.g.,
  albuterol)

Decongestants
Fenfluramine (weight-
  loss aid)
Insulin
Interferon
L-dopa
Lithium
Oral contraceptives
Steroids
Thyroid replacements
Yohimbine

➤ *DSM–IV–TR* diagnoses on Axis I for anxiety symptoms associated with substances
  - Alcohol-induced anxiety disorder (479)
  - Amphetamine-induced anxiety disorder (479)
  - Caffeine-induced anxiety disorder (479)
  - Cannabis-induced anxiety disorder (479)
  - Cocaine-induced anxiety disorder (479)
  - Hallucinogen-induced anxiety disorder (479)
  - Inhalant-induced anxiety disorder (479)
  - Phencyclidine-induced anxiety disorder (479)
  - Sedative-, hypnotic-, or anxiolytic-induced anxiety disorder (479)
  - Other (or unknown) substance-induced anxiety disorder (479)

Personality Change Symptoms

Drugs, Medications, and Toxins Associated With Personality Change Symptoms

Drugs (I = intoxication, W = withdrawal)

Alcohol (I/W)	Stimulants/ amphetamines (I)
Opioids (I)	Stimulants/cocaine (I)

Medications

Antidepressants	Steroids
Mood stabilizers	Stimulants
Neuroleptics/atypical antipsychotics	

➤ *DSM–IV–TR* diagnoses on Axis I for *personality change* symptoms associated with substances
  - Alcohol-related disorder not otherwise specified (NOS) (223)
  - Amphetamine-related disorder NOS (231)
  - Cocaine-related disorder NOS (250)
  - Opioid-related disorder NOS (277)
  - Other (or unknown) substance-related disorder NOS (295)

Delirium, Dementia, and Amnestic Symptoms

Drugs, Medications, and Toxins Associated With Delirium, Dementia, and Amnestic Symptoms

Drugs (I = intoxication, W = withdrawal)

Alcohol (I/W)	Sedatives, hypnotics,
Cannabis (I)	anxiolytics (I/W)
Hallucinogens (I)	Stimulants/
Inhalants (I)	amphetamines (I)
Opioids (I)	Stimulants/cocaine (I)
Phencyclidine (I)	

➢ *DSM–IV–TR* diagnoses on Axis I for delirium, dementia, and amnestic symptoms associated with substances
- Alcohol intoxication delirium (143)
- Alcohol withdrawal delirium (143)
- Alcohol-induced persisting dementia (168)
- Alcohol-induced persisting amnestic disorder (177)
- Amphetamine intoxication delirium (143)
- Cannabis intoxication delirium (143)
- Cocaine intoxication delirium (143)
- Hallucinogen intoxication delirium (143)
- Inhalant intoxication delirium (143)
- Inhalant-induced persisting dementia (168)
- Opioid intoxication delirium (143)
- Phencyclidine intoxication delirium (143)
- Sedative, hypnotic, or anxiolytic intoxication delirium (143)
- Sedative, hypnotic, or anxiolytic withdrawal delirium (143)
- Sedative-, hypnotic-, or anxiolytic-induced persisting dementia (168)
- Sedative-, hypnotic-, or anxiolytic-induced persisting amnestic disorder (177)
- Other (or unknown) substance-induced delirium (143)
- Other (or unknown) substance-induced persisting dementia (168)
- Other (or unknown) substance-induced persisting amnestic disorder (177)

Sexual Dysfunction

Drugs, Medications, and Toxins Associated With Sexual Dysfunction Symptoms

Drugs (I = intoxication, W = withdrawal)

Alcohol (I)
Opioids (I)
Sedatives, hypnotics, anxiolytics (I)

Stimulants/amphetamines (I)
Stimulants/cocaine (I)

> *DSM–IV–TR* diagnoses on Axis I for sexual dysfunction symptoms associated with substances
> - Alcohol-induced sexual dysfunction (562)
> - Amphetamine-induced sexual dysfunction (562)
> - Cocaine-induced sexual dysfunction (562)
> - Opioid-induced sexual dysfunction (562)
> - Sedative-, hypnotic-, or anxiolytic-induced sexual dysfunction (562)
> - Other (or unknown) substance-induced sexual dysfunction (562)

Sleep Disorder

Drugs, Medications, and Toxins Associated With Sleep Disorder Symptoms

Drugs (I = intoxication, W = withdrawal)

Alcohol (I/W)
Opioids (I/W)
Sedatives, hypnotics, anxiolytics (I/W)

Stimulants/amphetamines (I/W)
Stimulants/caffeine (I)
Stimulants/cocaine (I/W)

> *DSM–IV–TR* diagnoses on Axis I for sleep disorder symptoms associated with substances
> - Alcohol-induced sleep disorder (655)
> - Amphetamine-induced sleep disorder (655)
> - Caffeine-induced sleep disorder (655)
> - Cocaine-induced sleep disorder (655)
> - Opioid-induced sleep disorder (655)
> - Sedative-, hypnotic-, or anxiolytic-induced sleep disorder (655)
> - Other (or unknown) substance-induced sleep disorder (655)

Step 3: Differential Diagnoses of Psychological Symptoms After Ruling Out Those Due to a General Medical Condition or Substance Use

Once it has been determined that the client's presenting psychological symptoms are not the direct physiological effect of a general medical condition or of substance intoxication or withdrawal, the clinician may consider the various Axis I and Axis II psychological disorders defined in the *DSM–IV–TR*. The guidelines in the outlines that follow present the starting points for generating hypotheses about various possible diagnoses. The clinician also should use the decision trees cited previously and the *DSM–IV–TR* diagnostic criteria (see page references for the print *DSM–IV–TR* listed with the possible diagnoses listed subsequently; see also http://www.psychiatryonline.com to access diagnostic criteria online) for more detailed decision making and determination of the final diagnoses. (Note: Diagnoses are listed on Axis I unless otherwise indicated.)

If the client presents with symptoms of a developmental nature, consider these possible diagnoses.

> Mental retardation (coded on Axis II; 43–44)
  - Mild mental retardation (43)
  - Moderate mental retardation (43)
  - Severe mental retardation (43)
  - Profound mental retardation (44)
  - Mental retardation, severity unspecified (44)
> Borderline intellectual functioning (740)
> Learning disorders
  - Reading disorder (51)
  - Mathematics disorder (53)
  - Disorder of written expression (54)
  - Learning disorder NOS (56)
> Motor skills disorder
  - Developmental coordination disorder (56)
> Communication disorders
  - Expressive language disorder (58)
  - Mixed receptive–expressive language disorder (62)
  - Phonological disorder (65)
  - Stuttering (67)
  - Communication disorder NOS (69)

- ➢ Attention-deficit and disruptive behavior disorders
  - ▪ Attention-deficit/hyperactivity disorder (85)
    - ○ Combined type
    - ○ Predominantly inattentive type
    - ○ Predominantly hyperactive–impulsive type
  - ▪ Attention-deficit/hyperactivity disorder NOS (93)
- ➢ Conduct disorder (93)
  - ▪ Childhood-onset type
  - ▪ Adolescent-onset type
  - ▪ Unspecified onset
- ➢ Oppositional defiant disorder (100)
- ➢ Disruptive behavior disorder NOS (103)
- ➢ Feeding and eating disorders of infancy or early childhood
  - ▪ Pica (103)
  - ▪ Rumination disorder (105)
  - ▪ Feeding disorder of infancy or early childhood (107)
- ➢ Tic disorders
  - ▪ Tourette's disorder (111)
  - ▪ Chronic motor or vocal tic disorder (114)
  - ▪ Transient tic disorder (115)
  - ▪ Tic disorder NOS (116)
- ➢ Elimination disorders
  - ▪ Encopresis (116)
    - ○ With constipation and overflow incontinence
    - ○ Without constipation and overflow incontinence
  - ▪ Enuresis (not due to a general medical condition; 118)
- ➢ Relational disorders
  - ▪ Separation anxiety disorder (121)
  - ▪ Reactive attachment disorder of infancy or early childhood (127)
- ➢ Other behavior disorders
  - ▪ Selective mutism (125)
  - ▪ Stereotypic movement disorder (131)
- ➢ Pervasive developmental disorders
  - ▪ Autistic disorder (70)
  - ▪ Rett's disorder (76)
  - ▪ Childhood disintegrative disorder (77)
  - ▪ Asperger's disorder (80)
  - ▪ Pervasive developmental disorder NOS (84)
- ➢ Disorder of infancy, childhood, or adolescence NOS (134)

If the client presents with current positive psychotic symptoms (e.g., hallucinations, delusions) and/or negative symptoms (e.g., flat affect, poverty of speech), consider these possible diagnoses.

- ➢ Schizophrenia (297)
  - ▪ Paranoid type (313)
  - ▪ Disorganized type (314)
  - ▪ Catatonic type (315)
  - ▪ Undifferentiated type (316)
  - ▪ Residual type (316)
- ➢ Schizophreniform disorder (317)
- ➢ Schizoaffective disorder (319)
- ➢ Delusional disorder (323)
- ➢ Brief psychotic disorder (329)
- ➢ Shared psychotic disorder (332)
- ➢ Cognitive disorder (e.g., delirium, dementia) with psychotic features (136; 147)
- ➢ Mood disorder with psychotic features (345–348)
- ➢ Psychotic disorder NOS (343)

If the client presents with symptoms of depression (with no history of mania, hypomania, or mixed state), consider these possible diagnoses.

- ➢ Major depressive disorder (369)
  - ▪ With psychotic features
  - ▪ Without psychotic features
- ➢ Schizoaffective disorder (319)
- ➢ Dysthymic disorder (376)
- ➢ Adjustment disorder (679)
  - ▪ With depressed mood
  - ▪ With mixed anxiety and depressed mood
  - ▪ With mixed disturbance of emotions and conduct
- ➢ Bereavement (740)
- ➢ Depressive disorder NOS (381)

If the client presents with current (or a history of) manic or hypomanic symptoms, consider these possible diagnoses.

- ➢ Schizoaffective disorder, bipolar type (319)
- ➢ Bipolar I disorder (382)
  - ▪ Most recent episode hypomanic, manic, or mixed, with or without psychosis

- Most recent episode depressed, with or without psychosis
- Bipolar II disorder (392)
  - Most recent episode hypomanic
  - Most recent episode depressed
- Cyclothymic disorder (398)
- Bipolar disorder NOS (400)
- Mood disorder NOS (410)

If the client presents with anxiety (fear, worry, panic) symptoms, consider these possible diagnoses.

- Obsessive–compulsive disorder (456)
- Posttraumatic stress disorder (463)
- Acute stress disorder (469)
- Generalized anxiety disorder (472)
- Social phobia (450)
- Specific phobia (443)
  - Animal type
  - Natural environment type
  - Blood-injection-injury type
  - Situational type
  - Other type
- Agoraphobia without a history of panic disorder (441)
- Panic disorder (433)
  - With agoraphobia
  - Without agoraphobia
- Adjustment disorder (679)
  - With anxiety
  - With mixed anxiety and depressed mood
  - With mixed disturbance of emotions and conduct
- Anxiety disorder NOS (484)

If the client presents with cognitive functioning deficits (e.g., attention difficulties, memory loss, disorientation), consider these possible diagnoses.

- Dissociative amnesia (520)
- Dissociative fugue (523)
- Dissociative identity disorder (526)
- Dissociative disorder NOS (532)
- Depersonalization disorder (530)

➢ Posttraumatic stress disorder (463)
➢ Age-related cognitive decline (740)
➢ Delirium NOS (147)
➢ Dementia NOS (171)
➢ Amnestic disorder NOS (179)
➢ Cognitive disorder NOS (179)

If the client presents with substance abuse or dependence symptoms, consider these possible diagnoses.

➢ Alcohol dependence (213)
➢ Amphetamine dependence (224)
➢ Cannabis dependence (236)
➢ Cocaine dependence (242)
➢ Hallucinogen dependence (251)
➢ Inhalant dependence (258)
➢ Nicotine dependence (264)
➢ Opioid dependence (270)
➢ Phencyclidine dependence (279)
➢ Sedative, hypnotic, or anxiolytic dependence (285)
➢ Polysubstance dependence (293)
➢ Other (or unknown) substance dependence (192)
➢ Alcohol abuse (214)
➢ Amphetamine abuse (225)
➢ Cannabis abuse (236)
➢ Cocaine abuse (243)
➢ Hallucinogen abuse (252)
➢ Inhalant abuse (259)
➢ Opioid abuse (271)
➢ Phencyclidine abuse (279)
➢ Sedative, hypnotic, or anxiolytic abuse (286)
➢ Other (or unknown) substance abuse (198)

If the client presents with symptoms of other types of impulse-control problems, consider these possible diagnoses.

➢ Intermittent explosive disorder (663)
➢ Pathological gambling (671)
➢ Kleptomania (667)
➢ Pyromania (669)
➢ Trichotillomania (674)

> Impulse-control disorder NOS (677)
> Paraphilias
>> ■ Exhibitionism (569)
>> ■ Fetishism (569)
>> ■ Frotteurism (570)
>> ■ Pedophilia (571)
>> ■ Sexual masochism (572)
>> ■ Sexual sadism (573)
>> ■ Transvestic fetishism (574)
>> ■ Voyeurism (575)
>> ■ Paraphilia NOS (576)

If the client presents with fears or concerns about eating, weight, or body image, and/or maladaptive behaviors regarding food, consider these possible diagnoses. (Note: If the client is an infant or very young child, consider feeding and eating disorders of infancy or early childhood listed previously.)

> Anorexia nervosa (583)
> Bulimia nervosa (589)
> Eating disorder NOS (594)

If the client presents with sexual dysfunction symptoms, consider these possible diagnoses.

> Sexual desire disorder
>> ■ Hypoactive sexual desire disorder (539)
>> ■ Sexual aversion disorder (541)
> Sexual arousal disorder
>> ■ Female sexual arousal disorder (543)
>> ■ Male erectile disorder (545)
> Orgasmic disorder
>> ■ Female orgasmic disorder (547)
>> ■ Male orgasmic disorder (550)
>> ■ Premature ejaculation (552)
> Sexual pain disorder
>> ■ Dyspareunia (not due to a general medical condition; 554)
>> ■ Vaginismus (not due to a general medical condition; 556)
> Sexual disorder NOS (582)

If the client presents with gender identity concerns, consider these possible diagnoses.
> Gender identity disorder (576)
  ▪ In children
  ▪ In adolescents or adults
> Gender identity disorder NOS (582)

If the client presents with symptoms of disrupted sleep, consider these possible diagnoses.
> Primary insomnia (599)
> Primary hypersomnia (604)
> Narcolepsy (609)
> Breathing-related sleep disorder (615)
> Circadian rhythm sleep disorder (622)
> Dyssomnia NOS (629)
> Nightmare disorder (631)
> Sleep terror disorder (634)
> Sleepwalking disorder (639)
> Parasomnia NOS (644)
> Insomnia related to . . . (an Axis I or Axis II disorder; 645)
> Hypersomnia related to . . . (an Axis I or Axis II disorder; 645)

If the client presents with complaints about the body, including impaired perceptions, consider these possible diagnoses.
> Depersonalization disorder (530)
> Somatization disorder (486)
> Undifferentiated somatoform disorder (490)
> Conversion disorder (492)
> Pain disorder (498)
> Hypochondriasis (504)
> Body dysmorphic disorder (507)
> Somatoform disorder NOS (511)

If the client presents with a long-standing pattern (appearing before early adulthood) of maladaptive intra- and interpersonal experiences and behavior, consider a diagnosis of personality disorder.
  > Note: Personality disorders are coded on Axis II. Some clients exhibit maladaptive personality traits that do not meet the criteria for a diagnosis of a personality disorder.

The clinician may indicate those traits (e.g., borderline personality traits) on Axis II with no specific code.

➢ It is not uncommon for a client to have an Axis I and a separate Axis II disorder. The clinician must exercise caution when considering an Axis II diagnosis in a client already carrying an Axis I diagnosis because of the overlap of symptom criteria for each disorder. In fact, the *DSM–IV–TR* cautions against diagnosing a personality disorder when the client exhibits current acute symptoms of an Axis I disorder.

  ▪ Research indicates, however, some strong evidence of comorbidity between specific Axis I and Axis II disorders. The clinician's awareness of potential comorbid conditions is critical because the presence of a personality disorder can significantly impact the presentation, treatment, and course of an Axis I disorder. Some common comorbid Axis I disorders are included with each Axis II personality disorder listed in the outline that follows.

➢ Paranoid personality disorder (690)

➢ Schizoid personality disorder (694)

➢ Schizotypal personality disorder (697)

➢ Antisocial personality disorder (701)

  ▪ Common comorbid Axis I disorders

    ○ Substance use disorders, particularly alcohol dependence and/or cocaine dependence

➢ Borderline personality disorder (706)

  ▪ Common comorbid Axis I disorders

    ○ Major depressive disorder

    ○ Dysthymic disorder

    ○ Bipolar II disorder

    ○ Posttraumatic stress disorder

    ○ Other anxiety disorders

    ○ Substance use disorders

    ○ Bulimia nervosa

➢ Histrionic personality disorder (711)

  ▪ Common comorbid Axis I diagnoses

    ○ Obsessive–compulsive disorder

    ○ Other anxiety disorders

    ○ Somatization disorder

    ○ Dissociative disorders

○ Major depressive disorder
○ Dysthymic disorder
➢ Narcissistic personality disorder (714)
▪ Common comorbid Axis I diagnoses
○ Major depressive disorder
○ Dysthymic disorder
○ Bipolar disorder
○ Substance use disorders
○ Eating disorders
➢ Avoidant personality disorder (718)
▪ Common comorbid Axis I diagnoses
○ Social phobia
○ Obsessive–compulsive disorder
➢ Dependent personality disorder (721)
▪ Common comorbid Axis I diagnoses
○ Eating disorders
○ Anxiety disorders (e.g., obsessive–compulsive disorder)
○ Somatization disorder
➢ Obsessive–compulsive personality disorder (725)

References

American Psychiatric Association. (2000). *Diagnostic and statistical manual of mental disorders* (4th ed., text revision). Washington, DC: Author. (*DSM–IV–TR* criteria are also available at http://www.psychiatryonline.com)

Blaney, P. H., & Millon, T. (Eds.). (2009). *Oxford textbook of psychopathology* (2nd ed.). New York, NY: Oxford University Press.

First, M. B., Frances, A., & Pincus, H. A. (Eds.). (2002). DSM–IV–TR *handbook of differential diagnosis*. Washington, DC: American Psychiatric Press. doi:10.1176/appi.books.9781585622658

Kay, J., & Tasman, A. (2000). *Psychiatry: Behavioral science and clinical essentials*. Philadelphia, PA: W. B. Saunders.

Kupfer, D. J., Horner, M. S., Brent, D. A., Lewis, D. A., Reynolds, C. F., Thase, M. E., & Travis, M. J. (2008). *Oxford American handbook of psychiatry*. New York, NY: Oxford University Press.

Morrison, J. (1997). *When psychological problems mask medical disorders*. New York, NY: Guilford Press.

Morrison, J. (2007). *Diagnosis made easier: Principles and techniques for mental health clinicians*. New York, NY: Guilford Press.

Paniagua, F. A. (2001). *Diagnosis in a multicultural context*. Thousand Oaks, CA: Sage.

World Health Organization. (2007). *International statistical classification of diseases and related health problems* (10th ed.). Retrieved from http://apps.who.int/classifications/apps/icd/icd10online/

CHAPTER 12

Evidence-Based Interventions

The health professions have long been dedicated to improving medical and mental health care through the application of relevant empirical research findings to the treatment of the individual patient or client. The various mental health disciplines have struggled to translate that commitment into practice. This chapter provides a brief historical overview of how psychologists have addressed the issue and an outline of recommendations for the clinician based on the work of Norcross, Hogan, and Koocher (2008) and Jongsma and Bruce (2010). The chapter concludes with an annotated list of web and print resources for evidence-based practice.

In 1993, the president of Division 12 (Society of Clinical Psychology) of the American Psychological Association (APA), David Barlow, appointed the Task Force on Promotion and Dissemination of Psychological Procedures to review psychotherapy research and identify those interventions with established treatment efficacy and clinical utility. The task force published criteria for empirically supported treatments (ESTs), including "having been tested in randomized controlled trials (RCTs) with a specific population and implemented using a treatment manual" (APA Presidential Task Force on Evidence-Based Practice, 2006, p. 272). The group later listed interventions that met their criteria for various disorders (Chambless et al., 1998; Chambless et al., 1996). Other groups followed with articles and reports that highlighted additional ESTs for geriatric, adult, adolescent, and child clients (e.g., Chambless & Ollendick, 2001; Gatz et al., 1998; Lonigan, Elbert, & Johnson, 1998). These early publications sparked considerable discussion and controversy among psychologists. Many argued that the concept of ESTs was too narrow and failed to give adequate weight to other factors known to account for significant variance in the outcome of psychological treatment—specifically, clinician expertise and client characteristics, culture, and preferences. For example, APA Division 29 (Psychotherapy) formed its own task force and presented evidence for the impact of therapy relationship factors such as empathy and positive regard on treatment efficacy (Norcross, 2002).

In 2005, APA President Ronald F. Levant appointed a new APA Presidential Task Force on Evidence-Based Practice in Psychology (EBPP)—a broader concept than EST intended to incorporate therapist and client characteristics, treatment relationship qualities, and therapeutic method. The task force "was charged with defining and explicating principles of evidence-based practice in psychology" (APA Presidential Task Force on Evidence-Based Practice, 2006, p. 273). Their work culminated in a proposed APA policy statement and a report regarding the current status of EBPP. The task force members defined evidence-based practice in psychology as "the integration of the best available research with clinical expertise in the context of patient characteristics, culture, and preferences" (p. 273). They referred to clinical expertise as the "competence attained by psychologists through education, training, and experience that results in effective practice" (p. 275) and listed eight specific competencies. In addition, they discussed the importance of understanding the roles of the client's cultural context and individual differences in treatment process and outcome. The task force members concluded their report by stating that the

> central message of [the] . . . report—and one of the most heartening aspects of the process that led to it—is the consensus achieved among a diverse group of scientists, clinicians, and scientist-clinicians from multiple perspectives that EBPP requires an appreciation of the value of multiple sources of scientific evidence. . . . The scientific method is a way of thinking and observing systemati-

cally, and it is the best tool we have for learning about what works for whom. (p. 280)

And, in January 2010, a position statement of APA Division 12 was adopted by the APA; the statement underscored the importance of consideration of treatment methods, participant (clinician and client) variables, relationship elements, and contextual factors through a variety of research strategies (not only RCTs) in research on psychotherapy.

Recommendations for Engaging in Evidence-Based Practice

These recommendations are based on the work of Jongsma and Bruce (2010) and Norcross et al. (2008).

> Adopt a scientist–practitioner approach to treatment by creating, testing, and revising hypotheses about what intervention may work best with a particular client with a particular problem (or set of problems) in a particular context.
> Maintain current knowledge of the literature regarding ESTs, client variables, clinician expertise, relationship factors, and contextual elements for effective treatment.
> Conduct a careful and complete assessment of the client that allows for an accurate diagnosis and/or case conceptualization.
> Identify a specific clinical problem as a target for intervention.
> Access information about and guidelines for delivering specific ESTs that are relevant.
> Choose and implement an EST with consideration of client variables, clinician expertise, client variables, relationship factors and contextual elements.
> Monitor the client's response to the intervention throughout the process, making adjustments as necessary.

Web Resources for Empirically Supported Assessments and Treatments

> American Psychiatric Association practice guidelines
>> ■ The guidelines provide evidence-based recommendations for the assessment and treatment of a variety of

mental health issues including acute stress disorder, posttraumatic stress disorder, Alzheimer's disease and other dementias, bipolar disorder, borderline personality disorder, delirium, eating disorders, HIV/AIDS, major depressive disorder, obsessive-compulsive disorder, panic disorder, schizophrenia, substance use disorders, and suicidal behaviors.
- http://www.psych.org/MainMenu/PsychiatricPractice/ PracticeGuidelines_1.aspx

➤ Evidence-Based Mental Health Treatments for Children and Adolescents (created and maintained by APA Division 53 [Society of Clinical Child and Adolescent Psychology] and the Association for Behavioral and Cognitive Therapies)
- The website provides information to the public and to professionals and educators regarding empirically supported treatments for children and adolescents. EST options for 13 specific child and adolescent mental health symptoms and disorders are provided under the Professionals and Educators link.
- http://www.effectivechildtherapy.com

➤ Evidence-Based Behavioral Practice (funded by the National Library of Medicine from the Office of Behavioral and Social Sciences Research, National Institute of Health, to Northwestern University)
- The Evidence-Based Behavioral Practice organization offers training to inform behavioral health professionals working in a variety of disciplines about empirically supported practices. Training modules are available for continuing education credit for social workers, psychologists, physicians, nurses, and nurse practitioners. The website also contains references to key articles and a teaching resource library.
- http://www.ebbp.org

➤ Manuals for Empirically Validated Treatments (created in June 1995 by W. C. Sanderson and S. Woody as a task force report for APA Division 12)
- Part of the APA Division 12 website, this document lists references and training opportunities for empirically validated treatments for a variety of psychological disorders.

- http://www.apa.org/divisions/div12/est/MANUALS forevt.html
➢ National Institute for Health and Clinical Excellence (maintained by an independent organization in Great Britain)
  - The website provides national guidelines for treatment of specific psychological disorders based on empirical research (e.g., alcohol abuse, depression).
  - http://www.nice.org.uk
➢ National Registry of Evidence-Based Programs and Practices (maintained by the Substance Abuse and Mental Health Services Administration)
  - This is a searchable online reference listing of more than 180 evidence-based interventions addressing mental health and substance abuse problems. The reference for each intervention includes a description of the treatment and of the supporting research.
  - http://www.nrepp.samhsa.gov
➢ TherapyAdvisor
  - The website gives registered practitioners access to information on empirically supported treatments for a variety of disorders in geriatric, adult, and child clients as well as links to treatment manuals and training materials and institutes.
  - http://www.therapyadvisor.com
➢ Website on Research-Supported Psychological Treatments (managed by APA Division 12)
  - This website offers descriptions of and information about research-supported psychological treatments for 15 disorders.
  - http://www.psychologicaltreatments.org

Print Resources for Evidence-Based Treatments

➢ *Advances in Psychotherapy—Evidence-Based Practice Series*
  - The series includes several books by different authors on evidence-based practice for a variety of psychological disorders and problems, including suicidology, schizophrenia, elimination disorders in children and adolescents, substance use problems, alcohol use problems, nicotine and tobacco dependence, chronic pain, eating disorders, heart disease, attention-deficit/hyperactivity

disorder in children and adults, sexual violence, child-
hood maltreatment, hypochondriasis and health anxiety, and social anxiety disorder.
- Refer to publisher's website at http://www.hogrefe.com/
  program/factfinder/?q=Advances+in+psychotherapy%
  3A++Evidence-based+practice+series
➤ *Clinical Handbook of Psychological Disorders: A Step-by-Step
  Treatment Manual* (Barlow, 2008)
  - Includes 16 chapters by different authors on several
    Axis I disorders, borderline personality disorder, and
    couples distress
➤ *Clinician's Guide to Evidence-Based Practices: Mental Health
  and the Addictions* (Norcross et al., 2008)
  - Outlines the process of implementing evidence-based
    practice in clinical work
➤ *Evidence-Based Practices in Mental Health: Debate and Dia-
  logue on the Fundamental Questions* (Norcross, Beutler, &
  Levant, 2006)
  - Offers chapters that contain position papers by differ-
    ent authors regarding nine important questions regard-
    ing evidence-based practices (e.g., "What qualifies as
    evidence of effective practice?")
➤ *Evidence-Based Psychotherapies for Children and Adolescents*
  (Weisz & Kazdin, 2010)
  - Presents 24 chapters by different authors on empiri-
    cally supported treatments for internalizing and exter-
    nalizing disorders and problems as well as for other
    significant psychological conditions common in chil-
    dren and adolescents (e.g., autism, trauma)
➤ *Handbook of Evidence-Based Therapies for Children and Adoles-
  cents: Bridging Science and Practice* (Steele, Elkin, & Roberts,
  2008)
  - Provides 20 chapters by different authors on a variety
    of psychological disorders common in children and
    adolescents as well as a section of chapters on imple-
    mentation issues (i.e., consideration of therapist, client,
    relationship, and treatment context variables)
➤ *Practitioner's Guide to Evidence-Based Treatments* (Fisher &
  O'Donohue, 2006)
  - Offers chapters by different authors on 73 psychologi-
    cal and behavioral disorders, each describing the key

features of the disorder, assessment guidelines, and effective treatments (including self-help, therapist based, medical, and combinations)

> *Principles of Therapeutic Change That Work* (Castonguay & Beutler, 2006)
>   - Provides chapters by different authors that review critical participant, relationship, and technique factors (and the integration of the therapeutic factors) in the effective treatment of several Axis I and Axis II disorders
> *Psychotherapy Relationships That Work: Therapist Contributions and Responsiveness to Patients* (Norcross, 2002)
>   - Offers chapters by different authors that outline the effective and promising general elements of therapeutic relationships and present strategies for adapting the therapy relationship for the individual client

References

American Psychological Association Presidential Task Force on Evidence-Based Practice. (2006). Evidence-based practice in psychology. *American Psychologist, 61,* 271–285. doi:10.1037/0003-066X.61.4.271

Barlow, D. (Ed.). (2008). *Clinical handbook of psychological disorders: A step-by-step treatment manual* (4th ed.). New York, NY: Guilford Press.

Castonguay, L. G., & Beutler, L. E. (Eds.). (2006). *Principles of therapeutic change that work.* New York, NY: Oxford University Press.

Chambless, D. L., Baker, M. J., Baucom, D. H., Beutler, L. E., Calhoun, K. S., Crits-Cristoph, P., . . . Woody, S. R. (1998). Update on empirically validated therapies, II. *Clinical Psychologist, 51*(1), 3–16.

Chambless, D. L., & Ollendick, T. H. (2001). Empirically supported psychological interventions: Controversies and evidence. *Annual Review of Psychology, 52,* 685–716. doi:10.1146/annurev.psych.52.1.685

Chambless, D. L., Sanderson, W. C., Shoham, V., Bennett Johnson, S., Pope, K. S., Crits-Cristoph, P., . . . McCurry, S. (1996). An update on empirically validated therapies. *Clinical Psychologist, 49*(2), 5–18.

Fisher, J. E., & O'Donohue, W. T. (Eds.). (2006). *Practitioner's guide to evidence-based psychotherapy*. New York, NY: Springer Science+Business Media.

Gatz, M., Fiske, A., Fox, L. S., Kaskie, B., Kasl-Godley, J. E., McCallum, T. J., & Weatherall, J. L. (1998). Empirically validated psychological treatments for older adults. *Journal of Mental Health and Aging, 4*, 9–46.

Jongsma, A. E., & Bruce, T. J. (2010). *Evidence-based psychotherapy treatment planning DVD companion workbook*. Hoboken, NJ: Wiley.

Lonigan, C. J., Elbert, J. C., & Johnson, S. B. (1998). Empirically supported psychosocial interventions for children: An overview. *Journal of Clinical Child Psychology, 27*, 138–145. doi:10.1207/s15374424jccp2702_1

Norcross, J. C. (2002). *Psychotherapy relationships that work: Therapist contributions and responsiveness to patients*. New York, NY: Oxford University Press.

Norcross, J. C., Beutler, L. E., & Levant, R. F. (Eds.). (2006). *Evidence-based practices in mental health: Debate and dialogue on the fundamental questions*. Washington, DC: American Psychological Association. doi:10.1037/11265-000

Norcross, J. C., Hogan, T. P., & Koocher, G. P. (2008). *Clinician's guide to evidence-based practices: Mental health and the addictions*. New York, NY: Oxford University Press.

Steele, R. G., Elkin, T. D., & Roberts, M. C. (Eds.). (2008). *Handbook of evidence-based therapies for children and adolescents: Bridging science and practice*. New York, NY: Springer Science+Business Media.

Weisz, J. R., & Kazdin, A. E. (Eds.). (2010). *Evidence-based psychotherapies for children and adolescents* (2nd ed.). New York, NY: Guilford Press.

CHAPTER 13

Psychopharmacotherapies

Research suggests that most major psychological disorders are determined by multiple factors. As such, possible treatment approaches vary and need to be carefully chosen by the clinician following a thorough evaluation and diagnosis. Increasing evidence indicates that many major disorders involve complex neurochemical abnormalities and that those with the disorders often benefit from appropriate medication, prescribed or over-the-counter (herbal and dietary supplements). However, psychopharmacological treatments may also have adverse effects. For example, some medications or products may produce unpleasant side effects (e.g., weight gain, dry mouth, lowered libido). Further, some may induce serious or life-threatening medical complications (e.g., neuroleptic malignant syndrome, abuse or dependence, psychotic symptoms). Given that most mental health practitioners will encounter clients who either have a history of treatment with medication or who begin taking medication while in therapy, clinicians of all disciplines should be familiar with common psychopharmacotherapies.

The two tables in this chapter list several medications used to treat psychological disorders. Table 13.1 presents prescription medications. Typically, such tables group drugs by the disorders for which they are commonly prescribed and then list them by their generic names in alphabetical order. However, Table 13.1 is intended to assist the clinician who learns from a client (or the client's representative) that he or she is taking a medication. Because clients typically refer to their medications by trade names, the format of Table 13.1 is different; the drugs are listed by trade names in alphabetical order, followed by generic names and drug class. Disorders for which each medication may be prescribed and typical dosage levels for children, adolescents, adults, and elderly clients also are indicated as well as common side effects, serious complications, withdrawal warnings, and cautions. Table 13.2 presents over-the-counter products, noting disorders treated, evidence of research support, typical dosage levels for adults, common side effects, serious complications, withdrawal warnings, and cautions.

The information in Tables 13.1 and 13.2 is derived from a variety of sources, including Green (2001); Kupfer et al. (2008); Petersen (2008); Preston, O'Neal, and Talaga (2006, 2010); Salzman (2001); Thomson Healthcare (2007a, 2007b); and Thomson PDR (2010). The tables are not intended to be an exhaustive list of all psychotropic medications. For example, the list of prescribed medications does not include tricyclics or monoamine oxidase inhibitors because of their relatively less frequent use by practitioners. The tables are intended to provide clinicians with an initial quick reference guide for the assessment and treatment of their clients. Therapists should obtain further information regarding a specific client's use of any medication from the client's prescribing practitioner and/or consultation with a medical professional.

TABLE 13.1
Commonly Prescribed Pharmacotherapies for Child (C),
Adolescent (A), Adult (Ad), and Elderly (E) Clients

Trade name Generic name Drug class	Disorders or symptoms treated	Common daily maintenance dose levels (mg/day, unless noted)	Side effects	Withdrawal warnings and cautions
Abilify Aripiprazole Atypical antipsychotic	Psychosis/schizophrenia, bipolar disorder/manic or mixed, major depressive disorder (adjunct treatment), autistic disorder/irritability symptoms	C: 5–15 A: 10–30 Ad: 10–30 E: Lower than adult dose	Common: Sedation, nausea, confusion, headache, anxiety, constipation, orthostatic hypotension, dizziness, dry mouth, weight gain, extrapyramidal symptoms, tachycardia or bradycardia Serious: Increased depression or suicidality, seizures, tardive dyskinesia, neuroleptic malignant syndrome	Caution with elderly clients

(continued)

TABLE 13.1 (*Continued*)
Commonly Prescribed Pharmacotherapies for Child (C),
Adolescent (A), Adult (Ad), and Elderly (E) Clients

Trade name Generic name Drug class	Disorders or symptoms treated	Common daily maintenance dose levels (mg/day, unless noted)	Side effects	Withdrawal warnings and cautions
Adderall, Adderall XR Amphetamine mixed salts Stimulant	Attention-deficit/ hyperactivity disorder (ADHD)	C: 5–40 A: 5–40 Ad: 10–80 E: —	Common: Insomnia, decreased appetite, gastrointestinal (GI) distress, weight loss, agitation, dry mouth, headache, dizziness, emotional upset, palpitations, tachycardia, tremor, sexual dysfunctions Serious: Abuse or dependence, exacerbation of anxiety, tics, agitated depression, aggressive behavior, psychosis, mania, aggressive behavior, seizures, cardiac complications with misuse	Avoid abrupt withdrawal

Ambien, Ambien CR Zolpidem Atypical antianxiety	Insomnia (short- term treatment)	C: — A: — Ad: 5–10 (CR: 6.25–12.5) E: 5–10	Common: Sedation, headache, dry mouth, GI distress, dizziness, palpita- tions Serious: Increased depression or sui- cidality, physical or psychological dependence, hallu- cinations, aggression	Avoid abrupt withdrawal Caution with alco- hol use, caution with elderly clients
Antabuse Disulfiram	Alcohol abuse or dependence (abstinence aid)	C: — A: — Ad: 125–500 E: Similar to adult dose	Common: Sedation, headache, acne, impotence Serious: Psychosis, hepatoxicity	

(continued)

TABLE 13.1 (*Continued*)
Commonly Prescribed Pharmacotherapies for Child (C),
Adolescent (A), Adult (Ad), and Elderly (E) Clients

Trade name Generic name Drug class	Disorders or symptoms treated	Common daily maintenance dose levels (mg/day, unless noted)	Side effects	Withdrawal warnings and cautions
Aricept Donepezil	Alzheimer's and other dementias	C: — A: — Ad: 5–10 E: 5–10	Common: GI distress, headache, dizziness, decreased appetite, weight loss, unusual dreams, muscle cramping, insomnia, fatigue, bradycardia Serious: Depression, seizures	
Ativan Lorazepam Benzodiazepine	Primary insomnia, anxiety	C: 0.5 mg/kg every 4 to 8 hr, max. 2 mg/dose A: 1–6 Ad: 2–6 E: 0.125–0.5 (sleep), 0.25–2 (anxiety)	Common: Sedation, dizziness, weakness, hypotension, paradoxical activation reactions (e.g., acute excitation, aggression)	Avoid abrupt withdrawal, should be very gradual Caution with alcohol use, caution with elderly clients

BuSpar Buspirone Other antianxiety	Anxiety disorders, ADHD, pervasive developmental disorder (PDD) symptoms (e.g., anxiety, irritability), agitation in elderly clients with dementia	C: (6 and up) 15–60 A: 15–60 Ad: 20–60 E: 20–80 for agitation	Common: Dizziness, drowsiness, blurred vision, GI distress, headache, agitation, insomnia, dry mouth, confusion, extrapyramidal symptoms Serious: Depression, hostility, tardive dyskinesia, serotonin syndrome
			Serious: Abuse or dependence, respiratory depression or failure, seizures, increased depression or suicidality

(continued)

TABLE 13.1 (*Continued*)
Commonly Prescribed Pharmacotherapies for Child (C),
Adolescent (A), Adult (Ad), and Elderly (E) Clients

Trade name Generic name Drug class	Disorders or symptoms treated	Common daily maintenance dose levels (mg/day, unless noted)	Side effects	Withdrawal warnings and cautions
Celexa Citalopram Selective serotonin reuptake inhibitors (SSRI)	Depression, obsessive-compulsive disorder (OCD), panic disorder, social phobia, generalized anxiety disorder (GAD), PDD symptoms, bulimia nervosa, agitation in elderly clients with dementia	C: — A: 10–40 Ad: 20–60 E: 5–40	Common: Sedation, dry mouth, sweating, GI distress, decreased appetite, insomnia, agitation, sexual (ejaculatory) dysfunction, tremor, extrapyramidal symptoms Serious: Increased depression or suicidality, seizures, mania, serotonin syndrome, neuroleptic malignant syndrome	Avoid abrupt withdrawal Caution with alcohol use, caution with elderly clients

Cognex Tacrine	Alzheimer's and other dementias	C: — A: — Ad: 80–160 E: 80–160	Common: Dizziness, headache, GI distress, decreased appetite, weight loss, agitation, confusion, insomnia, fatigue, rash Serious: Seizures, hepatoxicity, heart block	
Concerta Methylphenidate Stimulant	ADHD	C: (> 6) 18–54 A: 18–72 or 2 mg/kg Ad: 18–72 E: —	Common: Insomnia, decreased appetite, GI distress, headache, dry mouth, dizziness, agitation, irritability, transient dysphoria Serious: Exacerbation of anxiety, tics, agitated depression, abuse or dependence, psychosis, mania, aggressive behavior, cardiac complications, neuroleptic malignant syndrome	

(continued)

TABLE 13.1 (*Continued*)
Commonly Prescribed Pharmacotherapies for Child (C), Adolescent (A), Adult (Ad), and Elderly (E) Clients

Trade name Generic name Drug class	Disorders or symptoms treated	Common daily maintenance dose levels (mg/day, unless noted)	Side effects	Withdrawal warnings and cautions
Cymbalta Duloxetine SNRI	Depression, GAD, fibromyalgia	C: — A: 40–60 Ad: 40–60 E: Lower than adult dose	Common: Sedation, dry mouth, GI distress, decreased appetite, orthostatic hypotension, dizziness, sexual dysfunction, agitation, insomnia, headache, increased sweating, fatigue, tremor, extrapyramidal symptoms	Avoid abrupt withdrawal Caution with elderly clients

			Caution with child and elderly clients
	Bipolar disorder or acute mania, conduct disorder or oppositional defiant disorder symptoms, agitation in elderly clients with dementia	C: 10–60 mg/kg A: 10–60 mg/kg Ad: 750–1,500 E: 600–1,200 (125–750 for agitation)	Serious: Increased depression or suicidality, hypomania or mania, seizures, hypertensive crisis, serotonin syndrome, neuroleptic malignant syndrome
Depakote, Depakene Divalproex sodium or valproic acid Anticonvulsant			Common: Sedation, dizziness, headache, blurred vision, tremor, GI distress, weight gain, agitation, emotional lability, insomnia, rash Serious: Increased depression or suicidality, psychosis/hallucinations, liver damage or hepatic failure, Stevens–Johnson syndrome

(continued)

TABLE 13.1 (*Continued*)
Commonly Prescribed Pharmacotherapies for Child (C),
Adolescent (A), Adult (Ad), and Elderly (E) Clients

Trade name Generic name Drug class	Disorders or symptoms treated	Common daily maintenance dose levels (mg/day, unless noted)	Side effects	Withdrawal warnings and cautions
Desyrel Trazodone Atypical antidepressant	Depression, initial insomnia, aggressive behavior, agitation in elderly clients with dementia	C: (6–12) 1.5–6 mg/kg A: 1.5–6 mg/kg Ad: 25–400 E: 25–100	Common: Sedation, dizziness, hypotension, dry mouth, confusion, insomnia, fatigue, nightmares, headache, palpitations, GI distress, agitation, sexual dysfunctions, tremor, extrapyramidal symptoms Serious: Psychosis/ hallucinations, hypomania or mania, increased depression or suicidality, seizures, cardiac complications, tardive dyskinesia	Avoid abrupt withdrawal Caution with elderly clients

| Dexedrine Dexoamphetamine Stimulant | ADHD | C: (> 6) 5–40
A: 5–40
Ad: 5–40
E: — | Common: Insomnia, dry mouth, decreased appetite, GI distress, weight loss, headache, dizziness, euphoria, tremor, mild dysphoria, palpitations, tachycardia, agitation, sexual dysfunction

Serious: Psychosis, mania, exacerbation of anxiety, tics, agitated depression, aggressive behavior, seizures, abuse or dependence, cardiac complications with misuse | Avoid abrupt withdrawal |

(continued)

TABLE 13.1 (*Continued*)
Commonly Prescribed Pharmacotherapies for Child (C),
Adolescent (A), Adult (Ad), and Elderly (E) Clients

Trade name Generic name Drug class	Disorders or symptoms treated	Common daily maintenance dose levels (mg/day, unless noted)	Side effects	Withdrawal warnings and cautions
Effexor XR Venlafaxine XR SNRI	Depression, GAD, panic disorder, social anxiety disorder, ADHD behavioral symptoms	C: 12.5–37.5 A: 25–75+ Ad: 75–225 or 375 if severely depressed E: 75–100	Common: Agitation, insomnia, initial weight loss, loss of appetite, GI distress, increased sweating, dry mouth, sedation, dizziness, unusual dreams, sexual dysfunction, tachycardia, tremor, extrapyramidal symptoms	Avoid abrupt withdrawal Caution with elderly clients

			Serious: Increased depression or suicidality, mania, seizures, cardiac complications, serotonin syndrome, neuroleptic malignant syndrome	Severe depression during withdrawal
Focalin Dexmethylphenidate Stimulant	ADHD		C: (> 6) 5–20 A: 5–20 Ad: 5–20 E: —	Common: Insomnia, reduced appetite, weight loss, headache, agitation, dizziness Serious: Abuse or dependence, exacerbation of anxiety, tics, agitated depression, psychosis, mania, aggressive behavior seizures, cardiac complications, neuroleptic malignant syndrome	

(continued)

TABLE 13.1 (*Continued*)
Commonly Prescribed Pharmacotherapies for Child (C),
Adolescent (A), Adult (Ad), and Elderly (E) Clients

Trade name Generic name Drug class	Disorders or symptoms treated	Common daily maintenance dose levels (mg/day, unless noted)	Side effects	Withdrawal warnings and cautions
Haldol Haloperidol Antipsychotic (high potency)	Psychosis/schizophrenia, Tourette's disorder, autistic disorder or atypical PDD, severe behavioral disorder, mania in elderly (combined with mood stabilizers)	C: 0.05–0.15 mg/kg A: 1–15 Ad: 1–15 E: 0.25–3	Common: Drowsiness, insomnia, hypotension, agitation, blurred vision, dry mouth or eyes, constipation, weight changes, extrapyramidal symptoms (severe) Serious: Seizures, cardiac complications, tardive dyskinesia, neuroleptic malignant syndrome	Avoid abrupt withdrawal Caution with elderly clients

| Inderal
Propranolol
Other antianxiety
(Beta blocker) | GAD (somatic symptoms of anxiety), posttraumatic stress disorder (PTSD) symptoms, severe behavior disorders | C: 2–4 mg/kg
A: 2–4 mg/kg
Ad: 20–160
E: Lower than adult dose | Common: Dizziness, hypotension, fatigue, depression, insomnia, vivid dreams and nightmares, GI distress, confusion, impotence
Serious: Arrhythmias; bradycardia (severe); dermatological reactions, including Stevens–Johnson syndrome | Avoid abrupt withdrawal |

(continued)

TABLE 13.1 (*Continued*)
Commonly Prescribed Pharmacotherapies for Child (C),
Adolescent (A), Adult (Ad), and Elderly (E) Clients

Trade name Generic name Drug class	Disorders or symptoms treated	Common daily maintenance dose levels (mg/day, unless noted)	Side effects	Withdrawal warnings and cautions
Klonopin Clonazepam Benzodiazepine	Panic disorder, anxiety symptoms, primary insomnia	C: 1–2 A: 1–2 Ad: 1–4 E: —	Common: Sedation, dizziness, GI distress, dry mouth, headache, sleep disruption, confusion, hypotension, slurred speech, impaired memory, paradoxical activation reactions (e.g., acute agitation, aggression) Serious: Abuse or dependence, increased depression or suicidality, seizure exacerbation, respiratory depression	Avoid abrupt withdrawal, should be very gradual Caution with alcohol use, caution with elderly clients

| Lamictal
Lamotrigine
Anticonvulsant | Bipolar disorder
maintenance | C: —
A: —
Ad: 75–200
E: 12.5–50 | Common: Sedation, dizziness, dry mouth, insomnia, headache, incoordination, tremor, agitation, GI distress, weight loss, dysmenorrhea
Serious: Increased depression or suicidality; seizures (withdrawal); serious dermatologic reaction, including Stevens–Johnson syndrome | Avoid abrupt withdrawal |

(continued)

TABLE 13.1 (*Continued*)
Commonly Prescribed Pharmacotherapies for Child (C),
Adolescent (A), Adult (Ad), and Elderly (E) Clients

Trade name Generic name Drug class	Disorders or symptoms treated	Common daily maintenance dose levels (mg/day, unless noted)	Side effects	Withdrawal warnings and cautions
Lexapro Escitalopram SSRI	Depression, panic disorder, social phobia, GAD, PDD symptoms, bulimia nervosa	C: — A: 10–20 Ad: 10–20 E: 10	Common: Agitation, dizziness, dry mouth, GI distress, decreased appetite, insomnia, drowsiness, sweating, sexual dysfunction, extrapyramidal symptoms Serious: Increased depression or suicidality, mania, seizures, serotonin syndrome, neuroleptic malignant syndrome	Avoid abrupt withdrawal Caution with alcohol use

| Lithobid
Lithium carbonate
Mood stabilizer | Bipolar disorder or mania, schizoaffective disorder, severe behavioral disorder, PDD symptoms | C: (2–11) 15–60 mg/kg
A: 15–60 mg/kg
Ad: 1,800–2,400 (acute mania) or 900–1,200 maintenance
E: Lower dose than adult dose | Common: Sedation, dry mouth, blurred vision, loss of appetite, GI distress, tremor, muscle weakness
Serious: Coma, seizures, lithium toxicity | Caution with child and elderly clients |
| Lunesta
Eszopiclone
Atypical antianxiety | Insomnia | C: —
A: —
Ad: 2–3
E: 1–2 | Common: Sedation, headache, dry mouth, dizziness, confusion, GI distress, agitation, changes in libido, dysmenorrhea
Serious: Increased depression or suicidality; aggressive behavior, hallucinations | Avoid abrupt withdrawal
Caution with alcohol or drug abuse or dependence history
Caution with elderly clients |

(continued)

TABLE 13.1 (*Continued*)
Commonly Prescribed Pharmacotherapies for Child (C),
Adolescent (A), Adult (Ad), and Elderly (E) Clients

Trade name Generic name Drug class	Disorders or symptoms treated	Common daily maintenance dose levels (mg/day, unless noted)	Side effects	Withdrawal warnings and cautions
Luvox CR Fluvoxamine SSRI	OCD, social anxiety disorder, panic disorder, GAD, childhood separation anxiety disorder, PDD symptoms, bulimia nervosa, agitation in elderly clients with dementia	C: (> 8) 25–200 A: 100–300 Ad: 100–300 E: 25–150	Common: Drowsiness, dizziness, headache, insomnia, dry mouth, agitation, tremor, GI distress, loss of appetite, sweating, sexual dysfunction, unusual dreams Serious: Increased depression or suicidality, mania, seizures, serotonin syndrome, neuroleptic malignant syndrome	Avoid abrupt withdrawal Caution with elderly clients

| Metadate, Metadate ER, Metadate CD Methylphenidate Stimulant | ADHD | C: (> 6) 20–60
A: 20–60
Ad: 20–60
E: — | Common: Initial insomnia, agitation, dizziness, reduced appetite, GI distress, headache, tachycardia, palpitations, drowsiness, mild dysphoria
Serious: Abuse or dependence, psychosis, mania, aggressive behavior, exacerbation of anxiety, tics, agitated depression, seizures, cardiac complications, neuroleptic malignant syndrome | |

(continued)

TABLE 13.1 (*Continued*)
Commonly Prescribed Pharmacotherapies for Child (C),
Adolescent (A), Adult (Ad), and Elderly (E) Clients

Trade name Generic name Drug class	Disorders or symptoms treated	Common daily maintenance dose levels (mg/day, unless noted)	Side effects	Withdrawal warnings and cautions
Methylin, Methylin ER Methylphenidate Stimulant	ADHD	C: (> 6) 10–60 A: 10–60 Ad: 10–45 E: —	Common: Initial insomnia, reduced appetite, stomach-ache, headache, lethargy, mild dysphoria Serious: Abuse or dependence, psychosis, mania, aggressive behavior, exacerbation of anxiety, tics, agitated depression, seizures, cardiac complications, neuroleptic malignant syndrome	

| Orap
Pimozide
Antipsychotic (high potency) | Tourette's disorder (treatment resistant), psychosis | C: (> 12) 1–10
A: 1–10
Ad: 2–10
E: 0.25–4 | Common: Sedation, extrapyramidal symptoms, orthostatic hypotension, dizziness, blurred vision, palpitations, dry mouth, constipation, amenorrhea, impotence
Serious: Parkinsonism, seizures, cardiac complications, tardive dyskinesia, neuroleptic malignant syndrome | Caution with elderly clients |

(continued)

TABLE 13.1 (*Continued*)
Commonly Prescribed Pharmacotherapies for Child (C), Adolescent (A), Adult (Ad), and Elderly (E) Clients

Trade name Generic name Drug class	Disorders or symptoms treated	Common daily maintenance dose levels (mg/day, unless noted)	Side effects	Withdrawal warnings and cautions
Paxil Paroxetine SSRI	Depression, premenstrual dysphoric disorder, OCD, panic disorder, social phobia, GAD, PTSD, PDD symptoms, bulimia nervosa, agitation in elderly clients with dementia	C: (> 7) 10–30 A: 20–60 Ad: 20–60 E: 5–40	Common: Sedation, agitation, tremor, insomnia, GI problems, sweating, decreased appetite, dry mouth, headache, dizziness, drowsiness, sexual dysfunction. Serious: Increased depression or suicidality, mania, seizures, serotonin syndrome, neuroleptic malignant syndrome	Avoid abrupt withdrawal Caution with alcohol use Caution with elderly clients

Prolixin Fluphenazine Antipsychotic (high potency)	Psychosis/schizophrenia, PDD, tic disorders, mania in elderly (combined with mood stabilizers)	C: 1.5–10 A: 1.5–10 Ad: 2.5–40 E: 0.25–3	Common: Extrapyramidal symptoms, sedation, orthostatic hypotension, blurred vision, GI distress, loss of appetite, headache, depression, weight gain, tachycardia, impotence, menstrual irregularities Serious: Seizures, cardiac complications, tardive dyskinesia, neuroleptic malignant syndrome	Caution regarding interaction with other central nervous system (CNS) depressant substances (e.g., alcohol, sedatives, antihistamines) Caution with elderly clients
ProSom Estazolam Other antianxiety	Insomnia	C: — A: — Ad: 1–2 E: 0.5–2	Common: Sedation, dizziness, confusion, pain, unusual thinking Serious: Suicidality, hallucinations, abuse or dependence, respiratory depression	Avoid abrupt withdrawal Caution with alcohol use Caution with elderly clients

(continued)

TABLE 13.1 (*Continued*)
Commonly Prescribed Pharmacotherapies for Child (C),
Adolescent (A), Adult (Ad), and Elderly (E) Clients

Trade name Generic name Drug class	Disorders or symptoms treated	Common daily maintenance dose levels (mg/day, unless noted)	Side effects	Withdrawal warnings and cautions
Prozac Fluoxetine SSRI	Depression, pre-menstrual dys-phoric disorder, OCD, bulimia nervosa, panic disorder, social phobia, GAD, ADHD, separation anxiety disorder	C: 5–40 A: 10–60 Ad: 20–80 E: 10–60	Common: Agitation, tremor, headache, dry mouth, GI dis-tress, loss of appe-tite, weight loss, insomnia, dizziness, excessive sweating, sexual dysfunction Serious: Increased depression or sui-cidality, mania, seizures, serotonin syndrome, neuro-leptic malignant syndrome	Avoid abrupt withdrawal Caution with alcohol use Caution with elderly clients

| Remeron
Mirtrazapine
Other antidepressant | Depression | C: 15–30
A: 15–45
Ad: 15–45
E: Lower dose than adult | Common: Sedation, orthostatic hypotension, dizziness, dry mouth, constipation, sexual dysfunction, increased appetite, weight gain, unusual dreams, unusual thinking, tremor, confusion
Serious: Increased depression or suicidality, hypomania or mania, seizures | Caution with elderly clients |

(continued)

TABLE 13.1 (*Continued*)
Commonly Prescribed Pharmacotherapies for Child (C), Adolescent (A), Adult (Ad), and Elderly (E) Clients

Trade name Generic name Drug class	Disorders or symptoms treated	Common daily maintenance dose levels (mg/day, unless noted)	Side effects	Withdrawal warnings and cautions
Restoril Temazepam Benzodiazepine	Primary insomnia	C: — A: — Ad: 7.5–30 E: Lower than adult dose	Common: Sedation, fatigue, headache, agitation, dizziness, GI distress, dry mouth, depression, confusion, blurred vision, nightmares, paradoxical activation reactions (e.g., acute excitation, aggression) Serious: Respiratory depression, seizures	Avoid abrupt withdrawal Caution with alcohol use or substance abuse or dependence history

Risperdal Risperidone Atypical antipsychotic	Psychosis/schizophrenia, bipolar I, PDD, severe behavior disorders, mania in elderly (combined with mood stabilizers), agitation in clients with dementia	C: 0.5–4 A: 1–6 Ad: 1–6 E: 0.25–3	Common: Sedation, increased appetite, weight gain, extrapyramidal symptoms, tremor, orthostatic hypotension, dizziness, agitation, tachycardia, insomnia, dry mouth, GI distress, visual disturbances, confusion Serious: Suicidality, seizures, tardive dyskinesia, neuroleptic malignant syndrome	Caution with elderly clients

(continued)

TABLE 13.1 (*Continued*)
Commonly Prescribed Pharmacotherapies for Child (C), Adolescent (A), Adult (Ad), and Elderly (E) Clients

Trade name Generic name Drug class	Disorders or symptoms treated	Common daily maintenance dose levels (mg/day, unless noted)	Side effects	Withdrawal warnings and cautions
Ritalin, Ritalin SR, Ritalin LA Methylphenidate Stimulant	ADHD, severe behavior disorder, apathy and withdrawal in non-depressed elderly clients	C: (> 6) 0.3–2 mg/kg A: 0.3–2 mg/kg Ad: 10–45 E: 2.5–20	Common: Initial insomnia, reduced appetite, agitation, stomachache, GI distress, headache, palpitations, dizziness, drowsiness, mild dysphoria Serious: Exacerbation of anxiety, tics, agitated depression, mania, aggressive behavior, psychosis, abuse or dependency, cardiac complications, seizures, neuroleptic malignant syndrome	Possible severe depression during withdrawal Caution with alcohol or drug abuse or dependence history

| Seroquel
Quetiapine
Atypical
antipsychotic | Psychosis/schizophrenia, bipolar disorder, PDD, mania in elderly (combined with mood stabilizers), agitation in clients with dementia | C: 100–550
A: 400–800
Ad: 150–800
E: 25–100 | Common: Sedation, orthostatic hypotension, appetite increase, weight gain, GI upset, dizziness, headache, dry mouth, insomnia, irritability, tremor, menstrual irregularities
Serious: Increased depression or suicidality, seizures, tardive dyskinesia, neuroleptic malignant syndrome | Caution with elderly clients |

(continued)

TABLE 13.1 (*Continued*)
Commonly Prescribed Pharmacotherapies for Child (C), Adolescent (A), Adult (Ad), and Elderly (E) Clients

Trade name Generic name Drug class	Disorders or symptoms treated	Common daily maintenance dose levels (mg/day, unless noted)	Side effects	Withdrawal warnings and cautions
Serzone Nefazodone Atypical antidepressant	Depression, mood disorder with comorbid ADHD	C: — A: — Ad: 300–600 E: 50–200	Common: Dry mouth, orthostatic hypotension, headache, GI distress, drowsiness, dizziness, blurred or abnormal vision, insomnia, confusion, increased appetite, impaired memory, tremor, unusual dreams	Caution with elderly clients

				Serious: Increased depression or suicidality, hypomania or mania, seizures, cardiac complications, hepatic toxicity or failure	
Sonata Zaleplon Other antianxiety	Insomnia		C: — A: — Ad: 5–20 E: 5–10	Common: Sedation, dizziness, amnesia, headaches, GI distress, dysmenorrhea, tremor Serious: Increased depression or suicidality, hallucinations, aggressive behavior	Avoid abrupt withdrawal Caution with alcohol or drug abuse or dependence history or current use of other (CNS) depressants

(continued)

TABLE 13.1 (*Continued*)
Commonly Prescribed Pharmacotherapies for Child (C),
Adolescent (A), Adult (Ad), and Elderly (E) Clients

Trade name Generic name Drug class	Disorders or symptoms treated	Common daily maintenance dose levels (mg/day, unless noted)	Side effects	Withdrawal warnings and cautions
Strattera Atomoxetine Other antidepressant	ADHD	C: (> 6, < 70 kg) 1.2–1.4 mg/kg A: (> 6, > 70 kg) 80–100 Ad: 80–100 E: —	Common: Sedation, orthostatic hypotension, dry mouth, dizziness, sweating, palpitations, GI distress, insomnia, unusual dreams, decreased appetite, sexual dysfunctions, dysmenorrhea Serious: Increased depression or suicidality, psychosis, mania, aggressive behavior, seizure, cardiac complications, hepatoxicity	

Tegretol Carbamazepine Anticonvulsant	Mania or bipolar disorder, agitation in elderly clients with dementia	C: 10–20 mg/kg A: 800–1200 Ad: 800–1,600 E: 300–600 (100–600 for agitation)	Common: Sedation, GI distress, dizziness, blurred vision, incoordination, rash, confusion, weakness, fatigue Serious: Suicidality; seizure exacerbation; cardiac complications; serious dermatologic reactions, including Stevens–Johnson syndrome; possible neurotoxicity with lithium	Avoid abrupt withdrawal Caution with elderly clients
Tenormin Atenolol Other antianxiety (Beta blocker)	Anxiety (somatic symptoms)	C: — A: — Ad: 25–100 E: —	Common: Drowsiness, dizziness, hypotension, fatigue, GI distress, depression Serious: Severe bradycardia or arrhythmias	Avoid abrupt withdrawal Caution with elderly clients

(continued)

TABLE 13.1 (*Continued*)
Commonly Prescribed Pharmacotherapies for Child (C),
Adolescent (A), Adult (Ad), and Elderly (E) Clients

Trade name Generic name Drug class	Disorders or symptoms treated	Common daily maintenance dose levels (mg/day, unless noted)	Side effects	Withdrawal warnings and cautions
Valium Diazepam Benzodiazepine	Anxiety symptoms, enuresis, primary insomnia, sleep terror disorder, sleepwalking disorder, alcohol withdrawal	C: 0.12–0.80 mg/kg A: 4–40 Ad: 4–40 E: 2–20	Common: Sedation, fatigue, weakness, headache, confusion, tremor, dry mouth, slurred speech, GI distress, dizziness, libido changes, paradoxical activation reactions (e.g., acute excitation, aggression) Serious: Depression, psychosis/ hallucinations, abuse or dependence, seizure exacerbation, respiratory depression, cardiac complications	Avoid abrupt withdrawal Caution with alcohol use Caution with elderly clients

	Anxiety, insomnia	C: (< 6) 2 mg/kg; (6–12) 12.5–100 A: 50–400 Ad: 50–400 E: 25–100	Common: Sedation, dry mouth, dizziness, weakness, slurred speech, headache, agitation, GI distress Serious: Seizures	Caution with elderly clients
Vistaril Hydroxyzine Antihistamine				
Wellbutrin, Wellbutrin SR Bupropion Other antidepressant	Depression, ADHD, Tourette's disorder	C: — A: 150–300 Ad: 150–300 E: 75–225	Common: Agitation, tremor, insomnia, dry mouth, headache, GI distress, dizziness, sweating, unusual dreams, decreased appetite, weight loss, palpitations, blurred vision Serious: Increased depression or suicidality, psychosis/hallucinations, paranoia, mania, agitation and other behavioral disturbances, seizures, cardiac complications	Contraindicated with alcohol use Caution with elderly clients

(continued)

TABLE 13.1 (*Continued*)
Commonly Prescribed Pharmacotherapies for Child (C),
Adolescent (A), Adult (Ad), and Elderly (E) Clients

Trade name Generic name Drug class	Disorders or symptoms treated	Common daily maintenance dose levels (mg/day, unless noted)	Side effects	Withdrawal warnings and cautions
Xanax Alprazolam Benzodiazepine	Anxiety, panic disorder, primary insomnia, alcohol withdrawal	C: — A: — Ad: 0.75–1.5 (anxiety), 1.5–9 (panic) E: 0.25–2	Common: Sedation, dry mouth, blurred vision, lightheadedness, incoordination, fatigue, insomnia, confusion, GI distress, libido changes, paradoxical activation reactions (e.g., acute excitation, aggression) Serious: Suicidal ideation, abuse or dependence, hypomania or mania, seizures, respiratory depression	Avoid abrupt withdrawal Caution with alcohol use Caution with elderly clients

Zoloft Sertraline SSRI	Depression, pre-menstrual dysphoric disorder, OCD, panic disorder, PTSD, social phobia, GAD, PDD symptoms, bulimia nervosa, agitation in elderly clients with dementia	C: (> 6) 25–200 A: 50–200 Ad: 50–200 E: 12.5–150	Common: Sedation, dry mouth, headache, agitation, tremor, sweating, insomnia, GI distress, decreased appetite, sexual dysfunction (ejaculatory delay, decreased libido), dizziness Serious: Increased depression or suicidality, mania, seizures, serotonin syndrome, neuroleptic malignant syndrome	Avoid abrupt withdrawal Caution with alcohol use

(continued)

TABLE 13.1 (*Continued*)
Commonly Prescribed Pharmacotherapies for Child (C),
Adolescent (A), Adult (Ad), and Elderly (E) Clients

Trade name Generic name Drug class	Disorders or symptoms treated	Common daily maintenance dose levels (mg/day, unless noted)	Side effects	Withdrawal warnings and cautions
Zyprexa Olanzapine Atypical antipsychotic	Psychosis/schizophrenia, bipolar disorder, PDD, mania in elderly (combined with mood stabilizers), agitation in clients with dementia	C: — A: 10–20 Ad: 5–20 E: 2.5–10	Common: Weight gain, increased appetite, sedation, extrapyramidal symptoms, dry mouth, headache, insomnia, orthostatic hypotension, dizziness, agitation, GI distress, tremor, speech disturbance, tachycardia Serious: Seizures, tardive dyskinesia, neuroleptic malignant syndrome	Caution with elderly clients

TABLE 13.2
Common Over-the-Counter Psychopharmacotherapies for Adults

Product	Disorders and symptoms treated	Research evidence of efficacy	Common daily dose levels (mg/day, unless noted)	Side effects	Withdrawal warnings and cautions
5-HTP (5-hydroxytrypto-phan)	Depression (adjunct for treatment-resistant depression), anxiety, alcohol withdrawal, fibromyalgia	—	150–300	Common: Drowsiness, dizziness, headache, loss of appetite, insomnia, gastrointestinal (GI) distress, palpitations Serious: Hypomania	
Folic acid (vitamin B9)	Mood disorders	—	0.4	Common: GI distress, decreased appetite, sleep problems, irritability, excitation, rash	

(continued)

TABLE 13.2 (*Continued*)
Common Over-the-Counter Psychopharmacotherapies for Adults

Product	Disorders and symptoms treated	Research evidence of efficacy	Common daily dose levels (mg/day, unless noted)	Side effects	Withdrawal warnings and cautions
Ginkgo biloba	Cognitive impairment Depression, seasonal affective disorder	Yes Inconclusive	120–240 (leaf extract)	Common: Dizziness, headache, GI distress, hypotension, palpitations, agitation, weakness Serious: Bleeding disorders, seizures	Avoid co-use with melatonin
Kava (*Piper methysticum*)	Anxiety Insomnia	Yes, but associated with toxicity Inconclusive	50–400 (70% standardized extract)	Common: GI distress, dizziness, sedation, headache, allergic skin reactions, weight loss Serious: Depression, enhanced effects of sedative substances (e.g., alcohol, benzodiazepines)	

L-tryptophan	Depression (as an adjunct to prescribed medication), sleep disorder	Inconclusive	3–6 g	Common: Drowsiness, headache, GI distress, dizziness Serious: Serotonin syndrome	
Melatonin	Jet lag Other sleep disturbances, chronic fatigue syndrome	Yes Inconclusive	0.5	Common: Sedation, GI distress, confusion, circadian rhythm disruption, dizziness, headache, hypotension, irritability. tachycardia Serious: Transient depression, paranoia, hallucinations, seizures	Avoid co-use with *Gingko biloba*
Omega-3 fatty acids (fish oils)	Depression, mood instability (as an adjunct to prescribed medication)	Inconclusive	1–9 g	Common: GI distress, hypotension, weight gain, rash Serious: Hypomania in clients with bipolar disorder	

(continued)

TABLE 13.2 *(Continued)*
Common Over-the-Counter Psychopharmacotherapies for Adults

Product	Disorders and symptoms treated	Research evidence of efficacy	Common daily dose levels (mg/day, unless noted)	Side effects	Withdrawal warnings and cautions
St John's wort (*Hypericum perforatum*)	Depression Attention-deficit/hyper-activity disor-der (ADHD), anxiety, obsessive–compulsive disorder, social pho-bia, pain	Yes Inconclusive	900–1,800 (with 300 mg hypericin 0.3% stan-dardized extract)	Common: Agitation, insomnia, unusual dreams, GI dis-tress, loss of appe-tite, dizziness, dry mouth, headache, fatigue, weakness, tachycardia	Avoid abrupt withdrawal Avoid co-use with mono-amine oxi-dase inhibi-tors (MAOIs), selective serotonin reuptake inhibitors (SSRIs), tri-cyclics, Zyprexa

	Avoid with Alzheimer's, bipolar disorder, psychosis/schizophrenia, suicidal ideation		Serious: Hypomania or mania; serotoninlike syndrome; negative interactions with several other psychotropic medications, including MAOIs, SSRIs, tricyclics, Zyprexa	
SAM-e (S-adenosylmethionine)	Depression, ADHD, fibromyalgia. Avoid with bipolar disorder. Caution with anxiety disorders	Inconclusive	400–1,600 (oral)	Common: Agitation, GI distress, dizziness, fatigue, headache, palpitations, irritability, tachycardia, sleep problems. Serious: Hypomania or mania	Avoid co-use with MAOIs

References

Green, W. H. (2001). *Child & adolescent clinical psychopharmacology* (3rd ed.). Philadelphia, PA: Lippincott Williams & Wilkins.

Kupfer, D. J., Horner, M. S., Brent, D. A., Lewis, D. A., Reynolds, C. F., Thase, M. E., & Travis, M. J. (Eds.). (2008). *Oxford American handbook of psychiatry.* Oxford, England: Oxford University Press.

Petersen, D. D. (2008). *Psych notes: Clinical pocket guide* (2nd ed.). Philadelphia, PA: F. A. Davis.

Preston, J., O'Neal, J. H., & Talaga, M. C. (2006). *Child and adolescent clinical psychopharmacology made simple.* Oakland, CA: New Harbinger.

Preston, J., O'Neal, J. H., & Talaga, M. C. (2010). *Handbook of clinical psychopharmacology for therapists* (6th ed.). Oakland, CA: New Harbinger.

Salzman, C. (2001). *Psychiatric medications for older adults: The concise guide.* New York, NY: Guilford Press.

Thomson Healthcare. (2007a). *PDR drug guide for mental health professionals* (3rd ed.). Montvale, NJ: Author.

Thomson Healthcare. (2007b). *PDR for nonprescription drugs, dietary supplements, and herbs, 2008.* Montvale, NJ: Author.

Thomson PDR. (2010). *The PDR pocket guide to prescription drugs* (9th ed.). New York, NY: Pocket Books.

CHAPTER 14

Termination

Although it may seem counterintuitive, termination of a professional relationship with a client is actually a process that begins with the first session and unfolds until the clinician and the client no longer meet. Some have suggested that the clinician's preparation for guiding the process of termination should take place before the first session with any client (e.g., Vasquez, Bingham, & Barnett, 2008). The ending of a professional relationship is typically the result of a mutual agreement between the clinician and the client. At times, however, the relationship may end as a result of a unilateral decision imposed on the other by the therapist or by the client. Regardless of the reasons, the clinician holds an ethical and clinical responsibility to ensure that the process promotes the welfare of clients and protects them from harm as much as reasonably possible.

Ideally, the outcome of the termination process is positive. The practitioner and client have the opportunity to review progress toward goals established at the outset, make plans for maintaining and enhancing that progress, and process emotional reactions to the ending of the relationship. Unfortunately, some terminations result in negative outcomes—some so negative that any benefit of the work accomplished before the final session is overshadowed.

This chapter includes a brief outline of some recommendations designed to promote positive termination outcomes and sustain the highest clinical and ethical standards of practice. The recommendations listed in the section that follows are based on the work of Davis (2008); Joyce, Piper, Ogrodniczuk, and Klein (2007); O'Donohue and Cucciare (2008); Vasquez et al. (2008); and Zuckerman (2008). Although the concept of termination can apply to any type of professional relationship, including psychological assessment and/or testing, brief consultations, and different levels of therapy intervention (e.g., individual, couples, family, group), the focus here is on termination of individual psychotherapy. See the references at the end of this chapter for more in-depth discussions of terminations with couples, families, and groups as well as special issues to consider in the process of termination with patients with specific disorders.

Recommendations for the Promotion of Positive Termination Outcomes

> ➤ Become familiar with your professional ethics codes (see Chapter 16, this resource) and state practice regulations regarding the standards for termination of psychotherapy.
> ➤ Review the professional literature (including other ethics codes) regarding the demands of the termination process, issues and effects of client abandonment, warning signs of client premature termination, and guidelines for therapist-initiated termination.
> ➤ Develop a professional will that outlines procedures to contact and triage clients to be followed by a designee in the event of your unexpected disability or death (see Chapter 17, this resource).
> ➤ Provide a complete description of your termination policies and procedures as part of the initial informed consent process with clients. Include a discussion of mutual and unilateral reasons for termination as well as a plan for the client should you or the therapy become unexpectedly unavailable (e.g., through the therapist's illness, injury, or death; through changes in the client's insurance coverage).
> ➤ Establish (and document) goals for therapy in collaboration with the client. This early discussion and mutual understanding of the client's problems and the plans for remediating them can prevent later disagreements and a sudden departure by the client. As clearly as possible, specify the

criteria for the accomplishment of those goals and for the ending of therapy. Adjust the goals and criteria as necessary during the treatment.

➤ Encourage clients to ask questions and voice any negative reactions to the therapy relationship.

➤ Initiate periodic discussions of the client's progress toward the goals.

➤ As the client reaches goals set for therapy or as either the client or therapist decides that the therapy must end, discuss and decide on the timeline and topics for discussion collaboratively with the client. Set a date for the final session.

➤ Assist the client in developing plans for promoting his or her psychological health after termination.

➤ If a client initiates the end of the therapy relationship unilaterally and prematurely (e.g., by leaving a session suddenly, in a phone message, by not showing up for an appointment and not making or keeping another appointment), the following actions are appropriate:

- Contact the client by telephone to encourage the client to return to discuss the decision in person. If the client agrees, the termination process may proceed as discussed previously.

- If you make contact on the telephone, but the client refuses to come in for another appointment, discuss the client's decision briefly, outline any concerns that you may have, and offer referrals as appropriate.

- If the client cannot be reached by telephone, send the client a letter suggesting a meeting in person to discuss the decision, expressing your concerns, and offering to assist with appropriate referrals.

➤ If you think that you may need to initiate termination unilaterally either because of personal circumstances, signs that the client is not benefiting (or even being harmed) by continued contact, or actual threats to your safety from the client, the following actions are appropriate:

- Consult with knowledgeable and experienced colleagues regarding your concerns; make a decision; and develop a plan for terminating therapy and, if necessary, for safeguarding your own welfare.

- Think through the client's previous experiences with loss, available support and coping resources, and emotional expressiveness so that you can anticipate the client's possible reactions.
- Assess the client's need for continued therapy.
- Tell the client (in person if possible and reasonable) your decision to terminate and the reasons.
- Allow the client to respond to your decision.
- Outline the plan for the termination process. Set a date for the final session. If the client is not threatening or endangering you, allow ample time for the termination process and involve the client with the determination of the date.
- Discuss with the client the progress made toward goals for therapy and your assessment of the need for continuing treatment.
- If you think that continuing treatment is indicated, provide the client with referrals to other mental health practitioners. To the degree possible, help facilitate the transfer.
- Discuss with the client where your records will be maintained and provide contact information should the client decide to have records or summaries available to subsequent therapists.

➢ Document discussions and actions regarding termination as they unfold.
➢ Maintain your awareness of current ethical, legal, and clinical standards regarding termination by attending continuing education workshops, reading current literature, and consulting with colleagues on the topic.

References

Davis, D. (2008). *Terminating therapy: A professional guide to ending on a positive note*. Hoboken, NJ: Wiley.

Joyce, A. S., Piper, W. E., Ogrodniczuk, J. S., & Klein, R. H. (2007). *Termination in psychotherapy: A psychodynamic model of processes and outcomes*. Washington, DC: American Psychological Association. doi:10.1037/11545-000

O'Donohue, W. T., & Cucciare, M. A. (Eds.). (2008). *Terminating psychotherapy: A clinician's guide.* New York, NY: Routledge; Taylor & Francis.

Vasquez, M. J. T., Bingham, R. P., & Barnett, J. E. (2008). Psychotherapy termination: Clinical and ethical responsibilities. *Journal of Clinical Psychology, 64,* 653–665. doi:10.1002/jclp.20478

Zuckerman, E. L. (2008). *The paper office* (4th ed.). New York, NY: Guilford Press.

CHAPTER 15

Records and Record Keeping

Psychologists and other mental health practitioners have the duty to appropriately create, maintain, disseminate, and dispose of records regarding their professional work according to clinical, ethical (e.g., ethics codes of national and state professional organizations), and legal standards and regulations (e.g., federal laws such as the Health Insurance Portability and Accountability Act of 1996 [HIPAA], state laws, and state regulations regarding the practice of mental health professions). Accurate and timely documentation is necessary to ensure the continuity of services to clients, communicate with other professionals, meet workplace and/or legal requirements, provide documentation of preservice agreements and contracts, make assessments and diagnoses, develop treatment plans and interventions, and conduct business transactions with the client. In addition, practitioners must safeguard the confidentiality of client records, whether they are written or electronic, unless mandated or permitted by law to disclose information contained in the records. The standards, laws, and regulations that apply to record content, retention, and release by a specific professional vary depending on the nature of the clinician's practice (e.g., whether the practice must be HIPAA compliant, whether the practitioner owes a heightened legal duty for disclosure or privacy given the client's diagnosis [e.g., HIV/AIDS status or substance use problems]), the state in which the professional practices, and the context of the clinician's work (e.g., whether the professional works in a hospital that participates in Medicare or Medicaid for inpatient or outpatient services). In addition to various ethical and legal requirements, some professional organizations have established aspirational guidelines for record keeping (e.g., the American Psychological Association [APA]).

Citations and Internet links for ethical guidelines and standards and federal legal requirements regarding the creation, maintenance, transfer, and disposal of mental health records are listed in the section that follows. Clinicians are reminded that they should be familiar with the specific laws and professional regulations in their own state. In some states, that is no small task because legal standards for records are included in several different statute sections. For example, in California, laws regarding medical and mental health records exist in the Health and Safety Code, the Civil Code, the Welfare and Institutions Code, the Business and Professions Code, and the Code of Regulations, to name a few. State laws vary regarding the areas of record keeping they address and the specificity of the standards. For example, in Florida, the codes regulating psychological services allow the licensing board to adopt rules defining the minimum requirements for client records, including content, which is not specified in other state laws.

This chapter ends with an outline of possible content elements for the clinician to consider when creating a client record. To safeguard the privacy and uphold the dignity of the client, the practitioner should take care to record only what is germane to the client's assessment or treatment within the requirements of the law. Given that many practitioners must now be compliant with HIPAA laws and the very real possibility that health care reform will demand that all records be electronic in the near future, the elements of the record delineated by HIPAA are marked with an asterisk (*). It is important to note two things here. First, although HIPAA standards include "summaries" of certain information (e.g., diagnosis, treatment plan), the term is not defined in the regulation. Second, one of the elements listed by HIPAA is "results of clinical tests." Spokespersons for some professional organizations have expressed their opinions that psychological test data should not be included in the progress notes because of the possibility that such sensitive materials may be released without the client's specific authorization. In addition, some test publishers have extended policy statements that the inclusion of psychological test materials in the progress notes may compromise test security and copyright (Zuckerman, 2006). Other elements listed are derived from those presented by Koocher and Keith-Spiegel (2008), and Zuckerman (2008) as well as those outlined in the APA's "Record Keeping Guidelines" (APA, 2007).

Ethical Standards and Aspirational Guidelines

> American Psychiatric Association (2009), *The Principles of Medical Ethics With Annotations Especially Applicable to Psychiatry:* Section 4, Annotation 1 and Annotation 2; http://www.psych.org/MainMenu/PsychiatricPractice/ Ethics/ResourcesStandards/PrinciplesofMedicalEthics.aspx

> American Psychological Assocation (2010), *Ethical Principles of Psychologists and Code of Conduct (2002, Amended 2010):* Standards 4.01, 6.01, 6.02, and 6.03; http://www.apa.org/ ethics/code/index.aspx

> American Psychological Association (2007), "Record Keeping Guidelines"; http://www.apa.org/practice/guidelines/ record-keeping.pdf

> National Association of Social Workers (2008), *Code of Ethics:* Standards 1.07(b), 1.07 (j), 1.07 (l), 1.07 (n), 1.08 (a–b), 3.04 (a–d), and 3.05; http://www.naswdc.org/pubs/code/ code.asp

> American Association of Marriage and Family Therapists (2001), *Code of Ethics:* Principle II, 2.2, 2.4, 2.5; Principle III, 3.6; and Principle VII, 7.6; http://www.aamft.org/imis15/ content/legal_ethics/code_of_ethics.aspx

Federal Legal Standards

> Health Insurance Portability and Accountability Act of 1996, Pub. L. No. 104-191: HIPAA Privacy and Security Rule, 45 C.F.R. 160-164; http://www.hhs.gov/ocr/hipaa

> Medicare and Medicaid: Medicare Conditions of Participation 42 C.F.R. § 482.24 (b & c); http://www.cms.gov/ CFCsAndCoPs/06_Hospitals.asp

Contents of Mental Health Records

As indicated previously, this list of content elements for a client's mental health record is derived from HIPAA standards, aspirational guidelines from the APA, and recommendations from experienced professionals. The list is not meant to be comprehensive or necessarily reflect the standard of care. Practitioners must determine what elements are consistent with their professional activities, ethical guidelines, and state and applicable federal laws and regulations.

- ➢ Basic identifying information and informed consent
    - Client information (e.g., name, age, date of birth, address, phone contact information), including parent or guardian information, and contact information for emergency situations and for other current treating professionals
        - ○ Formal authorizations signed by client authorizing the clinician to make the contacts noted previously as necessary
    - Referral source
    - Documentation that client (and/or parent or guardian) has received appropriate notices of office practice policies consistent with federal (e.g., HIPAA Notice of Privacy Practices*) and/or state law
    - Documentation that the client (and/or parent or guardian) has received, reviewed, and been allowed to ask questions about the clinician's policies, procedures, and intended services (i.e., the informed assent or consent process has been completed)
- ➢ Initial clinical assessment information (see Chapter 1, this resource)
    - Date and duration of initial assessment*
    - Psychosocial, medical, and psychological history (including current medications and response*)
    - Presenting problems or symptoms*
    - Mental status examination (see Chapter 4, this resource)
    - If indicated, full risk evaluation for nonsuicidal self-injury, suicide, and/or harm to others (see Chapter 7, this resource)

- Results of psychological testing (screening [see Chapter 2, this resource] or full measure [see Chapter 5, this resource])
- Initial diagnosis, including assessment of functional status (e.g., Global Assessment of Functioning scale)*
- Prognosis*
- Plan (for assessment or treatment) with short- and long-term goals, including modalities and frequencies of sessions*

➢ Subsequent sessions documentation
  - Cancellation or no show for subsequent appointed sessions
  - Dates and duration of subsequent sessions*
  - Nature of services (e.g., psychological testing, psychotherapy modalities*)
  - Intended frequency of services*
  - Subsequent risk evaluations or other assessments as necessary
  - Symptoms targeted for assessment or treatment (note any increase or decrease in symptoms noted previously, new symptoms)*
  - Diagnosis, including functional status (e.g., Global Assessment of Functioning scale)*
  - Client's response to current assessment or treatment plan
  - Subsequent assessment or treatment plan (e.g., any modifications such as consideration of a higher level of care)*
  - Prognosis*
  - Referrals made (e.g., for psychopharmacological assessment) with client's follow-up and response

➢ Consultations by clinician with other professionals or collateral persons regarding client, including formal authorization forms signed by client for release of information

➢ Records of other treating professionals requested as appropriate, including notation that the records were reviewed by the clinician

➢ Correspondence sent to or received from client or others regarding the client (e.g., letters, postcards, e-mails and text messages, including formal authorization forms signed by the client for release of information)

> Notes regarding clinically significant or unusual in-office or out-of-office incidents or contacts (e.g., home visit, chance encounter in community, appearance in court, client's request to audiotape session, client's request for a hug)
> Notes of telephone conversations with the client or others regarding the client, including formal authorization forms signed by the client for release of information
> Notes of termination planning and progress
> Discharge or termination summary
  - Date of termination
  - Who initiated termination and rationale
  - Clinician's assessment of progress toward assessment or treatment goals
  - Client's assessment of progress toward assessment or treatment goals
  - Referrals given for further assessment and/or treatment
> Billing information and records
  - Date, type, and length of each service session
  - Fee for session
  - Copies of third-party billing
  - Payments and balances

References

American Association of Marriage and Family Therapists. (2001). *Code of ethics*. Alexandria, VA: Author.

American Psychiatric Association. (2009). *The principles of medical ethics with annotations especially applicable to psychiatry.* Arlington, VA: Author.

American Psychological Association. (2007). Record keeping guidelines. *American Psychologist, 62,* 993–1004. doi:10.1037/0003-066X.62.9.993

American Psychological Association. (2010). *Ethical principles of psychologists and code of conduct (2002, Amended June 1, 2010).* Retrieved from http://www.apa.org/ethics/code/index.aspx

Koocher, G. P., & Keith-Spiegel, P. (2008). *Ethics in psychology and the mental health professions: Standards and cases* (3rd ed.). New York, NY: Oxford University Press.

National Association of Social Workers. (2008). *Code of ethics.* Washington, DC: Author.

Zuckerman, E. L. (2006). *HIPAA help: Health Insurance Portability and Accountability Act of 1996: A compliance manual for psychotherapists.* Armbrust, PA: Three Wishes Press.

Zuckerman, E. L. (2008). *The paper office* (4th ed.). New York, NY: Guilford Press.

CHAPTER 16

Resources for Clinicians I: Professional Standards

Mental health professionals engage in complex work. Over the course of their careers, they encounter a variety of challenging clinical, ethical, and legal issues regarding their clients. To best serve consumers and uphold the integrity of their profession, practitioners today must stay abreast of professional standards. This chapter provides available website access information for the national professional organizations and the state licensing boards and professional organizations that create, promote, and regulate those standards for psychologists, psychiatrists, marriage and family therapists, and social workers. Website citations to the ethics codes for each professional organization also are included. In addition, practice guidelines published by several professional organizations for the provision of psychological services to specific populations (e.g., forensic, girls and women, older adults) are referenced. The chapter concludes with some information to help the practitioner understand and implement federal Health Insurance Portability and Accountability Act of 1996 (HIPAA) laws in mental health practice.

National Professional Organizations

> ➤ American Association of Marriage and Family Therapists (AAMFT); http://www.AAMFT.org
> ➤ American Board of Professional Psychology; http://www.abpp.org/i4a/pages/index.cfm?pageid=3285

- ➢ American Psychiatric Association; http://www.psych.org
- ➢ American Psychological Association (APA); http://www.apa.org
- ➢ Association for Psychological Science; http://www.psychologicalscience.org/about/links.cfm
- ➢ Association of State and Provincial Psychology Boards; http://www.asppb.net
- ➢ National Association of Social Workers (NASW); http://www.naswdc.org

State Marriage and Family Therapy Regulatory Boards and Association of Marriage and Family Therapy (AMFT) Divisions

- ➢ Alabama
  - Alabama Board of Examiners in Marriage and Family Therapy; http://www.mft.state.al.us
  - Alabama AMFT Division; http://www.alamft.org
- ➢ Alaska
  - Alaska Board of Marital and Family Therapy/Division of Occupational Licensing; http://www.dced.state.ak.us/occ/pmft.htm
  - Alaska AMFT Division; http://www.akamft.org
- ➢ Arizona
  - Arizona Board of Behavioral Health Examiners; http://azbbhe.us
  - Arizona AMFT Division; http://www.azamft.org
- ➢ Arkansas
  - Arkansas Board of Examiners in Counseling; http://www.accessarkansas.org/abec
  - Arkansas AMFT Division; http://www.aramft.org
- ➢ California
  - California Board of Behavioral Sciences; http://www.bbs.ca.gov
  - California AMFT Division; http://www.aamftca.org
- ➢ Colorado
  - Colorado Board of Marriage and Family Therapist Examiners, Department of Regulatory Agencies; http://www.dora.state.co.us/mental-health/mft/index.htm
  - Colorado AMFT Division; http://www.coamft.org

- Connecticut
  - Connecticut Department of Public Health Services; http://www.ct.gov/dph/cwp/view.asp?a=3121&q=389370
  - Connecticut AMFT Division; http://www.ctamft.org
- Delaware
  - Delaware Board of Mental Health and Chemical Dependency Professionals; http://dpr.delaware.gov/boards/profcounselors/index.shtml
  - Delaware AMFT Division; http://www.middleatlanticaamft.org
- District of Columbia
  - District of Columbia Department of Health, Board of Marriage and Family Therapy; http://hpla.doh.dc.gov/hpla/cwp/view,A,1195,Q,490654.asp
  - District of Columbia AMFT Division; http://www.middleatlanticaamft.org
- Florida
  - Florida Board of Clinical Social Work, Marriage and Family Therapy and Mental Health Counseling; http://www.doh.state.fl.us/mqa.491
  - Florida AMFT Division; http://www.famft.org
- Georgia
  - Georgia Composite Board of Professional Counselors, Social Workers, and Marriage and Family Therapists; http://www.sos.state.ga.us/plb
  - Georgia AMFT Division; http://www.gamft.org
- Hawaii
  - Hawaii Professional and Vocational Licensing Division, Department of Commerce and Consumer Affairs; http://www.hawaii.gov/dcca/areas/pvl/programs/marriage
  - Hawaii AMFT Division; http://www.hamft.net
- Idaho
  - Idaho Board of Professional Counselor and Marriage and Family Therapists, Bureau of Occupational Licenses; http://www.ibol.idaho.gov/cou.htm
  - Idaho AMFT Division; http://www.idamft.org
- Illinois
  - Illinois Marriage and Family Therapist Licensing and Disciplinary Board, Illinois Department of Professional Regulation; http://www.idfpr.com/dpr/WHO/marfm.asp
  - Illinois AMFT Division; http://www.iamft.org

➢ Indiana
  ▪ Indiana Behavioral Health and Human Services Licensing Board; http://www.in.gov/pla/3031.htm
  ▪ Indiana AMFT Division; http://www.inamft.org
➢ Iowa
  ▪ Iowa Board of Behavioral Science Examiners, Bureau of Professional Licensure; http://www.idph.state.ia.us/licensure
  ▪ Iowa AMFT Division; http://www.iamft.com
➢ Kansas
  ▪ Kansas Behavioral Sciences Regulatory Board; http://www.ksbsrb.org/marriagefamily.htm
  ▪ Kansas AMFT Division; http://www.ksamft.org
➢ Kentucky
  ▪ Kentucky Board of Licensure of Marriage and Family Therapists; http://mft.ky.gov
  ▪ Kentucky AMFT Division; http://www.kamft.org
➢ Louisiana
  ▪ Louisiana Licensed Professional Counselors Board of Examiners; http://www.lpcboard.org
  ▪ Louisiana AMFT Division; http://www.lamft.org
➢ Maine
  ▪ Maine Department of Professional and Financial Regulation, Office of Licensing and Registration; http://maine.gov/pfr/professionallicensing/professions/counselors/marriage_family_therapist.htm
  ▪ Maine AMFT Division; http://www.meamft.org
➢ Maryland
  ▪ Maryland State Board of Examiners of Professional Counselors; http://dhmh.state.md.us/bopc
  ▪ Maryland AMFT Division; http://www.middleatlantic aamft.org
➢ Massachusetts
  ▪ Massachusetts Board of Regulation of Allied Mental Health and Human Services Professionals; http://www.state.ma.us/reg/boards/mh/default.htm
  ▪ Massachusetts AMFT Division; http://www.mamft.org
➢ Michigan
  ▪ Michigan Board of Marriage and Family Therapy; http://www.michigan.gov/mdch/0,1607,7-132-27417---,00.html

- Michigan AMFT Division; http://www.michiganfamily therapy.org
- Minnesota
  - Minnesota Board of Marriage and Family Therapy; http://www.bmft.state.mn.us
  - Minnesota AMFT Division; http://www.minnesota families.org
- Mississippi
  - Mississippi Board of Examiners for Social Workers and Marriage and Family Therapists; http://www.swmft. ms.gov/swmft/web.nsf
  - Mississippi AMFT Division; http://www.mamft.com
- Missouri
  - Missouri State Committee of Marital and Family Therapists; http://pr.mo.gov/marital.asp
  - Missouri AMFT Division; http://www.moamft.org
- Montana
  - Montana Board of Social Work Examiners and Professional Counselors; http://www.discoveringmontana. com/dli/bsd/license/bsd_boards/swp_board/board_ page.asp
- Nebraska
  - Nebraska Department of Health and Human Services; http://www.hhs.state.ne.us/crl/mhcs/mental/ CMFT.htm
  - Nebraska AMFT Division; http://www.nebraskaamft.org
- Nevada
  - Nevada Board of Marriage and Family Therapist Examiners; http://marriage.state.nv.us
  - Nevada AMFT Division; http://www.nevadaamft.org
- New Hampshire
  - New Hampshire Board of Mental Health Practice, Department of Health and Human Service; http://www.state. nh.us/mhpb
  - New Hampshire AMFT Division; http://www.nhamft.org
- New Jersey
  - New Jersey Board of Marriage and Family Therapy Examiners; http://www.state.nj.us/lps/ca/medical/family therapy.htm
  - New Jersey AMFT Division; http://www.aamftnj.org

➢ New Mexico
- New Mexico Counseling and Therapy Practice Board; http://www.rld.state.nm.us/Counseling/index.html
- New Mexico AMFT Division; http://www.nmamft.com

➢ New York
- New York State Board for Mental Health Practitioners; http://www.op.nysed.gov/mhpques-ans.htm
- New York AMFT Division; http://www.nyamft.org

➢ North Carolina
- North Carolina Marriage and Family Therapy Licensure Board; http://www.nclmft.org
- North Carolina AMFT Division; http://www.ncamft.org

➢ North Dakota
- North Dakota Marriage and Family Therapy Licensure Board; http://www.governor.state.nd.us/boards/boards-query.asp?Board_ID=144

➢ Ohio
- Ohio Counselor, Social Worker, and Marriage and Family Therapist Board; http://cswmft.ohio.gov
- Ohio AMFT Division; http://www.ohioamft.org

➢ Oklahoma
- Oklahoma Professional Counselor Licensing Division; http://www.ok.gov/health/Protective_Health/Professional_Counselor_Licensing_Division
- Oklahoma AMFT Division; http://www.okamft.org

➢ Oregon
- Oregon Board of Professional Counselors and Therapists; http://www.oblpct.state.or.us
- Oregon AMFT Division; http://www.oamft.org

➢ Pennsylvania
- Pennsylvania Board of Social Workers, Marriage and Family Therapists, and Professional Counselors; http://www.dos.state.pa.us/bpoa/socwkbd/mainpage.htm
- Pennsylvania AMFT Division; http://www.pamft.com

➢ Rhode Island
- Rhode Island Board of Marriage and Family Therapy; http://www.health.ri.gov/hsr/professions/mf_counsel.php
- Rhode Island AMFT Division; http://www.riamft.com

- South Carolina
  - South Carolina Board of Examiners for Licensure of Professional Counselors, Marital and Family Therapists, and Psycho-Educational Specialists; http://www.llr.state.sc.us/pol.asp
  - South Carolina AMFT Division; http://www.scamft.org
- South Dakota
  - South Dakota Board of Examiners for Counselors and Marriage and Family Therapists; http://dhs.sd.gov/brd/counselor
  - South Dakota AMFT Division; http://www.sdamft.org
- Tennessee
  - Tennessee Board of Professional Counselors and Marital and Family Therapists; http://health.state.tn.us/Boards/PC_MFT&CPT/index.htm
  - Tennessee AMFT Division; http://www.tnamft.org
- Texas
  - Texas State Board of Examiners of Marriage and Family Therapists; http://www.dshs.state.tx.us/mft
  - Texas AMFT Division; http://www.tamft.org
- Utah
  - Utah Division of Occupational and Professional Licensing; http://www.dopl.utah.gov/licensing/marriage_family_therapy.html
  - Utah AMFT Division; http://www.uamft.org
- Vermont
  - Vermont Board of Allied Mental Health Practitioners, Office of Professional Regulation; http://www.vtprofessionals.org/opr1/allied
- Virginia
  - Virginia Board of Counselors; http://www.dhp.state.va.us/counseling
  - Virginia AMFT Division; http://www.vamft.org
- Washington
  - Washington State Department of Health, Health Professions Quality Assurance; http://www.doh.wa.gov/hsqa/Professions/Marriage_Family_Therapist/default.htm
  - Washington AMFT Division; http://www.wamft.org

- ➤ West Virginia
  - West Virginia Board of Examiners in Counseling; http://www.wvbec.org
- ➤ Wisconsin
  - Wisconsin Joint Board of Marriage and Family Therapy, Professional Counseling, and Social Work, Department of Regulations and Licensing; http://drl.wi.gov/profession.asp?profid=24&locid=0
  - Wisconsin AMFT Division; http://www.relationshiphelp.org
- ➤ Wyoming
  - Wyoming Mental Health Professions Licensing Board; http://plboards.state.wy.us/mentalhealth/index.asp
  - Wyoming AMFT Division; http://uwacadweb.uwyo.edu/wmft

State Psychiatry Licensing Boards and Psychiatric Societies and Associations

- ➤ Alabama
  - Alabama State Board of Medical Examiners; http://www.albme.org
  - Alabama Psychiatric Society; http://www.alabamapsych.org
- ➤ Alaska
  - Alaska Division of Occupational Licensing, State Medical Board; http://www.commerce.state.ak.us/occ/pmed.htm
  - Alaska Psychiatric Association; http://www.psychiatryalaska.org
- ➤ Arizona
  - Arizona Medical Board; http://www.azmd.gov
  - Arizona Board of Osteopathic Examiners in Medicine and Surgery; http://www.azdo.gov
  - Arizona Psychiatric Society; http://www.azpsych.us
- ➤ Arkansas
  - Arkansas State Medical Board; http://www.armedicalboard.org
  - Arkansas Psychiatric Society; http://www.arkansaspsychiatricsociety.org

➢ California
  - Medical Board of California; http://www.medbd.ca.gov
  - Osteopathic Medical Board of California; http://www.ombc.ca.gov
  - California Psychiatric Association; http://www.calpsych.org
➢ Colorado
  - Colorado State Board of Medical Examiners; http://www.dora.state.co.us/medical
  - Colorado Psychiatric Society; http://www.coloradopsychiatric.org
➢ Connecticut
  - State of Connecticut, Department of Public Health; http://www.ct.gov/dph/site/default.asp
  - Connecticut Psychiatric Society; http://www.ctpsych.org
➢ Delaware
  - Delaware Board of Medical Practice; http://dpr.delaware.gov
  - Psychiatric Society of Delaware; http://www.medicalsocietyofdelaware.org/SpecialtySocieties/PSD.aspx
➢ District of Columbia
  - District of Columbia Board of Medicine; http://www.dchealth.dc.gov/doh/site/default.asp
  - Washington DC Psychiatric Society; http://www.dcpsych.org
➢ Florida
  - Florida Board of Medicine; http://www.doh.state.fl.us
  - Florida Board of Osteopathic Medicine; http://www.doh.state.fl.us/mqa
  - Florida Psychiatric Society; http://www.floridapsych.org
➢ Georgia
  - Georgia Composite State Board of Medical Examiners; http://medicalboard.georgia.gov/portal/site/GCMB
  - Georgia Psychiatric Physicians Association; http://www.gapsychiatry.org
➢ Hawaii
  - Hawaii Board of Medical Examiners; http://hawaii.gov/dcca/pvl/boards/medical
  - Hawaii Psychiatric Medical Association; http://hawaii.gov/ethics/lobby/orgexp/H/ORG-H0133

- Idaho
  - Idaho State Board of Medicine; http://bom.idaho.gov/BOMPortal/Home.aspx
- Illinois
  - Illinois Department of Professional Regulation; http://www.idfpr.com
  - Illinois Psychiatric Society; http://www.illinoispsychiatricsociety.org
- Indiana
  - Indiana Health Professions Bureau; http://www.in.gov/pla
  - Indiana Psychiatric Society; http://www.indianapsychiatricsociety.org
- Iowa
  - Iowa Board of Medicine; http://medicalboard.iowa.gov
  - Iowa Psychiatric Society; http://www.iowapsych.org
- Kansas
  - Kansas State Board of Healing Arts; http://www.ksbha.org
  - Kansas Psychiatric Society; http://kansas.psych.org/Pages/default.aspx
- Kentucky
  - Kentucky Board of Medical Licensure; http://kbml.ky.gov
  - Kentucky Psychiatric Medical Association; http://www.kypsych.org
- Louisiana
  - Louisiana State Board of Medical Examiners; http://new.dhh.louisiana.gov/index.cfm/directory/detail/520
  - Louisiana Psychiatric Medical Association; http://www.lpma.net
- Maine
  - Maine Board of Licensure in Medicine; http://www.docboard.org/me/me_home.htm
  - State of Maine Board of Osteopathic Licensure; http://www.maine.gov/osteo
  - Maine Association of Psychiatric Physicians; http://www.mainepsych.org

➢ Maryland
  ▪ Maryland Board of Physicians; http://www.mbp.state.md.us
  ▪ Maryland Psychiatric Society; http://www.mdpsych.org
➢ Massachusetts
  ▪ Massachusetts Board of Registration in Medicine; http://www.mass.gov/massmedboard
  ▪ Massachusetts Psychiatric Society; http://www.psychiatry-mps.org
➢ Michigan
  ▪ Michigan Board of Medicine; http://www.michigan.gov/mdch/0,1607,7-132-27417_27529_27541-58914--,00.html
  ▪ Michigan Board of Osteopathic Medicine & Surgery; http://www.michigan.gov/mdch/0,1607,7-132-27417_27529_27547-59176–,00.html
  ▪ Michigan Psychiatric Society; http://www.mpsonline.org
➢ Minnesota
  ▪ Minnesota Board of Medical Practice; http://www.state.mn.us/portal/mn/jsp/home.do?agency=BMP
  ▪ Minnesota Psychiatric Society; http://www.mnpsychsoc.org
➢ Mississippi
  ▪ Mississippi State Board of Medical Licensure; http://www.msbml.state.ms.us
➢ Missouri
  ▪ Missouri State Board of Registration for the Healing Arts; http://www.pr.mo.gov/healingarts.asp
  ▪ Eastern Missouri Psychiatric Society; http://www.emopsych.org
➢ Montana
  ▪ Montana Board of Medical Examiners; http://bsd.dli.mt.gov/license/bsd_boards/med_board/board_page.asp
➢ Nebraska
  ▪ Nebraska Health and Human Services System; http://www.hhs.state.ne.us
➢ Nevada
  ▪ State of Nevada Board of Medical Examiners; http://www.medboard.nv.gov

- Nevada State Board of Osteopathic Medicine; http://license.k3systems.com/LicensingPublic/app?page=main&service=page
- Nevada Psychiatric Association; http://www.nvpsychiatry.org

➤ New Hampshire
- New Hampshire Board of Medicine; http://www.nh.gov/medicine
- New Hampshire Psychiatric Society; http://www.nhpsych.org

➤ New Jersey
- New Jersey State Board of Medical Examiners; http://www.state.nj.us/lps/ca/medical.htm
- New Jersey Psychiatric Association; http://www.psychnj.org

➤ New Mexico
- New Mexico Medical Board; http://www.nmmb.state.nm.us
- New Mexico Board of Osteopathic Medical Examiners; http://www.rld.state.nm.us/Osteopathy/index.html

➤ New York
- New York State Board for Medicine; http://www.op.nysed.gov/prof/med
- New York State Psychiatric Association; http://www.nyspsych.org

➤ North Carolina
- North Carolina Medical Board; http://www.ncmedboard.org
- North Carolina Psychiatric Association; http://www.ncpsychiatry.org

➤ North Dakota
- North Dakota Board of Medical Examiners; http://www.ndbomex.com

➤ Ohio
- State Medical Board of Ohio; http://med.ohio.gov
- Ohio Psychiatric Physicians Association; http://www.ohiopsych.org

➤ Oklahoma
- Oklahoma State Board of Medical Licensure and Supervision; http://www.okmedicalboard.org

- Oklahoma Board of Osteopathic Examiners; http://www.ok.gov/osboe
- Oregon
  - Oregon Board of Medical Examiners; http://www.oregon.gov/OMB
  - Oregon Psychiatric Association; http://www.orpsych.org
- Pennsylvania
  - Pennsylvania State Board of Medicine; http://www.dos.state.pa.us/portal/server.pt/community/state_board_of_medicine/12512
  - Pennsylvania State Board of Osteopathic Medicine; http://www.portal.state.pa.us/portal/server.pt/community/state_board_of_osteopathic_medicine/12517
  - Pennsylvania Psychiatric Society; http://www.papsych.org
- Rhode Island
  - Rhode Island Board of Medical Licensure and Discipline; http://www.health.ri.gov/hsr/bmld
  - Rhode Island Psychiatric Society; http://www.psychri.org
- South Carolina
  - South Carolina Board of Medical Examiners; http://www.llr.state.sc.us/pol/medical
  - South Carolina Psychiatric Society; http://www.scpsych.org
- South Dakota
  - South Dakota State Board of Medical & Osteopathic Examiners; http://www.sdbmoe.gov/?aspxerrorpath=/boards/medicine/Default.aspx
- Tennessee
  - Tennessee Department of Health; http://health.state.tn.us/Boards/ME/index.htm
  - Tennessee State Board of Osteopathic Examiners; http://health.state.tn.us/Boards/Osteo
- Texas
  - Texas State Board of Medical Examiners; http://www.tmb.state.tx.us
  - Texas Society of Psychiatric Physicians; http://www.txpsych.org
- Utah
  - State of Utah Department of Commerce; http://www.dopl.utah.gov

- Utah Psychiatric Association; http://www.utahpsychiatric association.org
- Vermont
  - Vermont Board of Medical Practice; http://health vermont.gov/hc/med_board/bmp.aspx
  - Vermont Board of Osteopathic Physicians and Surgeons; http://vtprofessionals.org/opr1/osteopaths
- Virginia
  - Virginia Board of Medicine; http://www.dhp.virginia.gov
  - Psychiatric Society of Virginia; http://www.psva.org
- Washington
  - Washington State Department of Health Medical Quality Assurance Committee; http://www.doh.wa.gov/hsqa/MQAC/Default.htm
  - Washington Board of Osteopathic Medicine and Surgery; http://www.doh.wa.gov/hsqa/professions/Osteopath/default.htm
  - Washington State Psychiatric Association; http://www.wapsychiatry.org
- West Virginia
  - West Virginia Board of Medicine; http://www.wvbom.wv.gov
  - West Virginia Board of Osteopathy; http://www.wvbdosteo.org
- Wisconsin
  - State of Wisconsin Medical Examining Board; http://drl.wi.gov
  - Wisconsin Psychiatric Association; http://www.wapsychiatry.org
- Wyoming
  - Wyoming Board of Medicine; http://wyomedboard.state.wy.us

State Psychology Licensing Boards and Psychological Associations

- Alabama
  - Alabama Board of Examiners in Psychology; http://psychology.state.al.us

- Alabama Psychological Association; http://www.ala psych.org
➢ Alaska
  - Alaska Board of Psychologist and Psychological Associate Examiners; http://www.dced.state.ak.us/occ/ppsy.htm
  - Alaska Psychological Association; http://www.ak-pa.org
➢ Arizona
  - Arizona Board of Psychologist Examiners; http://www.psychboard.az.gov
  - Arizona Psychological Association; http://www.azpa.org
➢ Arkansas
  - Arkansas Board of Psychology; http://www.arkansas.gov/abep
  - Arkansas Psychological Association; http://www.arpa psych.org
➢ California
  - California Board of Psychology; http://www.psych board.ca.gov
  - California Psychological Association; http://www.cpa psych.org
➢ Colorado
  - Colorado Board of Psychologist Examiners; http://www.dora.state.co.us/mental-health/psy/index.htm
  - Colorado Psychological Association; http://www.coloradopsych.org/default.aspx
➢ Connecticut
  - Connecticut Board of Examiners of Psychologists; http://www.ct.gov/dph/cwp/view.asp?a=3143&q=388938&dphNav_GID=1830
  - Connecticut Psychological Association; http://www.connpsych.org
➢ Delaware
  - Delaware Board of Examiners of Psychology; http://www.dpr.delaware.gov/boards/psychology/index.shtml
  - Delaware Psychological Association; http://www.depsych.org
➢ District of Columbia
  - District of Columbia Board of Psychology; http://hpla.doh.dc.gov/hpla/cwp/view,A,1195,Q,488253,hplaNav,%7C30661%7C,.asp

- District of Columbia Psychological Association; http://www.dcpsychology.org
- Florida
  - Florida Board of Psychology; http://www.doh.state.fl.us/mqa/psychology
  - Florida Psychological Association; http://www.flapsych.com
- Georgia
  - Georgia State Board of Examiners of Psychologists; http://sos.georgia.gov/plb/psych
  - Georgia Psychological Association; http://www.gapsychology.org
- Hawaii
  - Hawaii Board of Psychology; http://hawaii.gov/dcca/pvl/boards/psychology
  - Hawaii Psychological Association; http://www.hawaiipsychology.org/default.aspx
- Idaho
  - Idaho Board of Psychologist Examiners; https://secure.ibol.idaho.gov/IBOL/BoardPage.aspx?Bureau=PSY
  - Idaho Psychological Association; http://www.idahopsych.org
- Illinois
  - Illinois Clinical Psychologists Licensing and Disciplinary Committee; http://www.idfpr.com/dpr/WHO/psych.asp
  - Illinois Psychological Association; http://www.illinoispsychology.org
- Indiana
  - Indiana State Psychology Board; http://www.in.gov/pla/psych.htm
  - Indiana Psychological Association; http://www.indianapsychology.org
- Iowa
  - Iowa Board of Psychology Examiners; http://www.idph.state.ia.us/licensure/board_home.asp?board=psy
  - Iowa Psychological Association; http://www.iowapsychology.org
- Kansas
  - Kansas Behavioral Sciences Regulatory Board (Psychologists); http://www.ksbsrb.org/psychologists.htm

- Kansas Psychological Association; http://www.ks psych.org
➢ Kentucky
  - Kentucky State Board of Examiners of Psychology; http://psy.ky.gov
  - Kentucky Psychological Association; http://www. kpa.org
➢ Louisiana
  - Louisiana State Board of Examiners of Psychologists; http://www.lsbep.org
  - Louisiana Psychological Association; http://www. louisianapsychologist.org
➢ Maine
  - Maine Board of Examiners of Psychologists; http://www. maine.gov/pfr/professionallicensing/professions/ psychologists/index.htm
  - Maine Psychological Association; http://www.mepa.org
➢ Maryland
  - Maryland Board of Examiners of Psychologists; http:// dhmh.maryland.gov/psych
  - Maryland Psychological Association; http://www. marylandpsychology.org
➢ Massachusetts
  - Massachusetts Board of Registration of Psychologists; http://www.mass.gov/?pageID=ocasubtopic&L=4& L0=Home&L1=Licensee&L2=Division+of+Professional +Licensure+Boards&L3=Board+of+Registration+of+ Psychologists&sid=Eoca
  - Massachusetts Psychological Association; http://www. masspsych.org
➢ Michigan
  - Michigan Board of Psychology; http://www.michigan. gov/mdch/0,1607,7-132-27417_27529_27552---,00.html
  - Michigan Psychological Association; http://www. michiganpsychologicalassociation.org
➢ Minnesota
  - Minnesota Board of Psychology; http://www.psychology board.state.mn.us
  - Minnesota Psychological Association; http://www. mnpsych.org

- ➤ Mississippi
  - Mississippi Board of Psychology; http://www.psychology board.state.ms.us/msbp/web.nsf
  - Mississippi Psychological Association; http://www. mpassoc.org
- ➤ Missouri
  - Missouri State Committee of Psychologists; http://pr. mo.gov/psychologists.asp
  - Missouri Psychological Association; http://www.mo psych.org
- ➤ Montana
  - Montana Board of Psychologists; http://bsd.dli.mt. gov/license/bsd_boards/psy_board/board_page.asp
  - Montana Psychological Association; http://wtp.net/ mpa
- ➤ Nebraska
  - Nebraska Board of Psychologists; http://www.hhs.state. ne.us/crl/mhcs/psych/psychlicense.htm
  - Nebraska Psychological Association; http://www.neb psych.org
- ➤ Nevada
  - State of Nevada Board of Psychological Examiners; http://psyexam.state.nv.us
  - Nevada Psychological Association; http://www.nv psychology.org
- ➤ New Hampshire
  - New Hampshire Board of Mental Health Practice; http://www.nh.gov/mhpb
  - New Hampshire Psychological Association; http:// www.nhpaonline.org
- ➤ New Jersey
  - New Jersey State Board of Psychological Examiners; http://www.njconsumeraffairs.gov/psy
  - New Jersey Psychological Association; http://www. psychologynj.org
- ➤ New Mexico
  - New Mexico Board of Psychological Examiners; http:// www.rld.state.nm.us/Psychology/index.html
  - New Mexico Psychological Association; http://www. nmpa.com

➢ New York
  - New York State Board for Psychology; http://www.op. nysed.gov/prof/psych
  - New York State Psychological Association; http://www. nyspa.org
➢ North Carolina
  - North Carolina Psychology Board; http://www.nc psychologyboard.org
  - North Carolina Psychological Association; http://www. ncpsychology.com
➢ North Dakota
  - North Dakota State Board of Psychologist Examiners; http://ndsbpe.org
  - North Dakota Psychological Association; http://www. ndpsych.org
➢ Ohio
  - Ohio State Board of Psychology; http://psychology. ohio.gov
  - Ohio Psychological Association; http://www.ohpsych. org
➢ Oklahoma
  - Oklahoma State Board of Examiners of Psychologists; http://www.ok.gov/OSBEP
  - Oklahoma Psychological Association; http://okpsych.org
➢ Oregon
  - Oregon State Board of Psychologist Examiners; http:// www.obpe.state.or.us
  - Oregon Psychological Association; http://www.opa.org
➢ Pennsylvania
  - Pennsylvania State Board of Psychology; http://www. portal.state.pa.us/portal/server.pt/community/state_ board_of_psychology/12521
  - Pennsylvania Psychological Association; http://www. papsy.org
➢ Rhode Island
  - Rhode Island Board of Psychology; http://www.health. ri.gov/hsr/professions/psych.php
  - Rhode Island Psychological Association; http://www. ripsych.org/mc/page.do;jsessionid=EA4582067FA8F76 787E736471B61B8E8.mc1?sitePageId=66045

➢ South Carolina
- South Carolina Board of Examiners in Psychology; http://www.llr.state.sc.us/POL/Psychology
- South Carolina Psychological Association; http://www.scpsychology.com

➢ South Dakota
- South Dakota Board of Examiners of Psychologists; http://dhs.sd.gov/brd/Psychologist/default.aspx
- South Dakota Psychological Association; http://www.psysd.org

➢ Tennessee
- Tennessee Board of Examiners of Psychology; http://health.state.tn.us/Boards/Psychology/index.htm
- Tennessee Psychological Association; http://www.tpaonline.org

➢ Texas
- Texas State Board of Examiners of Psychologists; http://www.tsbep.state.tx.us
- Texas Psychological Association; http://www.texaspsyc.org

➢ Utah
- Utah Psychologist Licensing Board; http://www.dopl.utah.gov/licensing/psychology.html
- Utah Psychological Association; http://www.utpsych.org

➢ Vermont
- Vermont Board of Psychological Examiners; http://vtprofessionals.org/opr1/psychologists
- Vermont Psychological Association; http://www.vermontpsych.org

➢ Virginia
- Virginia Board of Psychology; http://www.dhp.state.va.us/psychology/default.htm
- Virginia Psychological Association;http://www.vapsych.org

➢ Washington
- Washington State Examining Board of Psychology; http://www.doh.wa.gov/hsqa/Professions/psychology/licensure.htm
- Washington State Psychological Association; http://www.wapsych.org

➢ West Virginia
- West Virginia Board of Examiners of Psychologists; http://www.wvpsychbd.org
- West Virginia Psychological Association; http://www.wvpsychology.org

➢ Wisconsin
- Wisconsin Psychology Examining Board; http://drl.wi.gov/profession.asp?profid=44&locid=0
- Wisconsin Psychological Association; http://www.wipsychology.org

➢ Wyoming
- Wyoming State Board of Psychology; http://plboards.state.wy.us/psychology/index.asp
- Wyoming Psychological Association; http://www.wypsych.org

State Social Work Licensing Boards and National Association of Social Workers Chapters

➢ Alabama
- Alabama State Board of Social Work Examiners; http://www.abswe.state.al.us
- Alabama NASW Chapter; http://www.naswal.org

➢ Alaska
- Alaska Board of Social Work Examiners, Division of Occupational Licensure; http://www.dced.state.ak.us/occ
- Alaska NASW Chapter; http://www.naswak.org

➢ Arizona
- Arizona Board of Behavioral Health Examiners; http://http://azbbhe.us
- Arizona NASW Chapter; http://www.naswaz.org

➢ Arkansas
- Arkansas Social Work Licensing Board; http://www.arkansas.gov/swlb
- Arkansas NASW Chapter; http://www.naswar.org

➢ California
- California Board of Behavioral Science Examiners; http://www.bbs.ca.gov
- California NASW Chapter; http://www.naswca.org

➢ Colorado
- Colorado Board of Social Work Examiners; http://www.dora.state.co.us/mental-health
- Colorado NASW Chapter; http://www.naswco.org

➢ Connecticut
- Connecticut Department of Public Health—Social Work Licensure; http://www.ct.gov/dph/site/default.asp
- Connecticut NASW Chapter; http://www.naswct.org

➢ Delaware
- Delaware Board of Clinical Social Work Examiners; http://www.dpr.delaware.gov/boards/socialworkers/index.shtml
- Delaware NASW Chapter; http://www.naswde.org

➢ District of Columbia
- District of Columbia Board of Social Work, District of Columbia Department of Health; http://dchealth.dc.gov/doh/site/default.asp
- District of Columbia—Metro NASW Chapter; http://www.naswmetro.org

➢ Florida
- Florida Board of Clinical Social Work, Marriage and Family Therapy, and Mental Health; http://www.doh.state.fl.us/mqa/491/soc_lic_req.html
- Florida NASW Chapter; http://www.naswfl.org

➢ Georgia
- Georgia Composite Board of Professional Counselors, Social Workers, and Marriage and Family Therapists; http://sos.georgia.gov/plb/counselors
- Georgia NASW Chapter; http://www.naswga.org

➢ Hawaii
- Hawaii Department of Commerce and Consumer Affairs, Social Work Program; http://hawaii.gov/dcca/pvl/programs/socialworker
- Hawaii NASW Chapter; http://www.naswhi.org

➢ Idaho
- Idaho State Board of Social Work Examiners; http://ibol.idaho.gov/IBOL/BoardPage.aspx?Bureau=SWO
- Idaho NASW Chapter; http://www.naswidaho.org

➢ Illinois
  - Illinois Social Work Examining and Disciplinary Board, Department of Professional Regulation; http://www.idfpr.com/dpr/WHO/sw.asp
  - Illinois NASW Chapter; http://www.naswil.org
➢ Indiana
  - Indiana Social Worker, Marriage and Family Therapist, and Mental Health Counselor Board; http://www.in.gov/pla/2337.htm
  - Indiana NASW Chapter; http://www.naswin.org
➢ Iowa
  - Iowa Board of Social Work Examiners, Bureau of Professional Licensure; http://www.idph.state.ia.us/licensure
  - Iowa NASW Chapter; http://www.iowanasw.org
➢ Kansas
  - Kansas Behavioral Sciences Regulatory Board; http://www.ksbsrb.org
  - Kansas NASW Chapter; http://www.knasw.com
➢ Kentucky
  - Kentucky Board of Examiners of Social Work; http://http://bsw.ky.gov
  - Kentucky NASW Chapter; http://www.naswky.org
➢ Louisiana
  - Louisiana State Board of Social Work Examiners; http://www.labswe.org
  - Louisiana NASW Chapter; http://www.naswla.org
➢ Maine
  - Maine State Board of Social Work Licensure; http://www.maine.gov/pfr/professionallicensing/index.shtml
  - Maine NASW Chapter; http://www.naswmaine.org
➢ Maryland
  - Maryland State Board of Social Work Examiners, Department of Health and Mental Hygiene; http://dhmh.maryland.gov/bswe
  - Maryland NASW Chapter; http://www.nasw-md.org
➢ Massachusetts
  - Massachusetts Division of Registration; http://www.mass.gov/?pageID=ocasubtopic&L=4&L0=Home&L1=

Licensee&L2=Division+of+Professional+Licensure+
Boards&L3=Board+of+Registration+of+Social+Workers
&sid=Eoca
- Massachusetts NASW Chapter; http://www.naswma.org
➤ Michigan
  - Michigan Board of Social Work; http://www.michigan.
    gov/mdch/0,1607,7-132-27417_27529---,00.html
  - Michigan NASW Chapter; http://www.nasw-michigan.
    org
➤ Minnesota
  - Minnesota Board of Social Work; http://www.social
    work.state.mn.us
  - Minnesota NASW Chapter; http://www.naswmn.org
➤ Mississippi
  - Mississippi Board of Examiners for Social Workers and
    Marriage and Family Therapists; http://www.swmft.ms.
    gov/swmft/web.nsf
  - Mississippi NASW Chapter; http://www.naswms
    chapter.org
➤ Missouri
  - Missouri State Committee for Licensed Social Workers,
    Division of Professional Registration; http://www.pr.
    mo.gov/socialworkers.asp
  - Missouri NASW Chapter; http://www.nasw-mo.org
➤ Nebraska
  - Nebraska Credentialing Division; http://www.hhs.
    state.ne.us/crl/mhcs/mental/mentalhealth.htm
  - Nebraska NASW Chapter; http://www.naswne.org
➤ Nevada
  - Nevada Board of Examiners for Social Workers; http://
    www.socwork.nv.gov
  - Nevada NASW Chapter; http://www.naswnv.org
➤ New Hampshire
  - New Hampshire Board of Mental Health Practice; http://
    www.nh.gov/mhpb
  - New Hampshire NASW Chapter; http://www.nhnasw.org
➤ New Jersey
  - New Jersey State Board of Social Work Examiners;
    http://www.state.nj.us/lps/ca/social/swlic.htm
  - New Jersey NASW Chapter; http://www.naswnj.org

➢ New Mexico
  ■ New Mexico Board of Social Work Examiners; http://www.rld.state.nm.us/SocialWork/index.html
  ■ New Mexico NASW Chapter; http://www.naswnm.org
➢ New York
  ■ New York State Board for Social Work; http://www.op.nysed.gov/prof/sw
  ■ New York City NASW Chapter; http://www.naswnyc.org
➢ North Carolina
  ■ North Carolina Social Work Certification and Licensure Board; http://www.ncswboard.org
  ■ North Carolina NASW Chapter; http://www.naswnc.org
➢ North Dakota
  ■ North Dakota Board of Social Work Examiners; http://www.ndbswe.com
  ■ North Dakota NASW Chapter; http://www.naswnd.org
➢ Ohio
  ■ Ohio Counselor, Social Worker, and Marriage and Family Therapy Board; http://www.cswmft.ohio.gov
  ■ Ohio NASW Chapter; http://www.naswoh.org
➢ Oklahoma
  ■ Oklahoma Board of Licensed Social Workers; http://www.ok.gov/socialworkers
  ■ Oklahoma NASW Chapter; http://www.naswok.org
➢ Oregon
  ■ Oregon State Board of Clinical Social Workers; http://www.oregon.gov/BLSW
  ■ Oregon NASW Chapter; http://www.nasworegon.org
➢ Pennsylvania
  ■ Pennsylvania State Board for Social Workers, Marriage and Family Therapists, and Professional Counselors; http://www.portal.state.pa.us/portal/server.pt/community/state_board_of_social_workers,_marriage_and_family_therapists_and_professional_counselors/12524
  ■ Pennsylvania NASW Chapter; http://www.nasw-pa.org
➢ Rhode Island
  ■ Rhode Island Division of Professional Regulation/Department of Health; http://www.health.state.ri.us/hsr/professions/s_work.php
  ■ Rhode Island NASW Chapter; http://www.rinasw.info

> South Carolina
>> ■ South Carolina Board of Social Work Examiners; http://www.llr.state.sc.us/pol/socialworkers
>> ■ South Carolina NASW Chapter; http://www.scnasw.org
> South Dakota
>> ■ South Dakota Board of Social Work Examiners; http://dhs.sd.gov/brd/SocialWorker/default.aspx
>> ■ South Dakota NASW Chapter; http://www.naswsd.org
> Tennessee
>> ■ Tennessee Board of Social Work Certification and Licensure; http://health.state.tn.us/boards/sw/index.htm
>> ■ Tennessee NASW Chapter; http://www.naswtn.com
> Texas
>> ■ Texas State Board of Social Work Examiners; http://www.dshs.state.tx.us/socialwork
>> ■ Texas NASW Chapter; http://www.naswtx.org
> Utah
>> ■ Utah Social Work Licensing Board; http://www.dopl.utah.gov/licensing/social_work.html
>> ■ Utah NASW Chapter; http://www.utnasw.org
> Vermont
>> ■ Vermont Office of the Secretary of State, Licensing and Regulations; http://vtprofessionals.org
>> ■ Vermont NASW Chapter; http://www.naswvt.org
> Virginia
>> ■ Virginia Board of Social Work; http://www.dhp.state.va.us/social
>> ■ Virginia NASW Chapter; http://www.naswva.org
> Washington
>> ■ Washington State Department of Health; http://www.doh.wa.gov/hsqa/Professions/Social_Worker/default.htm
>> ■ Washington NASW Chapter; http://www.nasw-wa.org
> West Virginia
>> ■ West Virginia Board of Social Work Examiners; http://www.wvsocialworkboard.org
>> ■ West Virginia NASW Chapter; http://www.naswwv.org
> Wisconsin
>> ■ State of Wisconsin Department of Regulation and Licensing, Marriage and Family Therapy, Professional Counseling, and Social Work; http://drl.wi.gov/board_detail.asp?boardid=33&locid=0

- Wisconsin NASW Chapter; http://www.naswwi.org
➢ Wyoming
  - Wyoming Mental Health Professions Licensing Board; http://www.plboards.state.wy.us/mentalhealth
  - Wyoming NASW Chapter; http://www.wyomingnasw. com

National Professional Organization Ethics Codes

➢ American Association of Marriage and Family Therapists *Code of Ethics* (2001); http://www.AMFT.org/resources/LRM_ Plan/Ethics/ethicscode2001.asp
➢ American Counseling Association *Ethics & Professional Standards* (2005); http://www.counseling.org/Resources/ CodeOfEthics/TP/Home/CT2.aspx
➢ American Psychiatric Association *The Principles of Medical Ethics With Annotations Especially Applicable to Psychiatry* (2009); http://www.psych.org/MainMenu/Psychiatric Practice/Ethics/ResourcesStandards/PrinciplesofMedical Ethics.aspx
➢ American Psychoanalytic Association *Principles and Standards of Ethics* (2009–2010); http://www.apsa.org/About_ APsaA/Ethics_Code.aspx
➢ APA *Ethical Principles of Psychologists and Code of Conduct* (2010); http://www.apa.org/ethics/code/index.aspx
➢ APA *Guidelines for Ethical Conduct in the Care and Use of Animals* (2010); http://www.apa.org/science/leadership/ care/guidelines.aspx
➢ National Association of Social Workers *Code of Ethics* (1999); http://www.socialworkers.org/pubs/code/default.asp

Practice Guidelines

➢ American Psychology-Law Society *Specialty Guidelines for Forensic Psychologists* (2011); http://www.ap-ls.org/about psychlaw/SpecialtyGuidelines.php
➢ American Psychiatric Association *Practice Guidelines* (for a variety of specific disorders); http://www.psych.org/ MainMenu/PsychiatricPractice/PracticeGuidelines_1.aspx
➢ APA *Guidelines for Child Custody Evaluations in Family Law Proceedings* (2010); http://www.apa.org/practice/guidelines/ child-custody.pdf

> APA *Guidelines for the Evaluation of Dementia and Age-Related Cognitive Decline* (1998); http://www.apa.org/practice/guidelines/dementia.aspx
> APA *Guidelines for Psychological Evaluations in Child Protection Matters* (1999); http://www.apa.org/practice/guidelines/child-protection.pdf
> APA *Guidelines for Psychological Practice With Girls and Women* (2007); http://www.apa.org/practice/guidelines/girls-and-women.pdf
> APA *Guidelines for Psychological Practice With Older Adults* (2004); http://www.apa.org/practice/guidelines/older-adults.pdf
> APA *Guidelines for Psychotherapy With Lesbian, Gay, and Bisexual Clients* (2011); http://www.apa.org/pi/lgbt/resources/guidelines.aspx
> APA *Guidelines on Multicultural Education, Training, Research, Practice, and Organizational Change for Psychologists* (2002); http://www.apa.org/pi/oema/resources/policy/multicultural-guideline.pdf
> APA *Record Keeping Guidelines* (2007); http://www.apa.org/practice/guidelines/record-keeping.pdf

Health Insurance Portability and Accountability Act

> Health Insurance Portability and Accountability Act of 1996, Public Law 104-191: HIPAA Privacy & Security Rule, 45 CFR 160-164; http://www.hhs.gov/ocr/hipaa
> APA Insurance Trust (APAIT) and APA Practice Organization HIPAA Resources; http://www.apait.org/apait/resources/hipaa
> APA Practice Central HIPAA Compliance; http://www.apapracticecentral.org/business/hipaa/index.aspx
> BehaveNet HIPAA; http://www.behavenet.com
> National Association of Social Workers HIPAA Highlights for Social Workers; http://socialworkers.org/hipaa
> Zuckerman, E. L. (2006). *HIPAA help: A compliance toolkit for psychotherapists for maintaining records' privacy and security, managing risks, and operating ethically and legally under HIPAA* (Rev. ed.). Armbrust, PA: Three Wishes Press.

CHAPTER 17

Resources for Clinicians II: Strategies for Self-Care and Managing Adverse Events

Caring for mental health patients is a demanding occupation. Clinicians must have the core values, knowledge, skill, and emotional and physical strength to competently and ethically treat their clients. The demands of the profession require that practitioners engage in self-care; those who ignore or neglect caring for themselves risk negative consequences for themselves, their clients, and others. Self-care includes participating in a professional support network (e.g., an attorney, a peer consultation group, colleague assistance programs; Pope & Vasquez, 2011), developing and activating policies and procedures for managing unexpected adverse events (e.g., obtaining liability insurance, developing a professional will, responding to a subpoena or a notice of a malpractice claim, managing social media, responding to a patient suicide), and participating in activities that build and sustain emotional and physical well-being (e.g., mindfulness, volunteer work). Pope and Vasquez (2011) have advised mental health professionals to create "strategies for self-care as early as possible" (p. 69) in the course of their training and practice. This chapter provides some resources for creating those strategies.

> ➢ Colleague assistance
>> ■ American Psychological Association. (n.d.). *Colleague assistance and self-care.* Retrieved from http://www.apa.org/practice/resources/assistance/index.aspx

➢ Mindfulness resources
  ▪ Pope, K. S. (n.d.). *Mindfulness.* Retrieved from http://bit.ly/KenPopeMindfulness
➢ Professional liability (malpractice) insurance
  ○ Pope, K. S., & Vasquez, M. J. T. (2005). Finding professional liability coverage. In *How to survive and thrive as a therapist: Information, ideas, and resources for psychologists in practice* (pp. 57–63). Washington, DC: American Psychological Association.
  ○ Zuckerman, E. L. (2008). Professional liability ("malpractice") insurance. In *The paper office* (4th ed., pp. 86–100; also see p. 443 for sellers of insurance as of 2008). New York, NY: Guilford Press.
➢ Professional will
  ▪ Alban, A., & Frankel, A. S. (2010, January–February). So how's it feel to be in breach of the APA Ethics Code and California law? Professional wills: The ethics requirement you haven't (yet) met. *California Psychologist, 43*(1), 25. Retrieved from http://clinicallawyer.com/2010/01/professional-wills-some-concrete-steps-to-take
  ▪ Holloway, J. D. (2003). *Professional will: A responsible thing to do.* Retrieved from http://www.apa.org/monitor/feb03/will.aspx
  ▪ Pope, K. S., & Vasquez, M. J. T. (2011). Creating a professional will. In *Ethics in psychotherapy and counseling: A practical guide* (4th ed., pp. 78–84). Hoboken, NJ: Wiley.
  ▪ Steiner, A. (2003). *The empty chair: Making our absence less traumatic for everyone.* Retrieved from http://www.psychotherapy.net/article/psychotherapist-retirement
➢ Responding to a malpractice complaint
  ▪ Pope, K. S., & Vasquez, M. J. T. (2011). Responding to ethics, licensing, or malpractice complaints. In *Ethics in psychotherapy and counseling: A practical guide* (4th ed., pp. 110–116). Hoboken, NJ: Wiley.
  ▪ Zuckerman, E. L. (2008). What to do if you are complained against: A checklist. In *The paper office* (4th ed., pp. 83–86). New York, NY: Guilford Press.
➢ Responding to a patient suicide
  ▪ American Association of Suicidology Clinician Survivor Task Force available at http://mypage.iu.edu/~jmcintos/therapists_mainpg.htm

- Berman, A. L., Jobes, D., & Silverman, M. M. (2006). Survivors of suicide and postvention. In *Adolescent suicide: Assessment and intervention* (2nd ed., pp. 335–364). Washington, DC: American Psychological Association.
- Bongar, B. (2002). Risk management: Prevention and postvention. In *The suicidal patient: Clinical and legal standards of care* (2nd ed., pp. 213–261). Washington, DC: American Psychological Association.
- Campbell, F. R. (2006). Aftermath of suicide: The clinician's role. In R. I. Simon & R. E. Hales (Eds.), *The textbook of suicide assessment and management* (pp. 459–476). Washington, DC: American Psychiatric Publishing.
- Gitlin, M. (2006). Psychiatrist reactions to patient suicide. In R. I. Simon & R. E. Hales (Eds.), *The textbook of suicide assessment and management* (pp. 477–492). Washington, DC: American Psychiatric Publishing.

➢ Responding to a patient threat, attack, or stalking
- Pope, K. S. (n.d.) *Resources for vulnerable therapists.* Retrieved from http://bit.ly/KenPopeResourcesForVulnerableTherapists

➢ Responding to a subpoena
- American Psychological Association Committee on Legal Issues. (2006). Strategies for private practitioners coping with subpoenas or compelled testimony for client records or test data. *Professional Psychology: Research and Practice, 37,* 215–222.
- American Psychological Association Legal and Regulatory Affairs. (2008). *How to deal with a subpoena.* Retrieved from http://www.apapracticecentral.org/update/2008/12-17/subpoena.aspx

➢ Self-care
- Pope, K. S., & Vasquez, M. J. T. (2011). Creating strategies for self-care. In *Ethics in psychotherapy and counseling: A practical guide* (4th ed., pp. 69–77). Hoboken, NJ: Wiley.

➢ Social media management
- Kolmes, K. (2010). *A psychotherapist's guide to Facebook and Twitter: Why clinicians should give a tweet!* Retrieved from http://www.psychotherapy.net/article/psychotherapies-guide-social-media

- Tate, R. (2011). *How to keep Facebook from humiliating you today.* Retrieved from http://gawker.com/5729990/how-to-keep-facebook-from-humiliating-you-today
- Whittaker, Z. (2011). *January 2011: The definitive Facebook lockdown guide.* Retrieved from http://t.co/x4iqPRS

➢ Volunteer opportunities for mental health professionals
  - Pope, K. S. (n.d.). *Volunteering resources.* Retrieved from http://bit.ly/KenPopeVolunteeringResources

Reference

Pope, K. S., & Vasquez, M. J. T. (2011). *Ethics in psychotherapy and counseling: A practical guide* (4th ed.). Hoboken, NJ: Wiley.

CHAPTER 18

Resources for Clients and Their Significant Others

Consumers of mental health services often derive great benefit from contacting trained hotline personnel and/or reading specific information regarding their psychological problems. In addition, such resources can be extremely helpful to the significant others of those experiencing emotional distress. Resources for clients and their significant others are listed in the outline that follows by problem category (e.g., HIV/AIDS, schizophrenia), including national toll-free phone numbers and Internet contacts (when available). Although every effort was made to ensure that contacts were current at the time the list was constructed, the reader is advised that phone numbers and websites are updated or deleted periodically.

> ➢ AIDS, HIV, and sexually transmitted disease (STD)
>> ▪ National AIDS Hotlines; 1-800-342-2437, 1-800-232-4636
>> ▪ AIDS Treatment Information Services; 1-800-HIV-0440
>> ▪ Centers for Disease Control AIDS Information; 1-800-342-2437, http://www.cdc.gov/hiv
>> ▪ National STD Hotlines; 1-800-227-8922, 1-919-361-8488
>> ▪ Centers for Disease Control STD Information; http://www.cdc.gov/STD
>> ▪ Additional websites; http://www.aids.gov/, http://www.aids.org

> Attention-deficit disorder and attention-deficit/hyper-activity disorder
  - CHADD (Children and Adults With Attention-Deficit/ Hyperactivity Disorder); 1-800-233-4050, http://www. chadd.org
> Anxiety disorders
  - Anxiety Disorders Association of America; http://www. adaa.org
> Autism
  - Autism Speaks; http://www.autismspeaks.org
> Bipolar disorder
  - National Institute of Mental Health (NIMH): Bipolar Disorder; http://www.nimh.nih.gov/health/publications/ bipolar-disorder/complete-index.shtml
  - Child & Adolescent Bipolar Foundation; http://www. bpkids.org
  - U.S. National Library of Medicine, National Institutes of Health (NIH); http://www.nlm.nih.gov/medlineplus/ bipolardisorder.html
> Borderline personality disorder
  - NIMH: Borderline Personality Disorder; http://www. nimh.nih.gov/health/publications/borderline-personality-disorder-fact-sheet/index.shtml
> Cancer
  - American Cancer Society; http://www.cancer.org
  - Association of Cancer Online Resources; http://acor.org
  - Centers for Disease Control and Prevention Cancer Resources; http://www.cdc.gov/cancer/dcpc/resources
  - National Cancer Institute; http://www.cancer.gov
  - OncoLink; http://www.oncolink.org/index.cfm
  - Psychological intervention for people with cancer: Therapy and self-help; http://bit.ly/KenPopeCancer Resources
> Caregivers
  - Caregiver resources; http://bit.ly/KenPopeCaregiver Resources
> Child abuse
  - Childhelp Hotline; 1-800-4-A-CHILD (1-800-422-4453)
  - Incest Awareness Foundation; 1-888-547-3222
  - U.S. National Library of Medicine, NIH; http://www. nlm.nih.gov/medlineplus/childabuse.html

- Rape, Abuse, & Incest National Network; 1-800-656-HOPE, http://www.rainn.org
- ➢ Clergy abuse
  - Baylor University Clergy Sexual Misconduct Study; http://www.baylor.edu/clergysexualmisconduct
  - The Survivors Network for Those Abused by Priests; http://www.snapnetwork.org
- ➢ Community assistance and service
  - Red Cross; http://www.redcross.org
  - Salvation Army; http://www.salvationarmyusa.org/usn/www_usn_2.nsf
  - YMCA; http://www.ymca.net
  - YWCA; http://www.ywca.org/site/pp.asp?c=djISI6PIKpG&b=284783
- ➢ Consumer credit counseling
  - National Foundation for Credit Counseling; 1-800-388-2227, http://www.nfcc.org
- ➢ Cutting and other self-injury
  - HelpGuide: Cutting and Self-Injury; http://www.helpguide.org/mental/self_injury.htm
  - S.A.F.E. Alternatives; 1-800-DONTCUT, http://www.selfinjury.com
- ➢ Depression
  - NIMH: Depression; http://www.nimh.nih.gov/health/publications/depression-listing.shtml
  - U.S. National Library of Medicine, NIH; http://www.nlm.nih.gov/medlineplus/depression.html
- ➢ Disaster relief
  - Red Cross; http://www.redcross.org
  - Salvation Army; http://www.salvationarmyusa.org/usn/www_usn_2.nsf
- ➢ Domestic violence
  - The National Domestic Violence Hotline; 1-800-799-SAFE, http://www.ndvh.org
  - National Resource Center on Domestic Violence; http://www.nrcdv.org
  - Women's Law; http://www.womenslaw.org
- ➢ Eating disorders
  - Bulimia and Anorexia Self-Help Hotline; 1-800-227-4785
  - National Association of Anorexia and Associated Disorders; 1-630-577-1330, http://www.anad.org

- National Eating Disorder Referral and Information Center; http://www.edreferral.com
- ➢ Elder abuse
  - Eldercare Locator; 1-800-677-1116
  - National Center on Elder Abuse; http://www.ncea.aoa.gov/ncearoot/Main_Site/index.aspx
- ➢ Elderly client concerns
  - American Association of Retired Persons; http://www.aarp.org
- ➢ Gambling addiction
  - U.S. National Council on Problem Gambling Helpline; 1-800-522-4700 http://www.ncpgambling.org/i4a/pages/index.cfm?pageid=1
  - HelpGuide: Gambling Addiction; http://www.helpguide.org/mental/gambling_addiction.htm
- ➢ Gay, lesbian, bisexual, and transgender concerns
  - Gay, Lesbian, Bisexual, and Transgender National Hotline; 1-888-THE-GLNH (1-888-843-4564), http://www.glnh.org/hotline/index.html
  - Parents, Families, and Friends of Lesbians and Gays; http://community.pflag.org/Page.aspx?pid=194&srcid=-2
- ➢ General mental health organizations information
  - Canadian Psychological Association, *Your Health: "Psychology Works" Fact Sheets;* http://www.cpa.ca/publications/yourhealthpsychologyworksfactsheets
  - National Alliance on Mental Illness; 1-800-950-6264, http://www.nami.org
  - NIMH; http://www.nimh.nih.gov/index.shtml
  - Mental Health America; http://www.nmha.org
- ➢ Homelessness
  - Homelessness 24-hour Hotline; 1-800-654-8595
  - Homelessness Resource Center; http://www.nrchmi.samhsa.gov
  - Homeless Shelter Directory; http://www.homelessshelterdirectory.org
- ➢ Internet addiction
  - HelpGuide: Internet Addiction; http://www.helpguide.org/mental/internet_cybersex_addiction.htm
- ➢ Legal aid referrals
  - Law Help; http://lawhelp.org

➢ Medication information
- Medline Plus, *Drugs, Supplements, and Herbal Information;* http://www.nlm.nih.gov/medlineplus/druginformation.html

➢ Military service members, family, and friends
- Defense Centers of Excellence; http://www.dcoe.health.mil
- Military One Source; http://www.militaryonesource.com
- Real Warriors; http://www.realwarriors.net

➢ Obsessive–compulsive disorder
- National Obsessive–Compulsive Disorder Information Hotline; 1-800-NEWS-4-OCD
- NIMH: Obsessive–Compulsive Disorder; http://www.nimh.nih.gov/health/topics/obsessive-compulsive-disorder-ocd/index.shtml

➢ Panic disorder
- NIMH: Panic Disorder; http://www.nimh.nih.gov/health/topics/panic-disorder/index.shtml

➢ Pet loss
- American Society for the Prevention of Cruelty to Animals and Pet Loss; http://www.aspca.org/pet-care/pet-loss

➢ Posttraumatic stress disorder (PTSD)
- NIMH: PTSD; http://www.nimh.nih.gov/health/topics/post-traumatic-stress-disorder-ptsd/index.shtml
- U.S. Department of Veterans Affairs, National Center for PTSD; http://www.ptsd.va.gov

➢ Rape
- Rape, Abuse, & Incest National Network; 1-800-656-HOPE, http://www.rainn.org

➢ Runaways
- National Runaway Switchboard; 1-800-RUNAWAY (1-800-786-2929), http://www.1800runaway.org

➢ Schizophrenia
- National Alliance of Mental Illness: Schizophrenia; http://www.nami.org/Template.cfm?Section=By_Illness&template=/ContentManagement/ContentDisplay.cfm&ContentID=7416
- National Library of Medicine, NIH: Schizophrenia; http://www.nlm.nih.gov/medlineplus/ency/article/000928.htm

> Smoking cessation
>   - Quitline; 1-800-QUITNOW (1-800-784-8669)
>   - National Cancer Institute; http://www.cancer.gov/cancertopics/smoking
> Substance abuse
>   - Alcoholics Anonymous; http://www.aa.org/?Media=PlayFlash
>   - Al-Anon/Alateen Hotline; 1-888-425-2666, http://www.al-anon.alateen.org
>   - U.S. Department of Health and Human Services, Substance Abuse and Mental Health Services Administration; 1-800-662-HELP (1-800-662-4357), http://www.samhsa.gov
>   - National Institute on Drug Abuse; http://www.nida.nih.gov
>   - U.S. National Library of Medicine, NIH: Alcohol Abuse; http://www.nlm.nih.gov/medlineplus/alcoholism.html
>   - U.S. National Library of Medicine, NIH: Substance Abuse; http://www.nlm.nih.gov/medlineplus/drugabuse.html
> Suicide prevention
>   - American Association of Suicidology; http://www.suicidology.org/web/guest/home
>   - American Foundation for Suicide Prevention; http://www.afsp.org
>   - National Suicide Prevention Lifeline; 1-800-273-TALK, http://www.suicidepreventionlifeline.org
> Suicide survivors
>   - American Association of Suicidology; http://www.suicidology.org/web/guest/suicide-loss-survivors
>   - Jackson, J. (1984). *SOS: A Handbook for Survivors of Suicide;* http://www.suicidology.org/c/document_library/get_file?folderId=229&name=DLFE-73.pdf
> Therapist–client sexual abuse
>   - Advocate Web; http://www.advocateweb.org
>   - Therapy Exploitation Link Line; http://www.therapyabuse.org
> Veterans affairs
>   - U.S. Department of Veterans Affairs; http://www.va.gov

Index

AAMFT (American Association of Marriage and Family Therapists), 253, 285
Achievement measures, 30, 64–65
Actuarial measures, 106–107, 114
Actuarial risk evaluation, 100–101
ACUTE (Adolescent & Child Urgent Threat Evaluation), 106–107, 114
Acute stress disorder, 181
ADD. *See* Attention-deficit disorder
ADHD. *See* Attention-deficit/hyperactivity disorder
ADHD Symptom Checklist–4 (ADHD–SC4), 33–34
ADHDT (Attention-Deficit/Hyperactivity Disorder Test), 34
ADI–R (Autism Diagnostic Interview-Revised), 44–45
Adjustment disorder, 180, 181
Adolescent & Child Urgent Threat Evaluation (ACUTE), 106–107, 114
Adolescent clients
     behavioral assessment measures for, 69
     cognitive assessment measures for, 58–63
     evidence-based treatments for, 192, 194
     interpersonal violence assessment measures for, 93, 94, 113
     over-the-counter medications for, 239–243
     prescription medications for, 199–238
     resources for, 291–296
     safeguarding of, 115
     screening measures for, 30, 32, 34–40
     self-harm assessment of, 89
     with sexual orientation concerns, 294
     structured/semistructured interviews for, 44–46
     suicide risk evaluation for, 104–107
     symptom assessment measures for, 69, 70, 72
Adolescent Substance Abuse Subtle Screening Inventory–A2 (SASSI–A2), 40
Adolescent Symptom Inventory–4 (ASI–4), 30
Adolescent Symptom Screening Form, 32
ADS (Anger Disorders Scale), 91–92
ADS:S (Anger Disorders Scale: Short Form), 91–92

About the Author

Janet L. Sonne received her undergraduate degree in psychology from Stanford University, her master's degree in social and personality psychology research from the University of California, Santa Barbara, and her doctorate in clinical psychology from the University of California, Los Angeles. She is currently the coordinator of psychology training programs at the Loma Linda University Behavioral Medicine Center in Redlands, California, and she maintains an independent clinical and forensic practice. Dr. Sonne was a founding psychologist of the graduate clinical psychology programs at Loma Linda University; in 2005 she retired from her position there as professor of psychology and director of clinical training. Previously, she was a member of the faculty of the Department of Psychiatry at Loma Linda University School of Medicine, where she taught and supervised the psychotherapy training of psychiatry residents. In addition, she taught medical students and graduate students in the departments of nursing, social work, and marriage and family therapy. Dr. Sonne is a fellow of the American Psychological Association's (APA's) Division 42 (Independent Practice) and a member of the California Psychological Association (CPA). She is the former chair and a member of the CPA Ethics Committee, and she served twice on the APA Ethics Committee. Dr. Sonne is an expert consultant to the California Board of Psychology, and to attorneys, religious organizations, and practitioners regarding professional standards of care, competency issues, and perpetration and sequelae of childhood sexual abuse. She is the author of several publications on the topics of therapist–patient relationships, including a chapter, "Sexualized Relationships," in the recent *APA Handbook of Ethics and Psychology* and an article for which she was awarded a citation from Division 42, "Nonsexual Multiple Relationships: A Practical Decision-Making Model for Clinicians." She coauthored two books: *Sexual Feelings in Psychotherapy: Explorations for Therapists and Therapists-in-Training* with Ken Pope and Jean Holroyd, and *What Therapists Don't Talk About and Why: Understanding the Taboos That Hurt Us and Our Clients* with Ken Pope and Beverly Greene.